高等学校应用型特色规划教材 经管系列

市场营销学(双语教材)
Marketing

主 编 李志宏 梁 东

副主编 约翰·冈瑟(Johann Günther) 刘建堤

清华大学出版社
北京

内 容 简 介

市场营销学是一门建立在经济科学、行为科学和现代管理理论基础之上的应用科学，是工商管理类各专业的核心课程，其研究对象是以满足消费者需求为中心的企业市场营销活动的过程及其规律性。本书共十五章，主要内容包括现代市场营销理论的形成和发展、市场营销管理哲学的演变、经典的 4P 组合等基本理论以及市场营销环境对企业市场营销活动的影响、市场购买行为和市场营销战略与策略等基本知识，同时还包括营销工程、市场细分、目标市场选择、市场定位以及市场营销调查与预测等基本技能及其实际运用。

本书为中英文双语教材，以问题为导向组织编写，并配有丰富的案例，案例资料信息量大，选题新颖，通过案例问题讨论与案例点评，有助于读者更深入地体会市场营销理论在营销活动中的指导意义。

本书可作为高等院校工商管理、市场营销、物流管理、信息管理、会计学、财务管理及人力资源管理等专业应用型人才的教学用书，也可以作为相关从业人员的学习参考资料。

本书封面贴有清华大学出版社防伪标签，无标签者不得销售。
版权所有，侵权必究。侵权举报电话：010-62782989 13701121933

图书在版编目(CIP)数据

市场营销学(双语教材)/李志宏，梁东主编；冈瑟(Günther J.)，刘建堤副主编. —北京：清华大学出版社，2011.6（2020.3重印）
（高等学校应用型特色规划教材 经管系列）
ISBN 978-7-302-25504-8

Ⅰ. ①市… Ⅱ.①李… ②梁… ③冈… ④刘… Ⅲ. ①市场营销学—双语教学—高等学校—教材 Ⅳ. ①F713.50

中国版本图书馆 CIP 数据核字(2011)第 081293 号

责任编辑：温 洁 汤涌涛
封面设计：杨玉兰
版式设计：北京东方人华科技有限公司
责任校对：李玉萍
责任印制：沈 露

出版发行：清华大学出版社　　　地　址：北京清华大学学研大厦 A 座
　　　　　http://www.tup.com.cn　　邮　编：100084
　　　　　社 总 机：010-62770175　邮　购：010-62786544
　　　　　投稿与读者服务：010-62776969, c-service@tup.tsinghua.edu.cn
　　　　　质量反馈：010-62772015, zhiliang@tup.tsinghua.edu.cn
印 装 者：三河市龙大印装有限公司
经　　销：全国新华书店
开　　本：185mm×230mm　　印 张：18　　字 数：403 千字
版　　次：2011 年 6 月第 1 版　　印 次：2020 年 3 月第 10 次印刷
定　　价：46.00 元

产品编号：038780-03

出版说明

应用型人才是指能够将专业知识和技能应用于所从事的专业岗位的一种专门人才。应用型人才的本质特征是具有专业基本知识和基本技能，即具有明确的职业性、实用性、实践性和高层次性。加强应用型人才的培养，是"十一五"时期我国教育发展与改革的重要目标，也是协调高等教育规模速度与市场人才需求关系的重要途径。

教育部要求今后需要有相当数量的高校致力于培养应用型人才，以满足市场对应用型人才需求量的不断增加。为了培养高素质应用型人才，必须建立完善的教学计划和高水平的课程体系。在教育部有关精神的指导下，我们组织全国高校的专家教授，努力探求更为合理有效的应用型人才培养方案，并结合我国当前的实际情况，编写了这套《高等学校应用型特色规划教材 经管系列》丛书。

为使教材的编写真正切合应用型人才的培养目标，我社编辑在全国范围内走访了大量高等学校，拜访了众多院校主管教学的领导，以及教学一线的系主任和教师，掌握了各地区各学校所设专业的培养目标和办学特色，并广泛、深入地与用人单位进行交流，明确了用人单位的真正需求。这些工作为本套丛书的准确定位、合理选材、突出特色奠定了坚实的基础。

✧ 教材定位

- 以就业为导向。在应用型人才培养过程中，充分考虑市场需求，因此本套丛书充分体现"就业导向"的基本思路。
- 符合本学科的课程设置要求。以高等教育的培养目标为依据，注重教材的科学性、实用性和通用性。
- 定位明确。准确定位教材在人才培养过程中的地位和作用，正确处理教材的读者层次关系，面向就业，突出应用。
- 合理选材、编排得当。妥善处理传统内容与现代内容的关系，大力补充新知识、新技术、新工艺和新成果。根据本学科的教学基本要求和教学大纲的要求，制订编写大纲(编写原则、编写特色、编写内容、编写体例等)，突出重点、难点。
- 建设"立体化"的精品教材体系。提倡教材与电子教案、学习指导、习题解答、课程设计、毕业设计等辅助教学资料配套出版。

✧ 丛书特色

- ➢ 围绕应用讲理论，突出实践教学环节及特点，包含丰富的案例，并对案例作详细解析，强调实用性和可操作性。
- ➢ 涉及最新的理论成果和实务案例，充分反映岗位要求，真正体现以就业为导向的培养目标。
- ➢ 国际化与中国特色相结合，符合高等教育日趋国际化的发展趋势，部分教材采用双语形式。
- ➢ 在结构的布局、内容重点的选取、案例习题的设计等方面符合教改目标和教学大纲的要求，把教师的备课、授课、辅导答疑等教学环节有机地结合起来。

✧ 读者定位

本系列教材主要面向普通高等院校和高等职业技术院校，适合应用型人才培养的高等院校的教学需要。

✧ 关于作者

丛书编委特聘请执教多年且有较高学术造诣和实践经验的教授参与各册教材的编写，其中有相当一部分的教材主要执笔者是精品课程的负责人，本丛书凝聚了他们多年的教学经验和心血。

✧ 互动交流

本丛书的编写及出版过程，贯穿了清华大学出版社一贯严谨、务实、科学的作风。伴随我国教育改革的不断深入，要编写出满足新形势下教学需求的教材，还需要我们不断地努力、探索和实践。我们真诚希望使用本丛书的教师、学生和其他读者提出宝贵的意见和建议，使之更臻成熟。

清华大学出版社

前　言

随着经济的全球化以及全球市场经济的不断发展与完善，企业和社会组织的国际商业交往越来越频繁，市场营销学作为一门集经济学、管理学和行为科学等于一身的学科，以其独特的科学性、艺术性和应用性受到了经济社会的关注，并被企业和社会组织广泛用于生产经营与商务运作决策的制定过程中。同时，市场经济的提升性发展、全球经济一体化以及市场与商务往来的频繁性，对市场营销人员及其决策者提出了更高的要求，不但要求他们具备市场营销的基本理论知识和技巧，还要求他们了解市场营销发展的前沿领域及其在实践中的应用，同时对他们在专业实践领域的中英文沟通能力也提出了新的挑战。为适应市场发展需要，在清华大学出版社的支持与指导下，我们与奥地利的约翰·冈瑟教授(Johann Günther)合作编写了这本中英双语教材。

本教材具有如下特点。

一是编写形式的推陈出新。本书不但重视继承已有中文教材中的合理部分，而且重视按英文原版教材编写体例进行编写，以问题为导向，既突出内容结构与章节安排的系统性，又力求做到每章篇首问题与结尾的总结首尾呼应，以帮助学生更深入地了解全书的结构层次及每章的知识架构。

二是内容简洁明了。本书针对中国大学生对英文原版教材理解有限的现状，在充分吸取现有市场营销学教材经典理论观点的同时，增加了部分前沿性的营销知识，并以简单明了的英文表现形式对这些观点与知识进行整合，尽量避免英文原版教材因过于庞大繁琐而影响学生阅读和理解等问题，以便学生在使用本书的过程中，能轻松地掌握市场营销学科的理论结构，同时，还能了解到市场营销的专业知识与术语的中英文表达。

三是知识的实用性与针对性强。市场营销学是一门应用性很强的学科，随着市场营销环境的开放化，学科知识与学生在学校学到的英文知识在实践中无法很好衔接，影响了他们在实践中与相关专业人士的深层次沟通，鉴于此，本书将理论教学、案例分析与营销策划、理论知识与语言知识的运用有机融合在一起，有利于提高学生的动脑、动手及动嘴能力。

四是案例的专业性与时效性强。"专业性"主要体现在每章结尾都配备有与该章内容相匹配的案例，尽力做到案例与内容的同步；"时效性"则表现在所选择的案例大部分为近年来国内外市场知名企业的案例，以此帮助学生熟悉市场发展变化的前沿思想。

五是配套练习的可操作性强。每个案例后均配有一定数量的案例讨论题，学生在学完一章的内容后，可以通过案例的阅读、理解与讨论，把学习到的营销理论知识与案例中反映的实际营销活动紧密结合并展开讨论，提出自己的观点，这样，一方面能提高灵活运用所学知识的能力，另一方面则可以深化对案例现象的理解，从理论的高度去解释实践中的市场现象，以便今后更好地指导自己的实践活动。

本教材由江汉大学商学院李志宏博士和梁东教授负责总体设计并拟就编写大纲，参编人员按编写大纲分工撰写。李志宏博士和梁东教授担任主编，奥地利约翰·冈瑟教授(Johann Günther)和刘建堤副教授担任副主编。全书共十五章，各章参编人员如下：第一章，李志宏；第二章，梁东、王自晔；第三章和第四章，李莉；第五章，刘泉宏；第六章，李志宏、刘建堤；第七章，洪菲；第八章，李志宏、邹蔚；第九章，周红；第十章，约翰·冈瑟；第十一章，洪菲；第十二章，许以洪；第十三章，约翰·冈瑟；第十四章，周红；第十五章，梁东、约翰·冈瑟。本书最后由李志宏、梁东统稿并修改定稿。本书所有参编人员均来自江汉大学商学院(除约翰·冈瑟教授外)。

本书从立项到完成得到了江汉大学领导、老师和朋友的指导与帮助。在此，我们深表谢意，同时我们也非常感谢清华大学出版社编辑为本教材的编写提出的建设性意见，也对为本教材的顺利完成提供资料的各界同仁一并表示谢意。

另外，本书配有电子课件，以适应多媒体教学的需要。课件下载网址为www.tup.com.cn。

由于编写组水平有限，书中存在的各种错漏和不足在所难免，还请各位专家、学者批评指正，对此，我们编写组全体成员表示由衷的感谢！我们的联系方式为cockrabbit@hotmail.com。

编　者
于武汉经济技术开发区三角湖畔

Contents

Part I About Marketing

Chapter 1 Production and Development of Marketing 1

1.1 Production of Marketing 1
1.2 Development of Marketing 3
    1.2.1 Classical Schools 3
    1.2.2 Management Schools 9
    1.2.3 Behavior Schools 12
1.3 Connotation and Nature of Marketing ... 15
    1.3.1 Connotation of Marketing 15
    1.3.2 Nature of Marketing 15
1.4 Research Approaches of Marketing 16
    1.4.1 Commodity Research Approach 16
    1.4.2 Functional Research Approach 17
    1.4.3 Institutional Research Approach 17
    1.4.4 Managerial Research Approach 17
    1.4.5 Systematic Research Approach 17
1.5 Summary 18

Chapter 2 Marketing Philosophy 22

2.1 Production Concept 22
    2.1.1 Background of Production Concept 22
    2.1.2 Meaning of Production Concept 23
    2.1.3 Characteristics of Production Concept 23
2.2 Product Concept 24
    2.2.1 Background of Product Concept 24
    2.2.2 Connotation of Product Concept 24
    2.2.3 Characteristics of Product Concept 24
2.3 Selling Concept 25
    2.3.1 Background of Selling Concept 25
    2.3.2 Contents of Selling Concept 25
    2.3.3 Features of Selling Concept 25
2.4 Marketing Concept 26
    2.4.1 Background of Marketing Concept 26
    2.4.2 Contents of Marketing Concept 26
    2.4.3 Four Pillars of Marketing Concept 27
2.5 Social Marketing Concept 28
    2.5.1 Background of Social Marketing Concept 28
    2.5.2 Contents of Social Marketing Concept 29
    2.5.3 Features of Social Marketing Concept 30
2.6 Mega-Marketing Concept 31

2.6.1 Rise of Mega-Marketing Concept 31
2.6.2 Connotation of Mega-Marketing Concept 32
2.6.3 Features of Mega-Marketing Concept 32
2.7 Summary 33

Part II   Market Elements

Chapter 3   Analysis of Marketplace and Marketing Environment 37

3.1 Implications and Classification of Marketplace 37
    3.1.1 Concept of Marketplace 37
    3.1.2 Division of Marketplace 38
3.2 Implications and Features of Marketing Environment 38
    3.2.1 Concept of Marketing Environment 38
    3.2.2 Contents and Features of Marketing Environment 38
3.3 Analysis of Macro-Marketing Environment 40
    3.3.1 Population Factors 41
    3.3.2 Economic Factors 42
    3.3.3 Political and Legal Factors 43
    3.3.4 Cultural Factors 43
    3.3.5 Sci-Tech Factors 44
    3.3.6 Natural Environmental Factors .. 45
3.4 Analysis of Micro-Marketing Environment 47
    3.4.1 Enterprises 47
    3.4.2 Marketing Channel Institutions 47
    3.4.3 Buyer's Market 48
    3.4.4 Competitors 48
    3.4.5 General Public 48
3.5 Summary 49

Chapter 4   Analysis of Market Behavior 51

4.1 Analysis of Competitors 51
    4.1.1 Competition Types of Marketplace 51
    4.1.2 Classification of Competitors and Their Behavior Features 52
4.2 Analysis of Consumer Market Purchasing Behavior 54
    4.2.1 Characteristics of Consumer Market Purchasing Behavior 54
    4.2.2 Factors Affecting Purchasing Behavior of Consumers 55
    4.2.3 Consumer Purchasing Behavior Mode 59
    4.2.4 Process of Consumers' Purchasing Decision-Making 60
4.3 Purchasing Behavior Analysis of Organizational Market 61
    4.3.1 Concept and Types of Organizational Market 61
    4.3.2 Analysis of Producers' Market Purchase Behavior 61
    4.3.3 Analysis of Reseller and Government Purchase 66
4.4 Summary 69

Chapter 5 Market Segmentation, Targeting and Positioning 72

5.1 Market Segmentation 72
    5.1.1 Using Market Segmentation 74
    5.1.2 Levels of Market Segmentation 75
    5.1.3 Patterns of Market Segmentation 77
    5.1.4 Market-Segmentation Procedure 78
    5.1.5 Bases for Segmenting Consumer Market 79
    5.1.6 Bases for Segmenting Business Market 81
    5.1.7 Effective Segmentation 81

5.2 Market Targeting 82
    5.2.1 Evaluating Market Segments 82
    5.2.2 Selecting and Entering Market Segments 82
    5.2.3 Targeting Multiple Segments and Super-Segments 85
    5.2.4 Ethical Choice of Market Targets... 86

5.3 Market Positioning................................. 86
    5.3.1 Choosing a Positioning Strategy 87
    5.3.2 Communicating the Company's Positioning.............. 89

5.4 Summary 90

Part III Marketing Elements

Chapter 6 Marketing Strategies 92

6.1 Generalities 92
    6.1.1 Connotation of the Marketing Strategy 92
    6.1.2 Functions of the Marketing Strategy 93
    6.1.3 Difference Between the Marketing Strategy and the Overall Strategy 94

6.2 Business Determination Adapt to the Marketing Strategy 94
    6.2.1 Grand Strategy Model 94
    6.2.2 Determination of the Business by the Grand Strategy Approach 95

6.3 Varieties of the Marketing Strategy 96
    6.3.1 Strategy Readjusting the Business 96
    6.3.2 Growth Planning Strategy 98
    6.3.3 Integration Development Strategy 100
    6.3.4 Diversification Development Strategy 101

6.4 Summary 102

Chapter 7 Marketing Competitive Strategies 108

7.1 Five Basic Competitive Forces 108
    7.1.1 Threat of New Entrants............. 109
    7.1.2 Threat of Substitute Products or Services 110
    7.1.3 Bargaining Power of Buyers 110

- 7.1.4 Bargaining Power of Suppliers 111
- 7.1.5 Competitive Rivalry Among Current Members of the Industry 111
- 7.2 Basic Competitive Strategies 113
  - 7.2.1 Overall Cost Leadership 113
  - 7.2.2 Differentiation 114
  - 7.2.3 Focus 116
- 7.3 Competitor Ranking and Marketing Competitive Strategy 117
  - 7.3.1 Market Leaders 117
  - 7.3.2 Market Challengers 120
  - 7.3.3 Market Followers 123
  - 7.3.4 Market Niches 125
- 7.4 Summary 126

Chapter 8 Marketing Engineering 132

- 8.1 Origin and Development of the Marketing Engineering 132
- 8.2 Connotation and Elements of the Marketing Engineering 133
  - 8.2.1 Theoretic Bases of Marketing Engineering 134
  - 8.2.2 Marketing Decision Models 134
  - 8.2.3 Marketing Practice and Engineering Software 137
- 8.3 Marketing Engineering Methods 139
  - 8.3.1 Cluster Analysis 139
  - 8.3.2 Factor Analysis 140
  - 8.3.3 Decision Tree Analysis 140
  - 8.3.4 Hierarchy Processing Analysis 140
  - 8.3.5 Conjoint Analysis 140
  - 8.3.6 Advertisement Budget Methods 141
- 8.4 Summary 142

Chapter 9 Marketing Investigation and Market Forecast 148

- 9.1 Marketing Information Systems 148
  - 9.1.1 Functions of Marketing Information 148
  - 9.1.2 Types of Marketing Information 149
  - 9.1.3 Marketing Information Systems 150
- 9.2 Marketing Research 152
  - 9.2.1 Contents of Marketing Research 152
  - 9.2.2 Marketing Research Process 154
- 9.3 Marketing Forecasting 157
  - 9.3.1 Types of Marketing Forecasting 157
  - 9.3.2 Marketing Forecast Steps 157
- 9.4 Summary 162

Part IV Marketing Mix

Chapter 10 Product Strategies 166

- 10.1 Generalities 166
  - 10.1.1 Term "Product" 166
  - 10.1.2 Types of Products 167
- 10.2 Product Policies 168
  - 10.2.1 Product Innovation 168
  - 10.2.2 Product Variation 170
  - 10.2.3 Product Elimination 171
- 10.3 Product Positioning 173

	10.4	Product Strategies 175
		10.4.1 Strategy: Bringing Under Control 175
		10.4.2 Strategy: Defense 175
		10.4.3 Strategy: Expansion 176
		10.4.4 Strategy: Holding 176
		10.4.5 Strategy: Exit......................... 177
	10.5	Brands 177
	10.6	Summary 177

Chapter 11   Price Strategies 182

	11.1	Factors Affecting Pricing 182
		11.1.1 Pricing Objectives 182
		11.1.2 Product Costs 183
		11.1.3 Market Demands 184
		11.1.4 Competition............................. 184
		11.1.5 Legal Aspects of Pricing Policies.................................... 185
	11.2	Elementary Pricing Methods............... 185
		11.2.1 Cost-Oriented Pricing 185
		11.2.2 Demand-Oriented Pricing 188
		11.2.3 Competition-Oriented Pricing.................................... 190
	11.3	Basic Pricing Strategy 192
		11.3.1 Pricing Policies over the Product Life Cycle 192
		11.3.2 Discount and Allowance Pricing.................................... 194
		11.3.3 Geographical Pricing.............. 196
		11.3.4 Portfolio Pricing 197
		11.3.5 Psychological Pricing............. 198
	11.4	Summary 200

Chapter 12   Place Strategies 202

	12.1	Basic Types and Features of Place..... 202
		12.1.1 Concepts of Place................... 202
		12.1.2 Basic Types of Place 202
		12.1.3 Features of Place 205
	12.2	Choice Tactics of Place...................... 206
		12.2.1 Factors Impacting the Selecting of Channel Type...... 206
		12.2.2 Choosing Place....................... 210
	12.3	Wholesalers and Retailers................... 213
		12.3.1 Retailers and Marketing Decisions............. 213
		12.3.2 Wholesalers and Marketing Decisions............. 216
	12.4	Summary 219

Chapter 13   Promotional Strategies..... 221

	13.1	Generalities 221
		13.1.1 Communication...................... 221
		13.1.2 Term "Market Communication".................... 222
	13.2	Sales Promotion 222
		13.2.1 Staff Promotion 223
		13.2.2 Merchandising........................ 223
		13.2.3 Consumer Promotion 223
	13.3	Public Relations 224
		13.3.1 Position of Public Relations Within the Marketing Mix 224
		13.3.2 Target Groups of Public Relations 224
	13.4	Advertising... 229
		13.4.1 Media Concept 230
		13.4.2 Determining the Advertising Objectives 230
		13.4.3 Advertising Strategy 232
		13.4.4 Advertising Media 234
		13.4.5 Service Enterprises of Advertising 238
	13.5	Summary 240

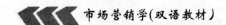

Part V Relative Marketing Issues

Chapter 14 Marketing Management ... 243
14.1 Marketing Planning ... 243
14.1.1 Generalities ... 243
14.1.2 Basic Process in Developing the Marketing Plan ... 243
14.2 Marketing Organization ... 244
14.2.1 Professional Marketing Organizations ... 244
14.2.2 Structural Marketing Organizations ... 247
14.3 Marketing Control ... 247
14.3.1 Annual-Plan Control ... 247
14.3.2 Profitability Capacity Control ... 248
14.3.3 Efficiency Control ... 249
14.4 Marketing Audit ... 250
14.4.1 Characteristics of Marketing Audit ... 250
14.4.2 Contents of Marketing Audit ... 251
14.5 Summary ... 252

Chapter 15 Other Marketing Orientations ... 255
15.1 Service Marketing ... 255
15.1.1 Contents of Service Marketing ... 255
15.1.2 Characteristics of Modern Service Marketing ... 256
15.2 Experiential Marketing ... 258
15.2.1 Connotation of Experiential Marketing ... 258
15.2.2 Features of Experiential Marketing ... 259
15.2.3 Analysis of the 6Es Mix of Experience Marketing ... 260
15.3 International Marketing ... 262
15.3.1 World Trade Triangle ... 263
15.3.2 Multinational or Global Marketing ... 263
15.3.3 Decision for International Activities ... 264
15.3.4 Framework of International Marketing ... 266
15.4 Social Marketing ... 269
15.5 Summary ... 270

参考文献 ... 274

Part I About Marketing

Chapter 1

Production and Development of Marketing

Focus on:

1. What are the connotation and features of marketing?

2. What is the main pathway on which marketing evolves?

3. Discuss the contributions to marketing by classical schools, management schools and behavior schools.

4. Analyze the concerns for marketing by commodity research approach, functional research approach, institutional research approach, management research approach and systematical research approach.

1.1 Production of Marketing

As an applied science, marketing is based both on such theories as management, psychology, and sociology and on the social practice. Its origin, development and application depend on the marketing practice of the firm and also react on it. The scholars at home and abroad have been making an extensive and deep study of the birth and growth of the marketing idea, of which the exploration of marketing by Peter Druke, a famous professor in management in the Western University of the United States is well established by many marketing experts.

Peter Druke thought that the marketing was originated in Japan during the 17th century. He also pointed out that until the mid of the 19th century, the marketing came into being in the United States, and that in the western countries, the first that regards the marketing as a distinctive function of the firm and the satisfaction of the customer's demands as the special task of management is Cyrus H. McCormick (1809-1884), the harvester inventor in the United States. Besides, Cyrus H. McCormick invested the basic tools of the modern marketing, i.e. market research and analysis, market positioning concepts, pricing policies, supplying parts and various services for customers and providing them with the payment credit by installments, etc.

Half century passed and the marketing has been studied systematically and used widely in the firms in the United States. By the end of 19th century, the scholars in the United States had started to issue and publish some theories as promotion, products, ads, pricing, product designs, brand business, package and physical distribution and so on. At the beginning of the early 20th century, "Marketing" had been up on the stage of the universities in the United States. For example, W. E. Kreusi taught a course named "The Marketing of Products" in the University of Pennsylvania in 1905; R. S. Butler in the University of Wisconsin taught "Marketing Methods" in 1910. Butler said that personnel promotion and ads must relate to the final outcome of the selling concept. In 1912, the Harvard University published the first teaching book of the marketing written by J. E. Hagertgy in the world, in which the issues about promotion, distribution, and ads, etc. were discussed comprehensively. As soon as the book was spread, a great response from the enterprise was made. Some of them established marketing departments in their organization such as Curtis Publishing Company in 1911, U. S. Rubber Company in 1916, etc.

However, the study on the marketing of this time is mostly based on the seller market which is quite different from the principles and concepts of modern marketing. Moreover, the content is narrow and limited in goods distribution and advertisement promotion, etc. So the principles, concepts and discipline systems of the modern marketing are still to be built.

From the 30s of the 20th century, marketing has been emphasized and different points and views and research approaches of various schools have been put forward successively. Then, the serious economic crisis broke out in the western world. The goods of the manufacturer couldn't be sold out, firms broke down one after another, and the unemployed increased greatly. All this led to grave problems in selling the products. So, some theoretic researchers in economy were engaged in solving these social economic problems. However, the scholars were still limited in studying the circulation field. Namely, they laid emphasis on the question how to promote the products produced in a larger scale and on the know-how of promotion, advertisements, and promoting tactics.

In this period, marketing organizations with various forms were set up one after another in the United States. In 1937, American Marketing Association (AMA) was founded, in which not only the learners who were engaged in the economic theory research but also the managers of all walks of life joined to make a conjoint study of the marketing theories and their application. At the same time, the special research class was established to teach the managers of enterprises the marketing course in order to train the promoter. In this way, the marketing was determined as a discipline. The theoretical systems of the marketing were initially constructed, too.

Chapter 1 Production and Development of Marketing

1.2 Development of Marketing

In forming and developing the marketing theories, classical schools, management schools and behavior schools, etc. were born gradually. Different schools have established their own views, features and specialties because of the research method, interests, importance, and the individual background. They have been accelerating the development and progress of the marketing theory jointly, promoting the set-up and improvement of the marketing system as a discipline. They have contributed much in establishing and upgrading the marketing.

1.2.1 Classical Schools

In the period of the founding of marketing theories the classical schools formed, namely the commodity school, the functional school, the regional school, the institutional school and so on. The classical schools played a historical role in establishing and developing the marketing. Although lots of new schools are coming up, the classical schools still remain well known in the academic field.

1. Commodity School

Among these schools, the commodity school enjoys a long history. It started at the entrance of the 20th century. Its basic principle is that since the marketing concerns the flow of the relative goods from producers to consumers, the marketing discipline should focus on the object (product) transaction. As the scholars of the early commodity school said, that if the products in the marketing exchange could be classified in a reasonable way, the marketing discipline would make more progress in science. So they pointed out that in a perfect classified system of merchandizes, each product was not isolated and sophisticated links existed among goods. Therefore, these goods can be arranged into the category with the relative homogeneity in which all the products can be marketed in the same methods and know-how. As for the commodity school, it is an important task to classify the merchandizes.

In the early stage of the commodity school, Charles Parlin first put forward the merchandize classification framework in 1912. According to his theory, women merchandizes can be divided into three categories: convenient goods, urgent goods and option goods. The convenient goods are those daily bought as food, groceries, etc. The urgent goods include medicines and those needed unexpectedly. The option goods refer to those that need to make a selection and that allow to be postponed buying.

In 1923, another famous classification of the merchandize was proposed by M. Cope. He classified the merchandize into convenience, option and peculiarity. The convenience can be found in the convenient shop and familiar to the customer; the option is the goods that the consumer always makes a careful comparison of price, quality and patterns of the product before buying decisions. After the birth of demands, the real buying behavior is often delayed and their satisfaction is less important than that of the convenience; the peculiarity is more attractive in distinctiveness than in price to consumers. The consumer pays more attention to the producer's and the retailer's brand or credit and service quality than the other elements in buying.

In 1958, L.V. Aspinwall, a famous scholar of the commodity school proposed a method of classifying the goods. He divided the goods into the red, the orange and the yellow and also ordered them in the light of the total relative value of the product features. These features were introduced as follows:

(1) turnover rate. The proportion that the customers choose and use a certain product is made to satisfy their needs.

(2) aggregate profits. The final difference is realized between the price and the cost.

(3) flexibility. The services are added to the product for the sake of better satisfying the consumer's needs.

(4) consuming time. It refers to the period needed in using the product.

(5) selection time. It means the average distance measured to the retailing shop. In the end, L.V. Aspinwall listed a system of classifying the product called "The Characteristics of Goods Theory" by him.

The early commodity school believed that the classification approach can overcome the difficulties faced by most marketing practices and in operation the following steps as classifying various products into the set system and then deploying the correspondent activities in light of their marketing standards of the kind could solve the problem.

In the late 50s to early 60s of the 20th century, considering the deficiencies of classifying the goods of the early commodity school, some scholars put forward that the method that the goods were defined as convenience, option and particulars should be modified and increased the preference on the existing classification.

These scholars thought that the differentiation between the convenience and the option should emphasize the role of consumers, for some products are the option for certain consumers but the convenience for other consumers. Only in the angle of the individual consumer can we precisely define the convenience and the option. With the ongoing development of the marketing and the introduction of the new concepts of other subjects, the marketing scholars kept on presenting the disputes and challenges to the existing classification framework. The commodity

Chapter 1 Production and Development of Marketing

school redefined the convenience, the option and the peculiarity.

The convenience refers to the product that the consumer little intervenes because of low prices, being easily damaged or the buying activities of no importance to him. Besides, the consumer often accepts the substituent for the functionality. The option means those that the consumer concerns much before buying and is afraid that the goods bought are unsuitable for him. These concerns can be eased by way of information collection and buying decisions afterwards. The peculiarities are those that can be sorted out into the option both in the economic importance and in the distinction of the product features, but their physical features have few relations with the performance nature sought by the consumer.

In the 70s of the 20th century, three principles were put forward as independent theoretic bases by the commodity school to make the classification system perfect. First, products should be regarded as a combination of the physical elements and the psychological reaction. Second, products should be defined through the consumer's behavior and the channel reaction and the correspondent measurements could be made between the delivery and the retailing time. Third, there exist links between the product communication structure and the buying behavior. On the basis of the principles, the commodity school added the 4th category of products to the existent categories: the preference goods.

In 1986, in order to apply their classification systems to the transaction, product selling, service, and ideas, the scholars of the commodity school further expounded the convenience, the option, the peculiarity, and the preference with the help of the buying efforts and risk norms related to the price. The detailed definition was presented as follows:

(1) The convenience is the lowest both in the buying efforts and in the risks. That's to say, the consumer is unwilling to spend too much time and money on these goods and no higher risks are felt in the decision-making.

(2) The preference has more buying efforts and risks than the convenience. In fact, the difference between the convenience and the preference lies in the perceptible risks. The reason that makes the consumer feel high risks usually comes from the marketing activities, especially from the brand and the ads.

(3) The option is the goods that the consumer is willing to spend more time and money in seeking for and evaluating. This high participation also makes the consumer perceive higher and higher risks.

(4) The peculiarity is very high in risks and efforts. The difference between the option and the peculiarity lies in the buying efforts, not in risks. The peculiarity is often priced high and needs much time to be bought. However, the buyer is not willing to accept any substituent for the peculiarity.

The scholars of the commodity school emphasized that the classification system of any products has the same target: to guide the decision of the managers. Although the commodity school has made a detailed study of various kinds of products and their classification and played an important role in the marketing advancement and practices, it lacks a further exploration of the marketing environment, the motivation of the consumer behavior and the specific needs of the different goods to the marketing.

2. Functional School

This school regards the marketing behavior as its focus. Being different from the commodity school, the functional school focuses on the "how to do" in the marketing while the commodity school on the "what the marketing is".

Arch Shaw was considered as the founder of the functional school. He first proposed the classification method in accordance with the marketing functions: (1) risk-taken; (2) goods delivery; (3) financing; (4) sales efforts; (5) making a centralization, arrangement and trans-shipping of the product.

In 1950, Edmund Mercalli improved his own classification framework based on the former categories, which consists of the following six functions:

(1) Communication functions. Seek for the latent consumer or supplier and making a connection with him.

(2) Merchandising functions. Take all kinds of activities relative to the production and to the satisfaction of the customer's needs.

(3) Pricing functions. Deal with the price issues as product supplying or acceptability.

(4) Publicity functions. Persuade the latent customer into buying some product and try to retain him.

(5) Logistic functions. Transport and stock the product.

(6) Terminal functions. Respond to the change of the management and responsibility of the product.

In 1960, McCarthy advanced the 4Ps theory, i.e. Product, Price, Place and Promotion, which was originated from the classification system of the early functional school as Weld, Leyen, especially Mercalli.

The functional school has assimilated the classification approach of the commodity school and mainly studied the marketing activities in the angle of the marketing functions, of which the classification outcomes of Mercalli are well established. They include such functions as communication, exchange, pricing, publicity, logistics and terminal, on the base of which Mercalli initially proposed the typical theory of 4Ps.

3. Regional School

The scholars of the regional school concern more the space role between the transaction parties on the base of accepting the research outcomes of the commodity and the functional schools. It was produced in the 1930s.

The commodity school and the functional school came into being in the 1920s. Until the 1930s, the regional school was born and its development was due to William J. Reilly, who tried to explain the relative attractiveness of the commercial areas in two different cities to the citizens living there in his book entitled "The Law of Retail Gravitation" in 1931 with the mathematical formula. Enlightened by him, P. D. Converse put forward the "New Laws of Retail Gravitation" in 1949 that was used to judge the limitation between the trade center and the trade area. As soon as the trade area was determined in the town, the merchants could decide where they should make their transaction activities and their advertisement. On the basis of the existent study, Hoover advanced a forecasting sales model, which showed more rationality in the analysis of the retail transaction.

Soon afterwards, some scholars of the regional school diverted their attention from the retail to the wholesale and made an analysis of the regional variable about the effects of the space distance on the sales organization. The regional structure was much connected with the wholesale system. The regional variable affecting the structure was first the space distance between the supplying place of the basic materials and the firm using them, in which the transportation system emphasized the initial influence. Then the next variable was the space distribution pattern of the intermediary wholesaler. The distribution of the retailer and the final consumers played a revised role in the above effects. To further establish the theory of the regional wholesales structure, they raised eight factors influencing the wholesales market scale: (1) product weights relative to the value; (2) easily corrosive; (3) technique of the product differentiation; (4) elements affecting the factory location; (5) price and its strategy; (6) efficiency and services of transport; (7) marketing means of the individual firm; (8) additional services.

Besides, the regional school made an analysis of the geographical variable on the ratio between the wholesales and the retails by using the statistical research data of the United States The scholars of the regional school thought that the business' behaviors such as the geographical location, the space expansion in selling and buying, and the relations among the supply and the demand in the marketing channel, should be considered not only from the price and sales, but also from the natural and social conditions. Recently, the regional school is focusing on the study of the mathematical model in the field of trade, for example, the models in assessing the coincidence of the boundaries between the two markets and the location selection of the retailing shops, etc.

The status, quantity and positions of the competitors among regions are often different, and the demands either of the final consumer, of intermediaries or of governments are various, too. In this way, the regional school bases its study on regional markets to explore the marketing issues such as regional competition and demands and the related strategies.

4. Institutional School

The institutional school was born at the beginning of the 20th century and dominated the same position as the commodity school and the functional school. However, the institutional school laid its more emphasis on the research of the marketing organization.

L. D. H. Weld was regarded as the founder of the institutional school and he raised an issue on the marketing channel efficiency in the book "The Marketing of Farm Products" published in 1916. In 1923, Ralph Starr Butter, manager of the Publicity Development in the U. S. Rubber Company published a book called "Marketing and Merchandising" which contributed much to the early development of the structure school. He laid emphasis on the effectiveness of the intermediary to the producer and the consumer. He thought that an important role of the intermediary was to create effectiveness, namely, the basic effectiveness, the form effectiveness, the place effectiveness and the time effectiveness. The market organization could do nothing to the basic and the form effectiveness, but played an important role in the place and the time effectiveness. That's to say, the intermediary could create them and bring the goods from the production place to the consuming area and sell the product to the consumer when it was needed. In this period, many scholars joined in the Institutional School and aired their own opinions. Ralph Frederick Breyer in the University of Pennsylvania explained the process forming the marketing structure in his book "The Marketing Institutions". He proposed that it was necessary to construct huge and complicated commercial mechanisms so as to achieve the marketing activities. We had found that the marketing function had something to do with the overcoming the difficulties of merchandize exchange, which needed us to spend much time and work in combining such elements as land, labor forces, capitals and other sources and in reasonably allocating and coordinating them in the light of quality and quantity in order to set up a work organ, of which all the parts should be considered commercially and linked to the marketing.

Some scholars of this school also made a study of the vertical integration. They thought that the firm could play more roles in production and distribution, which both reduced the marketing cost and insured the output of the finished products and the supplying of the raw materials. The reduction of the marketing cost could be realized through cutting down the process of continuous buying and selling due to the vertical integration in the firm's operation. The integration is an

Chapter 1   Production and Development of Marketing

effective approach to reduce the marketing cost, but causes grave problems in management and coordination.

From 1954 to 1973, the institutional school began to analyze the production of the marketing channel, the evolution of the channel structure and the design of the framework with high efficiency by way of the principles of economics.

During this period, F. C. Bauldston attempted to explain how to design marketing channels that could make the marketer obtain more profitability. He had explored an approach how an individual firm designed its channel. He believed that the individual firm faced channel-designing problems in some aspects and not in the whole marketing systems. Besides, the Institutional School had done some research in the integration theory that said the central channel coordinating system included three categories, i.e. the firm's marketing system, the management strategy and contracts. The firm's marketing system was a successive stage of production and distribution under the single property while the management strategy was able to co-operate the flow of goods and services so as to get the systematic thriftiness. The contracts could influence the channel, too.

In 1965 and 1973, some theories explained and foresaw the channel structure, and pointed out the deficiencies of the institutional school said. Besides, they made a deep study of the connotation about the deferring and speculation.

If the distribution channel was regarded as postponement, it was a tool for an independent organization to transfer the risks of all goods to another independent one. For manufacturers, he would refuse production unless he received no orders and then the correspondent risks were passed to the buyer; as for the intermediary, two kinds of postponement existed: one was called backward postponement, i.e. refusing to buy and the other was forward postponement, i.e. buying when he was sure to be able to sell out; the consumer realized the postponement by buying in the retailer.

The speculation theory meant that all the changes of the physical forms of goods or the move of the product in the inventory should be done in the marketing process as early as possible in order to reduce the cost of the marketing system.

In light of the deferring and speculation theories, the production of the inventory stage can be explained as follows: as for buyers and sellers, only if the net revenue surpasses the additional cost in the period of retardation, the inventory will be sure to happen.

1.2.2   Management Schools

Management schools came out from the 1940s to 1950s, and included the management school, the systematic school, the social exchange school, etc. They were lying in the transition period when the western countries were transformed from the seller market to the buyer market. In the new situation of the buyer market, the decision-makers of firms must think it over how to cater to the buyer's needs in the marketing. That's to say, they must learn how to face the market, adapt to the market and expand the market.

1. Management School

Since the end of the 1950s, as the buyer market was becoming bigger and bigger, the marketing research has been further extended so as to meet the needs of the marketing practice. Such concepts as "marketing myopia", "marketing mix", and "market segmentation", etc. were fabricated. These concepts laid their emphasis on consumers in the marketing research, which played an important role in the marketing theory and practice. From then on, the marketing management thoughts have begun to be grown up.

Initially, the management school advanced the marketing concept, which explained that seeking for the production efficiency alone was possibly myopic. The marketer should pay more attention to the consumer's wants and demands before making the production decision. If it wants to win in the changing competitive market, the firm must take the competitive role and efficiency into consideration correctly before the use of the marketing activities and understand all sorts of knowledge about consumers. Managerially, the primary task of the marketing would rather make the commercial behavior suitable for the consumer's benefits than master the know-how to let the consumer behave as the commercial benefits.

Besides, the management school has proposed many theories and views that are still being used substantially in the nowadays marketing textbooks.

Considering the different aims of the consumer buying behavior, the management school insisted for the first time in 1956 that marketers should segment the market and strive to establish various marketing combinations so as to satisfy the different demands of the consumer.

In light of the market segmentation theory, to better satisfy the consumer's demands, the market should be divided into some small homogeneous niches among which the differentiation exists. The main contribution of this school lies in: telling the market segmentation from the product differentiation; the application of the market segmentation in the industrial market; the quantitative analysis of the market segmentation. Besides, the scholars of this school had put forward the principles of how the marketing manager should deal with various elements as products, price, place and promotion in the marketing combination.

In the product decision, the most important achievement is the introduction of the product life cycle. Its application is embodied in the following: in one hand, its systematic framework like

Chapter 1   Production and Development of Marketing

production, development, maturation and decline can be used to explain the market impetus; on the other hand, it can be applied as a forecasting model to interpret when changes happen and when the take-over from one stage to another comes.

In pricing, the school strives to change the economic theory into the normalized rules so that the marketing management can easily make practices. The management school advocates that marketers can adopt the multi-stage analyzing method as pricing tools. This method divides the main factors to be considered in the pricing decision into six successive steps: (1) choose the target market; (2) select the brand image; (3) determine the marketing combination; (4) formulate the pricing policies; (5) establish the pricing strategy; (6) decide the price. The calculation in each step should simplify the work of the next step and reduce the possibility of the error in the pricing decision according to the above-said steps. In other words, this method translates the pricing decision into several parts of the management and logically, each part comes before the next part of which the decision can make the following less complicated.

In the field of promotion, the scholars of the management school advanced some suggestions on the personnel promotion and the advertisement decision. They insisted that the ads should aim at making the consumer buy the product through a series of marketing activities and that the seller should abandon the deceitful tactics and change the view that explores the market in the compelling personal promoting approach. Recently, they have laid more emphasis on the management of the personal promotion and of the selling field. The issues studied by them include the communication between promoters and consumers, the selling effects, the supervision to the selling forces, and the motive of the promoter, etc.

2. Systematic School

In the 1960s, the systematic school came into being. As the other schools of the marketing, the systematic school appeared with the market environment changing. In the meanwhile, its birth was due to the development of the other disciplines in studying technology, which advanced the scholars to explore the marketing and its activities in the angle of the systematic theory. Particularly, the extensive use of computers makes the word "systematic" more popular in the management literature.

The systematic school holds that a firm should be considered as an integrated system of different functions. In the system, the strength produced in the information, raw materials, human resources, capital, equipments and the flow of funds decides the basic trend of the growth, fluctuations and decline of the firm. The school also points out that production, marketing and consumption should be combined together and analyzed by way of the systematic framework. The marketing issue belongs to the systematic scope that is featured of communication and adaptation in the social organization. The decision maker can spot a series of problems when inspecting the market in the systematic theory and the correspondent feasible solutions are available, which are the reference when he encounters handicaps in solving the relative problems.

The systematic school has explored the systematic theory on the marketing and raised three types of systems: the atomic system, the mechanic system and the biological system. In the atomic system, no single element can influence the whole system and all the elements inter-move and inter-act. Some aspects of the marketing function as the mechanic system acts, such as inventories and distributions. Biology concerns the study of the organic body related to the natural environment and the organized behavior system is the reflection of the biology in the marketing.

The systematic school has made a classification and organization of the marketing thoughts in the micro-analysis method. This method emphasizes some tiny structure as ads and distribution of the sub-system while the macro-analysis method focuses on the systematic behavior of the overall system. Different from the micro-analysis method, the macro-analysis method pays more attention to the behavior patterns under the different conditions though it doesn't ignore completely the particular marketing phenomenon.

1.2.3 Behavior Schools

Behavior schools composed of the organizational power school, the consumerism school and the buyer behavior school. They paid more attention to the effects of the organizational activities, the individual behavior and the social actions on the marketing and tended to study the issues in a way of multi-disciplines combining the psychology, sociology, and organizational behavior science. The views put forward by them have contributed much in raising the consumer's satisfaction, safeguarding the consumer's rights and valuing the marketing in the social economical development.

1. Organizational Power School

The organizational power school is relatively new in the marketing and starts in the 1950s and has grown up in the 1970s and 1980s. In some degree, the organizational power school is the successor of the structural school. The main difference between these two schools is that of the different angle to study the issue. The structural school analyzes the effectiveness of the distribution channel in the angle of economy so as to increase the welfare for the consumer while the organizational power school diverts its concerns from the consumer's welfare to the target and demands of the distribution member as manufacturers, wholesalers and retailers. In the

Chapter 1   Production and Development of Marketing

article "Management of the Manufacturer-Distributor System", the organizational power school pointed out that manufacturers and distributors form a competitive system that needs management like a single system. The book "Distribution Channels: Behavior Perspective" published in 1969 makes it come to the front stage in the marketing. Its primary topics being discussed include the following:

(1) What is the source of the rights? These rights include coercion and non-coercion.

(2) How should the members of the distribution channel use the obtained rights? Correspondently, how should the marketing manager use his rights?

(3) Measurement methods of the rights. Some scholars are engaged in developing correct and reliable methods to measure the rights and consider that the rights have direct relations with the roles.

(4) What are relations between rights and conflicts?

(5) How should the conflicts be measured? They have analyzed the efficacy of the method measuring the conflicts.

(6) What is the cooperation in the inner organization system? They think that the cooperation refers to a joint action of two or more conductors in the hope that they exchange the resources with equilibrium to realize the targets inside and among the organization.

(7) How does the right influence the bargaining process?

2. Consumerism School

The consumerism school focused its importance on studying the consumer welfare and satisfaction in experience and concepts. For example, it mainly probed the problems as imbalance between buyers and sellers, malpractices of private enterprises in the marketing. Another issue it concerned is the morality in the marketing.

The consumerism school has made a study of the following topics: the product security and the consumer information; the discriminatory issue of the consumer; the satisfaction and dissatisfaction of the consumer.

Some scholars attempted to form the concept of the consumerism school, of which the consumer protectionism was included. Therefore, Peter Druke thought that the consumer regarded the manufacturer as the entity that was interested in the consumer and didn't really understand him. It is impossible to differentiate the consumers if the manufacturer has not made a deep research of them.

In this school, the most persuasive idea is proposed by Philip Kotler. He considered that the marketing concept on the customer-oriented idea could better cater to the commercial activities to realize the profit of the customer and that the marketing responsibility was to innovate new products that could both satisfy the recent demand of the consumer and upheld the long-term interests of him. So Kotler presented a case on the basis of the recent satisfaction and the long-term interests to differentiate the existent products (see Table 1.1).

Table 1.1 Product Classifications by Kotler

Short-term satisfaction Long-term interests	High	Low
High	Ideal products	Profitable products
Low	Pleasant products	Flaw products

Besides, the scholars of this school had expounded the nature and role of the marketing ethics, especially the ethical issues in advertisement, personal promotion, pricing, marketing research and international marketing. Overall, the school has turned to the tenet how the marketing encourages the ethical behavior by way of ethical training, orientation, management principles and encouragement in the marketing organization instead of pure criticism to the abnormal marketing activities.

3. Buyer Behavior School

The buyer behavior school is mainly engaged in the research of target customers, customer sizes, customer's buying incentives, and so on. In their study, the scholars inquires into the buyer's buying behavior with the aid of methodology of the behavior science, of experimental methods of the applied science, those related to physiology and psychology, and of mathematics, operational research and managerial technology as stochastic process, control on line and optimization, etc. The buyer behavior school has opened up research methodology of modern marketing and made it more matured, more serious and more scientific.

The buyer behavior school emphasizes the customer in the market and has made a study of such issues as who the customer is, how many exist and why the customer buys, etc. This school has the following characteristics:

(1) The consumer behavior is considered as part of the human behavior, and not as the unnatural and abnormal behavior phenomenon. This school tends to understanding and explaining the consumer behavior based on the human behavior and then many theories about the consumer behavior are born. Every theory is built on certain views of psychology, sociology and anthropology, and has raised various explanations to the consumer behavior patterns.

(2) The buyer behavior school has been focusing the package product and the durable consumption goods and is becoming more and more interested in the study of the buying behavior of the industrial and service industries.

Chapter 1 Production and Development of Marketing

(3) This school defines its research field as the choice of brands and not as the others, and thinks that its study aims at the buying behavior and not at the consuming or distributing behavior.

1.3 Connotation and Nature of Marketing

1.3.1 Connotation of Marketing

Marketing is a science to study the marketing activities and their rules of the firm. It absorbs both the principles and techniques of western economy, economical management and econometrics and the theories and methods of sociology, philosophy, politics, behavior psychology and mathematics, etc. In some aspects, it is an integrated and comprehensive applied economy.

1.3.2 Nature of Marketing

Marketing, as a discipline, has its own development tracks and regularity. Its primary features are defined as following:

1. Applicability

Marketing studies not only the basic theory of the market, but also the marketing activities and their rules of the firm. Its purpose is to guide the market operation effectively. Therefore, as a product of the development of the commodity economy to cater to the demands of modern enterprises, the marketing has been highly emphasized and widely used for the decision and practices of the firm's operation.

2. Comprehensiveness

Modern marketing was initially set up on the theory of economy and further developed into a brand-new science with the absorption and use of the theories and approaches of modern management, behavior science, mathematics, psychology, sociology, biology, package, trademark, and advertisement, etc. As Philip Kotler pointed out that marketing was an applied science based on economy, behavior science, and modern management theory. He also said that economy was the father of marketing; its mother was behavior science; mathematics was the grandfather of it; philosophy, grandmother of it.

3. Practicality

The theory and the contents of the marketing are originated in the marketing experience of the firm and the correspondent study is for the purpose of instructing the marketing practices. With the marketing practices deepened, modern marketing as a science will see a continuous advancement, too.

4. Artistry

The theoretic systems and approaches of modern marketing are easy to be understood and practicable. However, this doesn't mean that learning some theories and approaches can easily solve the marketing problems, for the linkage between theory and practice is the key to the solution. So we should learn the marketing theory as an art and flexibly use it in the marketing practice.

1.4 Research Approaches of Marketing

Marketing aims at probing the external environments of firms, the consumer behavior and the influence of them on the marketing activities, and the regularity of the whole marketing process in firms. Moreover, the research approaches keep on changing with the reform of the research object and the richness of the research content in the development of the marketing.

1.4.1 Commodity Research Approach

The commodity research approach is also called the product research approach. Its objects are usually some kinds of products and it mainly analyzes the marketing issues. The scholars are always interested in the study of the marketing of certain products, especially that of the non-farming product and the industrial finished outcome. For example, W. E. Krueusi wrote a book "The Marketing of Products" by using the product research approach (in 1905), in which he had demonstrated the marketing theory with the aid of many cases. Considering that people paid less attention to the marketing of non-farming products, he designed an analysis pattern applied for the marketing of oil, minerals, steel rolling, voyage car and telephone services and so on, and made a deep study of their supply and demand conditions, product features, places, agencies, pricing, distribution costs and trade management, etc.

Chapter 1 Production and Development of Marketing

1.4.2 Functional Research Approach

In 1940, R. Alexander, Sarfare, Ilder and W. Alderson expounded in the book "Marketing" that marketing was a management function. Being Different from the product research approach, they more concern marketing plans, investigation and budget controls and generalize some management functions included in the traditional marketing as merchandized functions, namely, all sorts of activities that regulate commodity production or selling so as to satisfy the consumer demands. They thought that three categories of the marketing function exist: exchange function like buying and selling; supply function like transport and stock; service function like financing, risk taking, and market information, etc.

1.4.3 Institutional Research Approach

The institutional research approach highlights the marketing activities of the various organizations and of all levels like producers, agents, wholesalers, and retailers, etc. in the marketing channel. Its drawbacks mainly lie in the fact that it neglects the consumer demands and still centers around the goods.

1.4.4 Managerial Research Approach

The managerial research approach takes the firm as its main body and synthesizes the elementary demands of the commodity research approach, the institutional research approach and the functional research approach in the angle of marketing management decisions, analyzes the market environment in the light of the target market, and formulates the concerned marketing strategy in accordance with the firm's resources and aims in order to satisfy the needs of the target market and to reach the firm's aim.

1.4.5 Systematic Research Approach

The systematic research approach was first proposed in the book entitled "Basic Marketing: Systematic Approach" (1971) written by George S. Downing. Marketing is a total framework of such activities as pricing, promotion, distribution, which can provide the current and latent customers with products and services through all kinds of channels. In the process of marketing, the firm keeps on observing the market, spotting and evaluating various change agents, then, makes a feedback to the managerial level for the sake of elaborating the new strategy and plans of the firm, does away with the handicaps that hinder the realization of the aim by means of the revised action and assesses the response of the customer and of the competitor to the revision, and further formulates the revised strategic plans. So marketing is one function no more, but a process going through the firm's operation and management.

1.5 Summary

现代的市场营销学不是简单的产品推销和广告，而是为了实现组织和个人的目标所进行的关于构思、货物和劳务的观念、定价、促销分销的策划与实施等一系列与市场有关的活动。现代营销学研究内容主要包括6个方面：市场、顾客、产品、价格、商品流通过程以及促销。

在市场营销学的发展过程中产生了很多学派，但归纳起来看，有古典学派、管理学派和行为学派等，各个学派从不同角度展开了对市场营销相关方面的研究，对市场营销理论的发展与市场营销实践发挥了不可磨灭的作用。

市场营销研究方法从商品研究法、功能研究法、机构研究法、管理研究法到系统研究法，由浅入深、由对营销某一方面进行研究到整个营销系统研究，充分显示了市场营销这一科学领域发展的复杂性与广泛性，学者们对市场营销方法的研究为进一步研究市场营销活动提供了基本的研究框架。

Key Terms

Marketing   Buyer Behavior School   Consumerism School   Organizational Power School   Systematic School   Management School   Institutional School   Regional School   Functional School   Commodity School

【案例】 日本企业的成功

许多获得成功的日本企业，都花费许多时间、精力和资金去分析市场机遇，并对目标市场作深入的了解，研究消费者心理，摸清组织市场营销的活动规律。

例如，索尼公司在进入美国市场之前，就先派出设计人员、工程师以及其他人员组成专家组去美国考察，研究如何设计产品以适应美国消费者的爱好。然后招聘美国工业专家、顾问和经理等人员，帮助索尼分析如何进入市场。

在仔细地研究分析市场机遇，确定目标市场后，日本企业会着手制定以产品、价格、分销、促销、公共关系和政治权力运用等内容的市场营销战略规划。

Chapter 1　Production and Development of Marketing

一、产品策略

日本企业最初进入国际市场时,遇到了许多困难,首当其冲的是来自美国和欧洲国家的强大竞争者的对抗,因为那时世界市场主要由美国和欧洲国家霸占。其次,就当时的日本产品而论,无论是技术上,还是全球性销售网络上,都比不上美国和欧洲的产品。此外,日本还要努力消除人们在二战前所形成的日本产品质量低劣的印象。但是,日本企业寄希望于利用其劳动力便宜的优势,在产品的价格上可以与欧美抗衡。为此,在20世纪50年代后期和60年代期间,为了打入世界市场,日本各企业特别强调产品设计的低成本、高质量和创新性。从目前日本进入国际市场的情况看,也可以证明他们仍然着重突出这三点。

日本企业以产品开发战略和市场开发战略为重点,进行目标市场渗透,一旦在某国市场取得了立足点,就努力扩大其产品的生产线,以便增加产量,扩大销售额,逐步增加对整个市场的控制范围。以丰田公司向美国市场渗透为例,即表现为产品推出的连续性和不断扩大生产线。

日本的许多企业,一向以增加产品的花色品种的方式进行市场开发。他们根据消费者的不同口味、爱好和收入水平,不断地变换产品型号、花色和品种。例如,坝农公司以AE-135单镜反光照相机为基础机型,生产出种类繁多、特点功能不同的相机,使其销售额猛增。坝农公司这种向市场纵深不断猛烈推进的策略,是日本许多企业的共同特点。每当一种新产品投入市场,就会有另一种新产品进入研发。此外,日本各企业的产品更新换代非常快,其速度几乎是德国(德国是产品更新换代比较快的国家之一)的两倍。如20世纪70年代期间,丰田汽车公司可以同时向美国汽车市场提供82种产品,而其他国家则只能提供48种或31种型号的汽车。

不断地改进产品质量,是日本企业获得成功的又一大特征。日本企业对不断改进产品的质量倾注了大量的心血,他们经常与消费者保持联系,甚至不惜花费大量的钱财和许多宝贵的时间,通过各种渠道,不断地了解和虚心听取顾客关于改进产品质量的意见。把质量当作企业的生命,已成为日本企业全体员工的群体意识。一项研究表明,日本产品质量已胜过美国产品。20世纪70年代中期,美国执世界计算机工业之牛耳时,日本尚属无名之辈。但近几年,日本却成为美国在计算机工业发展上的主要威胁者。

二、价格策略

日本企业在进入国际市场时,一直采用一种所谓的"市场份额"价格策略。这种策略就是采用较低的进入市场价格,以便取得一部分市场并进一步达到长期控制该市场。为此,日本总是将价格定得比竞争者低。他们乐于在最初几年里受点损失,把这种损失视为对长远市场发展的一种投资。这样做使日本在过去几年中被指责为进行"产品倾销",此情形在美国的小汽车等产品市场上表现得尤为明显。日本的小汽车以省油、低价等优点大量涌进美国市场,1990年已占美国小汽车市场约30%,使美国的汽车工业招架不住。最后,美日双方都以官方身份进入"对抗阶段",对簿公堂,美国做出了对小汽车限量进口的决定。

三、分销策略

日本企业想打进美国市场，但当初日本的产品质量形象低劣，声誉不佳。而且，许多企业没有产品销售渠道。何况，即使了解美国的销售渠道，也不能公开地加以利用。为此，日本企业采取了以下几种措施。

(1) 集中全力选好进入市场的突破口。他们不是采取全线出击，一下子占领全部市场，而是选中该市场的某一地区、某个批发商或某种类型的消费者，先打进去，站稳脚跟后再逐步扩大。如丰田汽车公司首先选择了加州，通过该地区了解美国市场的特点、消费者爱好以及与美国批发商和经销商打交道的经验。在突破口取得成功，尔后全面进入美国市场。日本电视机进入中国市场的步骤则是先找经销商销售12寸、16寸黑白电视机，尔后销售彩色电视机，最后在中国合资建厂。

(2) 精心挑选有效的销售渠道和能干的批发商。

(3) 对某种特殊产品，直接与用户联系，建立独立的销售机构。

(4) 利用竞争者的销售网络进行销售，即在打入某国市场后，利用该国中间商或生产者的牌号或商标销售日本产品。当其产品打入市场并占有一定地位时，就逐步建立自己的产品品牌形象，形成自己的销售渠道，最后取而代之。

四、销售策略

日本企业在进入某个市场时，十分注意与批发商的友好合作，向他们提供各种帮助，付给较优厚的酬金，激发中间商经营日本产品的积极性。日本企业坚持"经销商利益第一，本企业利益第二"的原则，始终与中间商保持友好商务关系。日本企业还大量投入金钱和精力，开展广告宣传，推进和提高产品的市场声誉，扩大销售额。

五、公共关系策略

日本企业的公共关系开展得颇具风格，有力地扩大了企业的知名度。例如，日本汽车公司在进入美国市场后，所有的公司都积极地致力于美国的社会服务，抽出人力、物力和资金，从事那些看起来和本职工作毫不相干的社会服务工作，并与当地社区建立了亲密关系。日本汽车公司在田纳西州自建立工厂的那一天起，便成立了义务活动小组和研究西方问题的捐款委员会，经常向当地的慈善机构捐赠钱物，还组织当地的居民到工厂参观和组织当地中学生每学期到工厂体验一天的工厂生活等。这许许多多的活动和亲善态度颇得当地社区居民的好感。这也是日本企业打入美国市场的竞争策略的重要因素。美惊呼日汽车商竞争有方，而美国的汽车公司却对此无能为力！

六、政治权力策略

历史记录表明，日本的企业在打进美国市场初期，很少与美国的公司进行正面冲突，而是寻找薄弱环节，甚至从美国公司尚未到达的市场先行突破，求得一席之地。然后，他们就像"滚雪球"一样，进行战略推进，建立他们的产品基地和巩固市场阵地，以便在将来某时与美国竞争者进行正面对抗或直接竞争。随着正面进攻"猛烈战斗"的日益加剧，必然遭到美国公司的强烈反击，于是就产生了"贸易摩擦"。日本企业或是周旋于当地社团、政府，或是吸引大量本来属于美国企业的零售网及小企业，或是改善工厂中美国员工的待遇等。采用各种方式和途径，以减弱美国竞争者的反击力量，减少乃至消除摩擦。有时也通过种种骚扰，使对手士气低落，以便最后迫使对手做出让步。当"贸易摩擦"激烈到企业无法运用自己的力量来消除时，最后只有通过政府的外交手段来解决。近两年来，日美进行的"东京回合"谈判就是一个有力的佐证。

(资料来源：宋小敏等. 市场营销案例实例与评析. 武汉：武汉工业大学出版社, 1992.)

【案例分析】

许多日本企业之所以能获得成功，主要得益于他们花费大量时间、精力和资金去分析市场机遇，并对目标市场进行深入了解，研究消费者心理，掌握了组织市场营销活动的规律。在仔细研究分析市场机遇并确定目标市场后，日本的企业会根据目标市场特点制定能适应目标市场需求的以产品、价格、分销、促销、公共关系和政治权力运用等为内容的市场营销战略规划。

【思考题】

1. 日本企业产品策略的主要特点是什么？
2. 日本企业公共关系策略的特点是什么？
3. 结合该案例及本章所学内容，谈谈中国企业进入世界市场应注意的问题及其对策。

Chapter 2

Marketing Philosophy

Focus on:

1. Evolution and background of the marketing philosophy.
2. Difference between the marketing concept and the promotion concept.
3. Discuss the statement: the establishment of the marketing concept is a radical reform of the marketing idea.
4. Discuss the roles of the marketing concept to the firms in China.

Marketing concept refers to the guidelines and standards of conduct based on marketing activities of enterprises organized and planned by the business operators. Marketing concept is the attitudes and perceptions of the business operators to the activities of market, but also the business concept and the method of thinking.

The formation of the marketing concept is not people's subjective imagination, but is gradually formed and developed with the development of social production and the changes of supply and demand conditions in the market. The certain marketing philosophy is a production of certain socio-economic development, which comes from business practice and develops from the practice. Looking at the history of the world commodity economy development, the evolution of the marketing concept has experienced generally six stages, which include production concept, product concept, selling concept, marketing concept, social marketing concept and mega-marketing concept.

2.1 Production Concept

2.1.1 Background of Production Concept

The production concept stemmed from the late 19th century to 1920s. In this stage, the capitalist production was still at a relatively low level because of the shortage of materials after experiencing the World War II, and their products could not fully meet the market demand. In the

Chapter 2 Marketing Philosophy

seller's market conditions, the market demand can only passively submit to the production. What the consumers care about is whether they can buy goods, the price is cheap or not and the main features of products without paying attention to some small differences of products. Therefore enterprises will be able to profit from a large number of production and sales by delivering a single line of products in the market.

2.1.2 Meaning of Production Concept

Production concept is a marketing concept which centers on the production, and focuses on improving efficiency, increasing productivity, lowering costs (see Figure 2.1). Under the environment of undeveloped commodity economy and the product in short supply, the operators tend to guide corporate marketing activities with production ideas. The main task of enterprise management is to improve the production technology, labor organizations, labor productivity, reduce costs and increase sales.

Production concept is supported by the marketers who think that the market needs our products, consumers like those with low price they can buy at any moment. Therefore, the production concept is a kind of "basing sales on production" concept, which attaches importance to the production and quantity, but contempt the marketing and characteristics.

Production concept is one of the oldest ideas to guide the seller to act. The production concept is generally regarded as that the enterprise is able to sell out what it has produced.

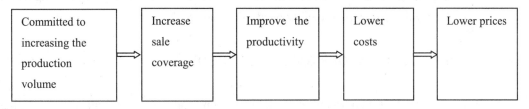

Figure 2.1 Production Concept Diagram

2.1.3 Characteristics of Production Concept

(1) Enterprises mainly focus on the production of products, and pursue the high efficiency, high-volume, low-cost; single variety of products, long life-cycle.

(2) The enterprises mainly care the existence and the number of products in the market, rather than consumer's demands to the market.

(3) The production sector is considered as the main sector in the management.

2.2 Product Concept

2.2.1 Background of Product Concept

The product concept comes from the 1920s to 1930s, which also was produced under the situation of "seller's market" like the production concept. However, with the further development capitalism productivity, the market situation of short supply had been eased. Companies not only concerned about production, but also began to focus much more on improving the product, that is, to change their importance from "quantity" to "quality".

2.2.2 Connotation of Product Concept

The product concept is based on enhancing products and improving the quality and functionality of existing products as the marketing concept. The basic assumption is that customers like the best quality and most powerful products.

The marketers holding the product concept think that consumers like the products with fine quality, complete functions and distinctive features. Therefore, companies should strive to improve the product's quality, increase the product's functionality, and constantly make the product better. At the same time, they insist on that they do not worry about sales as long as the product is good, only those with poor quality need to be marketed.

2.2.3 Characteristics of Product Concept

The product concept is also a kind of "basing sales on production" concept, which attaches importance to production and quality, but ignore product sales and customer's demands. Its main features are as follows:

(1) Enterprises focus on improving and producing the products, pursuing high quality and multifunctional products;

(2) Enterprises neglect marketing, simply attract customers by the emphasis on the product itself, and completely reject other promotion methods;

(3) Enterprises still make the productive sector as the main sector, but they promote quality control in the production process.

Chapter 2 Marketing Philosophy

2.3 Selling Concept

2.3.1 Background of Selling Concept

Selling concept arose during the late 20s to the early 50s in the 20th century, and was generated in the process which the capitalist economy changed from a "seller's market" to "buyer's market". At that time, the production of products increased rapidly, and the supply and demand situation had changed. Also, a buyer's market was not finally formed, but the competition among vendors became increasingly fierce. Marketing problems were exposed. And even more serious economic crisis in 1929 broke out and business failures occurred frequently. The selling of products became an issue of business survival and development. Such an objective situation made enterprises realize that it was not enough only to produce the products with fine quality and low price, and that the enterprises must pay attention to and strengthen the product selling efforts so as to obtain more profits in the competition.

2.3.2 Contents of Selling Concept

The selling concept is also known as marketing concept, which is centered on the production and sales of products in order to stimulate sales and promote the purchase. In the situation of products oversupplied, enterprises will consciously or unconsciously use the selling concept to guide the marketing activities of enterprises.

At this point, the primary task facing the company is no longer how to expand the production scale or improving producfivity, but how to market their products. So, enterprises begin to improve marketing systems and sales techniques to draw customers' attention. And enterprises set up special selling agencies, increase sales staff, pay great efforts on advertising, and gradually form a merchandising-centered marketing concept.

The basic assumptions of selling concept suggest that consumers are generally not based on subjective desires when purchasing products, and can be induced only by selling so that their buying behaviors were produced. Whether the sale of products succeeds or not lies in the selling ability of enterprises. This concept can be summarized as "try to sell what has been produced, and then customers will buy them."

2.3.3 Features of Selling Concept

The selling concept is still a "sales depends on production" marketing concept, its main features are as follows:

(1) Products are unchanged. Enterprises still decide the production direction and production as required according to their own conditions.

(2) Strengthen marketing. Focus on the sales of products, research and application of marketing and promotion methods and techniques.

(3) Begin to pay attention to the customers. Mainly look for potential customers, and study the ways and means to attract customers.

(4) Begin to set up the sales departments. But they are still in a subordinate position.

2.4 Marketing Concept

2.4.1 Background of Marketing Concept

Marketing concept came into being in the 50s of 20th century. After the World War II, because of capitalism's rapid economic recovery and development, as well as science and technology's wide range of applications in production, companies' production efficiency was continuously improved, and market supply was greatly increased and market competition became more intense; on the other hand, due to economic prosperity, consumers had more income which could be used to select consumption, and this made consumers more demanding.

Faced with these circumstances, many entrepreneurs realized that the traditional marketing concepts could not adapt to the new economic environment. Only sale promotion could not fundamentally solve the contradictions of oversupply. And it was essential to put needs of the consumers first, take the initiative to understand and recognize the reality demands of consumers and potential demands, thereby to determine their own production.

2.4.2 Contents of Marketing Concept

Marketing concept is based on consumer-centric idea. The idea suggests that all plans and strategies of enterprises should center on customers, and correctly identify the needs and desires of target market. It is more effective than identifying what competitors supply to satisfy the target market. Marketing concept requires that enterprise implement the "customer first" principle in marketing management, be good at discovering and understanding the needs of target customers, and do everything possible to satisfy it, make customers satisfied so as to achieve business goals.

The emergence of the marketing concept is a real revolution in the history of business idea.

Chapter 2 Marketing Philosophy

It has the following differences when compared with the traditional marketing concepts: Firstly, the traditional orientation is based on the production and sales, while marketing concept is customer-centric; secondly, the traditional concept strengthens the functions of sales and achieves profits by selling products, while the marketing concept achieves profits through meeting customers' needs; thirdly, the traditional marketing concepts are short-term marketing tools which can only gain profits from a large number of sales and have characteristics with the short-term, while the marketing concept is to satisfy customers' needs comprehensively, to earn long-term and stable profits.

2.4.3 Four Pillars of Marketing Concept

Marketing concept has four pillars: target market, customers' needs, integrated marketing and win-win profit model.

1. Identifying the Target Market

Marketing concept puts forward the idea that the enterprise must define its own target market. The so-called target market refers to the selected customer groups which the marketing firms will provide services to. The definition of the target market is to clear where the target market of a business is. It is the only way to better study the characters of the target market demands, and then better meet the needs of customers.

2. Driven by Customers' Demands

Marketing concept also means that business activities should be customers' demands-oriented. The correct understanding of customers' needs and satisfaction is the focal point for all the work. In the modern market environment, the reasonableness of enterprises' existence is their ability to meet the needs of the customers. A concept that the enterprise should "produce and operate what the customer wants" is to be established. Enterprises should not only see customers' demands as the starting point of corporate marketing, but also meet the needs of customers throughout the entire process of corporate marketing. This idea should permeate all sectors of corporate marketing as the criteria for the work of various departments. The enterprises should understand and meet not only the customer's actual demands, but also the potential needs, adjust the company's marketing strategies according to market demand trends in order to adapt to market changes, and to determine the survival and development of enterprises.

3. Integrated Marketing Approach

All sectors in the enterprises will be integrated into customer interests, and this is called integrated marketing. The integrated marketing has two meanings: firstly, the integration of various marketing functions; secondly, the integration of the various departments.

The marketing concept requires enterprises base corporate marketing objectives on marketing, take advantage of products, prices, channels, promotion, public relations and other factors, and meet the customer's overall demands from all aspects.

4. A Win-Win Profit Model

The marketing concept stresses that the marketing activities must achieve a win-win business of customers and marketing. Only in this way can marketing make the transactions between business and customers continue, otherwise, it can only be a short-term transaction.

The marketing concept requires enterprises to focus not only on current interest, but also on long-term ones of the enterprises. In marketing the enterprises should both meet customers' needs and make customers satisfied to establish a good corporate image and win re-buyers through customer satisfaction. Therefore, the enterprises must pay attention to the production, sales, and the marketing services in marketing. The service runs through the entire process of production and operation. The end of a cycle is the beginning of another new cycle, thus promoting the improvement of the enterprise management.

2.5 Social Marketing Concept

2.5.1 Background of Social Marketing Concept

Social marketing concept came into being in the 70s in the 20th century when the new situation of energy shortages, inflation, rising unemployment, serious environmental pollution, consumer protection movement prevalently emerged in the western capitalist. The marketing concept evaded the reality that there is implied conflict among the consumer needs, consumer interests and long-term social welfare. The development of marketing, on the one hand brought enormous benefits to the community and the consumers, on the other hand caused environmental pollution, destruction of social ecological balance. There had been fake and shoddy products and deceptive advertising, which made the majority of consumers not satisfied, and set off a movement to protect consumer rights and protection of ecological balance movement, forcing the corporate marketing activities to take into account long-term interests of consumers and the community.

2.5.2 Contents of Social Marketing Concept

The basic view of the social marketing concept is as follows: enterprises should ensure customer satisfaction and the consumers' and the public's long-term benefits, looking them as their fundamental purpose and the responsibility for the social marketing decision-making. At the same time, the enterprises should also take into account the needs of consumers, consumer desire, consumer's interests and social welfare (see Figure 2.2). On this premise, the enterprises can obtain profits.

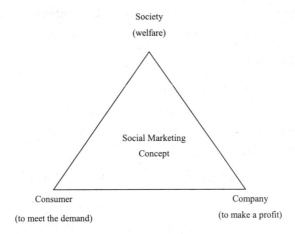

Figure 2.2 Three Factors of the Social Marketing Concept

The social marketing concept required marketers to consider interests of three parties, namely, corporate profits, satisfaction of customers' needs and social benefits in the development of making marketing policy.

As it is shown in the picture, the triangle diagram is a focus in business under the guidance of the social marketing concept. Therefore, the enterprises must do a good job in market research, not only to investigate and understand the reality of consumer practical and potential demand, but also to understand the satisfaction of consumers' demands, so it can avoid the waste of social resources due to the repeat of introduction and production. The enterprises should both look into consumers' demands and understand the effects of corporate marketing. Moreover, the enterprises ought to pay attention to the analysis of the competitor's strengths and weaknesses, take their advantages to do a good job of marketing. At the same time they must concern the social benefits of corporate marketing analysis, consider the overall interest, develop services which are beneficial to social development and people's physical and mental health, give up those services which are high energy consumption, high pollution, and harmful to people's physical and mental health in order to contribute to the economic and social development and benefit the future generations.

2.5.3 Features of Social Marketing Concept

1. Concerns of Interests

The social marketing concept requires business managers to consider consumers' needs and interests, business interests and social interests, immediate interests and the overall interests when making economic decisions and make the best marketing plan.

2. Tasks of the Business

The social marketing concept suggests that the task of business is to determine the needs, desires and interests of various target markets, to provide the target market products or services to meet their needs and demands, and to enhance consumer and social welfare in a more effective way than their competitors can.

3. Being the Changes and Additions of the Marketing Concept

The center of the marketing concept is to meet consumers' needs and demands, and thus to achieve corporate profit targets. But often this phenomenon occurs: there is a conflict of interest between the individual needs and social public interests in the process of meeting the individual's needs. The enterprise's marketing efforts may be unconsciously cause social losses.

4. Stresses of the Social Marketing Concept

Although the marketing concept also stresses the interests of consumers, it believes the interests of consumers must be based on the premise of achieving corporate profit targets. When the two are in conflict with each other, protecting the profits of an enterprise should be in priority. Meanwhile, the social marketing concept sees achieving customer satisfaction as well as consumer's and the public's long-term benefits as their fundamental purpose and responsibilities.

5. Decision-Making

Under the guidance of the marketing concept, decision-making process is usually to decide profit targets first, and then possible ways to achieve profit targets will be explored; the social marketing concept requires the decision-making should first consider the interests of consumers and society, seek for effective ways to meet consumers' demands and to promote the interests of

Chapter 2 Marketing Philosophy

consumers, and then consider the profit targets.

The proposal of the social marketing concept is another big step forward of the marketing concept. China's state-owned enterprise marketing activities regard the interests of society as the fundamental purpose of business, reflecting the interests of enterprises and social interests with great consistency. Chinese enterprises should consciously use the social marketing concept as a guide, considering the organic combination of points of the market demands, business strengths and interests of society as bases for the business decisions; they should improve the marketing effectiveness of enterprises comprehensively, and implement the social responsibilities of enterprises in the process of seeking the marketing profits.

2.6 Mega-Marketing Concept

2.6.1 Rise of Mega-Marketing Concept

The mega-marketing concept was an entirely new marketing concept which was proposed by Professor Philip Kotler in United States in the 1980s. In his view, the commodity economy has been developed to the current stage when the protectionism in the world trade, trade barriers and trade frictions increasingly happen from time to time. If companies want to successfully enter into a particular market, and to engage in marketing activities, relying solely on traditional 4Ps of marketing is hard to work, but they must be accompanied by political, economic, psychological and public relations and other means to win the cooperation of a number of participants in order to enter the market.

Philip Kotler first extended E. J. McCarthy's 4Ps theory (Product, Price, Place, Promotion) to 6Ps portfolio, which added 2Ps: Political Power and Public Relations. Later, he developed it into a 10Ps portfolio theory, in which he added a new combination of 4Ps on the basis of 6Ps portfolio, namely Probing, Partitioning, Prioritizing, and Positioning. Soon, Kotler added the 11th P on the basis of the above 10Ps combination, which was named People. It means understanding and providing services to people. The 11th P runs through the whole process of marketing activities, and it is the implementation guarantee of the success of the previous 10Ps. This P makes internal marketing theory incorporated into the mixture of the marketing theories and advocates that managers should understand and grasp the trends and patterns of staff needs to overcome the practical difficulties of workers and appropriately meet the material and spiritual needs of the workers in order to motivate employees' enthusiasm for work. The mega-marketing concept is of great significance for its transformation from tactical marketing to strategic marketing, which is known as the "Second Revolution" of the marketing.

2.6.2 Connotation of Mega-Marketing Concept

The mega-marketing concept was a new development of the marketing concept since the 1980s. It is a new strategic marketing theory which can guide the business to conduct marketing in a closed market. The core content is to emphasis that it is necessary to effectively adapt to the external environment, but also it should be able to play in some respects a subjective dynamic role and to make the external environment favorable to the business direction.

The so-called mega-marketing means the process of activities that enterprises strategically use economic, psychological, and political and public relationship means in order to successfully enter a particular market, where they are engaged in business operations so as to win the support and cooperation of all parties concerned.

The mega-marketing idea suggests the marketing problems that enterprises are facing are no longer just how to meet the needs of the existing target markets since the trade protectionism and government intervention are strengthened. In the marketing, the first thing enterprises do is to obtain the support from the authorities, the legislative branch, executive decision makers with the use of political power and public relations, inspire and guide the specific market needs and establish a good corporate reputation and brand image among the consumers in the market in order to open the market and enter the market. Then the traditional 4Ps (Product, Price, Place, Promotion) portfolios are adopted to meet the needs of the market to further consolidate market position.

2.6.3 Features of Mega-Marketing Concept

Compared with the common marketing concepts, the mega-marketing concept has the following two characteristics:

(1) The mega-marketing idea breaks through the dividing line between the "control elements" and "non-control elements", and stresses that corporate marketing activities can have an important impact on the environment to make the environment conducive to the direction of achieving business goals.

(2) The mega-marketing concept stresses the need of dealing with a lot of relationships in order to successfully carry out the regular marketing activities, thereby expanding the scope of the enterprise marketing.

2.7 Summary

市场营销观念是企业的管理人员对其营销活动的根本态度和看法，是企业开拓市场、实现经营管理和销售目标的根本指导思想，它概括了一个企业的经营态度和思维方式。

企业的市场营销观念作为一种企业经营活动的指导思想，是随着企业经营实践的变化而不断发生变化的。迄今为止，企业的市场营销观念经历了 6 个发展阶段：生产观念、产品观念、推销观念、营销观念、社会市场营销观念和大市场营销观念。

从市场营销观念演变过程可以看出，从推销观念到营销观念的发展是至关重要的一环，在此之前是以生产者为中心，不重视消费者的需求和欲望；在此之后则是以消费者和顾客为中心，企业以满足消费者的需求作为其生存的基础。社会市场营销观念和大市场营销观念都是以对市场为中心的市场营销观念的完善和发展。

Key Terms

Marketing Concept   Production Concept   Product Concept   Selling Concept   Marketing Concept   Social Marketing Concept   Mega-Marketing Concept

【案例】 "德力西"引出温州新模式

浙江有个温州，中国人大概没有不知道的。温州有个柳市镇，是全国低压电器生产基地。柳市镇有个德力西集团公司，德力西不仅是温州民营企业创新的"典范"，还在短短 16 年内创造出经济腾飞的奇迹，被经济界、理论界誉为"德力西现象"，新闻界更把"德力西现象"上升为一种"新温州模式"。

1999 年底，作为民营企业的德力西整体并购了作为国有企业的杭州西子集团公司，用"温州新模式"对其进行改造，半年后就实现了扭亏为盈。那么，"德力西现象"与"温州新模式"有什么联系？德力西集团成功的经验又是什么？

传统的温州模式已经走到了尽头

传统温州模式的基本特点是，以家庭经营为基础，以市场为导向，以小镇为依托，以农村能人为骨干。它的局限性主要表现在以下几个方面。

一是产权有障碍。分散经营的民营中小企业难以通过联合、重组、兼并、合并以及股份制改造等形式得以迅速扩张。

二是家族管理制度不适应现代企业制度。以血缘、亲缘为基础的家族管理制度随着企业规模的壮大，弊端愈加明显，特别是在人力资源的引进、配置、培养、储备等方面，家族管理制已成了严重的障碍。

三是经营方式落后。以产品经营为主要特征的传统经营模式，已在强大的竞争对手，尤其是世界强手面前显得软弱无力。

四是营销模式落后。专业市场和购销员包打天下的时代已一去不复返,日趋衰落的专业市场正是其真实的写照。

五是产品结构调整能力低,自主开发能力弱。以仿制为主的传统劳动密集型产品将面临更为激烈的竞争。

六是经营理念有局限性。以赢利为目的的经营理念已不适宜于现代社会的发展。一句话,温州模式的局限性归根结底还是观念的落后。

改革开放20多年后的今天,温州早已不是当年的温州,曾经缔造了温州模式的民营企业家们也不再满足于旧模式带给他们的利益,开始探索突破的途径,他们以温州人特有的开拓创新精神改写着温州模式,于是,一种新温州模式出现了,"德力西现象"就是"温州新模式"的代表。

和大多数温州民营企业的崛起一样,德力西也曾经历过那种旧的温州模式,但是,随着企业规模的壮大,弊端也愈加明显,德力西集团公司总裁胡成中痛感过去的经营方式行不通了,要继续发展就必须对自己和德力西过去一些非理性的成分进行否定,这也就是他要著书立说《企业集团创新论》的重要原因。

温州新模式——德力西现象的核心是什么

德力西现象的核心其实就是创新,一是不断创新,二是系统创新。纵观德力西的创新历程,比较温州其他民营企业,德力西在温州新模式的形成和发展过程中完全突破了原温州模式那种以家庭经营为基础的限制,走向了企业联合、兼并、重组、优化的集团化规模发展的道路。

调整了单纯以市场为导向的经营方式,走向了资产经营、资本经营的综合发展道路。改变了单纯以小城镇为依托的营销方式,走上了网络营销的道路。以农村"能人"为骨干的员工素质普遍得以提高,逐渐造就了一支具有现代智慧和理性思考的管理队伍。

业内专家称,"新温州模式"的本质特征可以概述为:以观念创新为核心,以网络营销为依托,以理性管理为基础,以规模效益求发展的一种新的经济运行模式。

先进生产力的发展常常要打破原有的模式。胡成中说:"德力西是在创新中发展起来的,还要通过创新来取得新的发展。"

他把德力西的创新归纳为6个方面。

一是产权制度创新。德力西的产权制度历经4个阶段的变革。

1984年到1990年,以家庭合伙制为主要形式,凭借"以质取胜"的经营理念和"船小好调头"的灵活机制,初步完成了原始积累。

1991年到1993年,进行股份制改造,实现了企业股份化,并正式启用德力西品牌,企业开始上规模,产品开始上档次,质量开始上水平。

1994年至1998年,将热销产品从车间中分离出来,进行专业化生产,并开始兼并企业,推进股份合作企业的战略性改组。

1998年至今,实现产权跨区域大规模延伸,主动参与国企改革,由母公司全资整体并购杭州西子集团，盘活了 2.5 亿元资产，使产权制度在集团化的基础上走向了社会化。

二是管理运行机制创新。德力西先后经历了从粗放的家庭工厂式管理到总厂式管理，再到股份合作制的公司化管理，进而到集团化管理的过程。

特别是自 1998 年开始，采用集团公司代表集团行使职权，推出董事局事业部制的"扁平式管理"体制，实行董事局领导下的总裁负责制，按照"高度集权、充分授权、有效监控、良性互动"的原则运行，有效缩短了管理半径，大大提高了工作效率。

三是技术与质量创新。德力西自进入 90 年代开始便逐步摆脱仿制国外知名产品的做法，注重加大技改投入和新产品开发力度，每年按销售额 5%的比例提取科技开发资金，结果每年均有几十个具备知识产权的新产品问世。同时，积极建立企业内部技术创新体系，目前已是国内同行中率先通过 ISO9001 产品质量体系和 ISO14001 环境体系双认证的企业。

四是营销模式创新。随着品牌声誉的不断提高，1994 年以后，德力西改变了传统的"游击战"、"运动战"的销售方式，把品牌资源与营销精英的优势互相嫁接，采取网络营销战略，快速推动企业产供销的良性循环，现已形成总部营销中心、省级销售总公司、地(市)级分销公司三级销售与管理的"金三角"产业构架体系。

五是经营方式创新。随着产权制度的变革和营销模式的转变，德力西的经营方式也在不断地升级，现已初步形成生产经营、资产经营、资本经营和品牌经营并举的格局。特别是 1999 年对国有杭州西子集团公司的并购成功以及上海高低压成套元件生产基地的建设投产，使德力西积累了进行大规模资本运作的经验。

六是企业文化创新。随着温州经济的不断发展，温州民营企业家的价值观也在不断发展的过程中出现蜕变，赢利不再是唯一的目标。德力西提出的"德报人类，力创未来"理念，说明胡成中已不满足于自我要求的目标，更加注重回报社会。

(资料来源：曹刚，李桂陵，王德发等. 国内外市场营销案例. 武汉：武汉大学出版社, 2003.)

【案例分析】

一些经济学家认为，"新温州模式"代表着中国经济体制改革的重要取向，是实施西部开发战略可以借鉴的重要方式。

随着民营企业参股、控股、并购国有企业的数量和规模越来越大，更多的国有中小困难企业将可以通过民营企业参与的方式走出困境。而国有企业民营化和民营企业社会化的趋势，也将使社会化的民营企业成为国民经济活动的主体。

在北京举行的一次记者座谈会上，胡成中曾说，德力西集团正在向中西部挺进，但今天的中西部开发不应再走当年温州的老路，应该站在一个更高的起点上。目前的西部犹如当年的温州，基础薄、条件差，因此，国家给予必要的支持是应该的，但中西部地区的群众应该学习温州人自力更生、奋发图强的精神，摆脱等、靠、要等陈旧观念，只有通过不断进取，才能抓住这一千载难逢的机会，实现经济的起飞和持续发展。

学者们也认为，温州的民营企业正在走向集团化、规模化和资产社会化，产品的档次和质量有了很大的提升，其中成功的经验不仅能够在中西部开发中发挥作用，而且可以成为实施西部开发战略的重要途径。

德力西的可贵之处在于摆脱了等、靠、要的陈旧观念，自力更生地实现了经济的快速持续发展。我国国有企业的改革正在向建立现代企业制度的纵深发展，德力西集团对产权制度、管理制度、经营方式和营销模式等方面进行的改革创新，为国有企业改革提供了很好的经验。

开发中西部地区，大批的温州民营企业家正在向那里进军，他们在温州成功的经验不仅能够在中西部开发中发挥作用，而且会带去温州人发展市场经济的经验和吃苦耐劳的精神。

【思考题】
1. 温州模式的转变反映了营销观念的哪些变化？为什么会发生这些变化？
2. 德力西现象的核心是什么？
3. 你从德力西现象中领悟到什么道理？

Part II Market Elements

Chapter 3

Analysis of Marketplace and Marketing Environment

Focus on:

1. Definition and classification of marketplace.
2. Contents and features of the marketing environment.
3. Elements of the macro-marketing environment.
4. Elements of the micro-marketing environment.

3.1 Implications and Classification of Marketplace

3.1.1 Concept of Marketplace

Viewing from the angle of modern marketing, the marketplace refers to the sum of demand for some kind or category of commodity. The demand for a commodity is always set by a buyer. Therefore we may say the marketplace is a group composed of all the real and potential buyers of some commodity.

When people say the auto marketplace in China is very large, it doesn't refer to the size of the auto trading place. Instead it refers to the great demand for automobiles in China with numerous real and potential buyers.

An enterprise has to face the market, which actually means to satisfy consumers' demands. Where there is an unsatisfied demand, there is a market.

To sum up, the marketplace is the sum of buyers' demands, namely, the comprehensive embodiment of three factors: population, purchasing power and purchasing motivation. It can be expressed in the following formula: Market = population + purchasing power + purchasing motivation.

3.1.2　Division of Marketplace

With the needs of marketing management in mind, we can analyze the market from different angles. Hence diversified methods of dividing the market are available.

1. Division by Circulation Area

It can be divided into domestic market and international market. The domestic market can also be subdivided into urban market and rural market, local market and non-local market.

2. Division by Form of Product

It can be divided into tangible market, intangible market and monetary capital market.

3. Division by Basic Situation of Market Operation

It can be divided into seller's market, buyer's market and equilibrium market.

4. Division by Mode of Market Transaction

It can be divided into spot market, futures market and credit market.

5. Division by Buyers and Purchase Motivation

It can be divided into consumer market and organizational market. The organizational market covers producer market, intermediary market and government market.

3.2　Implications and Features of Marketing Environment

3.2.1　Concept of Marketing Environment

By marketing, environment is meant the generic name of external factors and conditions related to the marketing activities of an enterprise, which refers to the scope of actions and influences of all the factors associated with and affected by an industrial and commercial enterprise in its marketing activities.

3.2.2　Contents and Features of Marketing Environment

Many internal and external environmental factors influence and restrict the marketing

Chapter 3 Analysis of Marketplace and Marketing Environment

activities of an enterprise and these are very complicated. Different factors exert different effects upon each aspect of marketing activities and similar environmental factors also produce different effects upon various enterprises. As a rule the marketing environment of an enterprise is divided into two parts, i.e., micro-environment and macro-environment.

The macro-environment refers to all the social binding forces that directly affect marketing activities of an enterprise, including population environment, economic environment, natural environment, sci-tech environment, political and legal environment and cultural environment (see Figure 3.1).

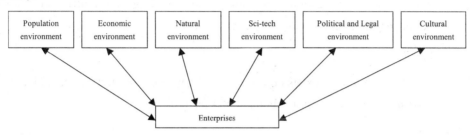

Figure 3.1 Marketing Macro-Environment Factors for Enterprises

The micro-environment refers to the relationship between the departments within an enterprise as well as the relationship between the enterprises that cooperate and compete with, or provide services for, the marketing activities of an enterprise. It includes factors within an enterprise and other factors, such as suppliers, customers, rivals and the general public outside an enterprise (see Figure 3.2).

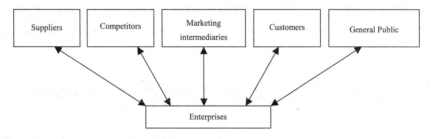

Figure 3.2 Marketing Micro-Environment Factors for Enterprises

All the micro-environmental factors have to be influenced and restricted by the macro-environment, which will produce an indirect effect upon the marketing activities of an enterprise by using the micro-environment as a medium in most cases. Sometimes it also exerts a direct effect upon the marketing activities of an enterprise.

The marketing environment of an enterprise is very complicated and many-sided, but is not without any regularity. To sum up, it has the following main features:

1. Complexity

The marketing environment is composed of many factors and in a given economic condition various combinations can be formed. When one is rising, the other is falling. They can melt each other too, thereby creating a complicated marketing environment.

2. Dynamics

A society always develops and the marketing environment of an enterprise is also changing constantly, thereby creating a changing situation of the marketing environment and leading to a dynamic marketing environment.

3. Objectivity

The marketing environment exists objectively and can be known and understood through the efforts of an enterprise. This is the most fundamental feature.

4. Uncontrollability

Here it mainly means that macro-factors in the marketing environment and the macro environmental factors confronted with by an enterprise are uncontrollable. We can only adapt ourselves to them or look for countermeasures to suit them. Only by doing so can an enterprise be in an invincible position.

5. Correlation

The marketing environment is a system, in which every influencing factor depends, acts and checks upon one another. Therefore full attention should be paid to the mutual influence of various factors.

3.3 Analysis of Macro-Marketing Environment

The macro-environmental factors of an enterprise's marketing activities will exert an effect upon the micro-environmental ones; thereby producing an indirect or direct effect upon the enterprise's marketing activities. These macro-environmental factors refer to all the forces that can bring business opportunities to enterprises and at the same time may be a menace to the enterprise's marketing activities. These include population factors, economic factors, political and legal factors, cultural factors, sci-tech factors and natural environmental factors.

Chapter 3 Analysis of Marketplace and Marketing Environment

3.3.1 Population Factors

The market as referred to by marketing is the congregation of a group of people with the intention and power to purchase. Population of a given quantity is the foundation of carrying out marketing activities. The population factors include such sub-classified determinants as population size, structure, move and growth.

1. Population Size

Population size means total population, which refers to the total amount of population in a country or region. The majority of population in the world is concentrated in the low- and medium-income countries and this ratio is about 80% while the population of high-income developed countries account for about 20%. Statistics show that total population is closely related to the economic development of a country and developed countries usually have a lower total population than developing countries.

2. Population Growth

For a decade or so, the world population has grown at an annual average rate higher than 1.5%. In ten years the world population has increased by about 900 million. According to estimation, it will take 41 years to double the world's population, 178 years to redouble the Europe's population, 95 years for North America, 40 years for Asia and 24 years for Africa.

The continual growth of the world's population means continuous development of world market and total market demand will be expanded further. The difference lies in the fact that population growth in developing countries is too fast. Low income, great market demand, short supply of commodities and rising price offers good opportunities to enterprises to carry out marketing activities. In contrast developed countries have slow population growth with ample supply of commodities and high income. People there set higher demand for products and labor services. This indicates the marketing in developed countries will become increasingly difficult.

3. Population Structure

Population structure often determines product structure, consumption structure and type of product demand.

Population structure mainly covers age composition, sex composition, educational attainment and family features, which are major factors that decide the final purchasing behavior.

4. Population Move

Population move in the world shows two trends: among countries, population in developing countries (especially senior talent) moves to developed countries; within one country or region, simultaneously coexist the phenomena of population move from rural area to urban area and from urban area to suburbs and rural area.

3.3.2 Economic Factors

Economic factors are major determinants to achieve demand. Without a population of a given quantity there would be no market. Likewise no demand will be generated without a purchasing power. The concentrated expression of economic factor in marketing is the purchasing power, which depends upon income, savings and credit.

1. Income

Economic income has multiple weighing indicators and different weighing indicators have different meanings for analysis of market demand. These indicators cover national income, personal income, disposable personal income and discretionary personal income.

2. Savings and Credit

With income remaining unchanged, the greater the amount of savings, the smaller the real expenditure and market purchasing power will become; on the contrary, the smaller the amount of savings, the greater the real expenditure and market purchasing power will become, offering more business opportunities to enterprises. To weigh the savings of one country, region or family, three indicators are usually used: total savings deposits, savings ratio and savings growth rate. The trend of changes in consumption and savings, consumer's income and expenditure during a given period can be analyzed through these three indicators.

3. Expenditure Pattern of Disposable Income

Marginal propensity to consume (MPC) is the ratio between consumer expenditure increment and income increment, namely:

MPC = Consumer expenditure increment / income increment

Judging by absolute quantity, a consumer's expenditure usually increases with income. However, after income has come to a given amount, the consumer expenditure increment will be smaller than income increment, namely, increase in consumption increases less fast than that in income, that is to say, MPC presents a decreasing trend.

3.3.3 Political and Legal Factors

Marketing is influenced and restricted by political and legal environmental factors to a large extent.

Political environment mainly refers to the political power of the home country an enterprise is in, political situation, relevant government policies and all the political factors that directly affect marketing activities.

Legal environment refers to all the decrees and regulations formulated by the state and locality of the home country an enterprise resides in.

Political and legal factors often restrict the marketing activities of an enterprise, but newly-formulated policies and regulations can also bring business opportunities to relevant enterprises.

3.3.4 Cultural Factors

Cultural factors include cultural and sub-cultural groups, religion, consumer habits, aesthetic interest and values.

1. Culture and Sub-Culture

Culture is the most fundamental determinant of human requirement and desire and also the most extensive environmental factor that affects a consumer's behavior. In the book of *Consumer Behavior*, culture is defined as the sum of faith, values and habits acquired through learning in a given society and used as a guide to consumer behaviors.

The culture of a society, especially cultural values, can influence the purchasing and consumption pattern of the people in this society.

Not everyone in a country or a specific society has the same cultural values. Sub-culture may exist within a group of different age ranges, areas and nationalities. The members of these secondary groups have some common peculiar faith, values and living habits. Different sub-cultural groups vary greatly in consumer behavior while the same sub-cultural group may exhibit similarity in consumer taste and purchasing behavior. Marketing personnel can select different sub-cultural groups as their own target market in light of different demand and consumer behavior of different sub-cultural groups.

2. Religious Belief, Consumer Habits, Aesthetic Interest and Values

Religion is the cultural layer through which people see cultural behavior or spiritual behavior clearly and influences people's customs, outlook on life, purchasing behavior and consumer mode.

Consumption custom is people's pattern of consumption shaped over a long time. As part of social cultural environment, consumption custom is formed over a long time with relative stability. Aesthetic interest is people's appreciation of and preference to music, art, drama, dance, shape and color. Differences in the national custom, social environment, educational attainment and sci-tech and legal system lead to different aesthetical ideas in different countries and regions. Formation of values has much to do with the society consumers live in, psychological state, and notion of time, attitude towards reform, life and work. With the improvement of people's living standards and acceleration of rhythm of life, people's notion of time is changing and the demand for clock workers, cooked food and automobiles is expanding.

3.3.5 Sci-Tech Factors

Science and technology exerts an extensive and profound effect upon social and economic life, business management and consumer's purchasing behavior and way of life.

(1) Development of science and technology creates business opportunities.

Development and reform in science and technology may bring about sharp changes in demand. For example, the invention of contraceptive drugs leads to smaller families, more professional women and higher disposable income, causing great changes in market demand and offering new business opportunities to such sectors as fast food, daily out-of-home child care, auto manufacturing and tourism.

(2) Development of science and technology poses a threat to some enterprises.

In some sense science and technology is a double-edged sword as it may bring a suffering to some enterprises while offering business opportunities to others. The development and reform in science and technology is a tragedy-comedy in the history of enterprise development in the petroleum industry.

The invention of electric light by Thomas Addison changed people's demand for kerosene lamp and almost shattered the fond dream of petroleum enterprises. The invention of internal combustion engine changed the fate of petroleum enterprises once again. The sharp increase in the demand for auto and air fuel saved the petroleum industry. However, the invention and industrialization of new energy and substitute energy will also cast a shadow on the fate of

Chapter 3 Analysis of Marketplace and Marketing Environment

petroleum businesses.

(3) Science and technology has changed each link and mode in marketing activities.

Development of science and technology has sped up replacement of the old by the new and shortened life cycle. For example, computer chip is upgraded once every 18 months. Under this new situation enterprises have to be always on the alert, seize market information, know the changes in consumer demand and preference, meet their requirements and guide consumer demand with innovative products.

In the epoch of knowledge-based economy the networking of market information has produced a great impact upon the pricing strategy of an enterprise. Consumers in the network market respond to price change rapidly and price elasticity of demand may be increased. Simultaneously the network also provides a tool for an enterprise to know the cost acceptable to customers. An enterprise provides a flexible product design and production program to be selected by users in light of the customer's cost till the customer identifies and confirms them before making arrangements for production and sale.

In the epoch of knowledge-based economy the traditional marketing mode may give way to online marketing based on information technology. High automation and networking of business process transplanted distribution to the Internet for realization of real virtual marketing. E-commerce has changed the conventional and materialized distribution system in the industrial times. To adapt to B-to-B or B-to-C service, enterprises must set up a brand-new distribution pattern on the Internet.

Development of and reform in science and technology has also boosted the change in enterprise promotion mode. The traditional promotion mode relies on enterprises only and carries out intensive one-way promotion to customers through some media or tools. The customers are in a passive position and promotion cost is very high. Online marketing is an interactive and person-to-person two-way communication and a customer is in an active position and can directly participate in the corporate marketing activities. He can have a dialogue with marketing personnel so that the enterprise may know his demand directly and seize the business opportunity promptly.

3.3.6 Natural Environmental Factors

Development of and changes in natural environment will also bring business opportunities or pose a menace to enterprises. Corporate managerial personnel should keep an eye on the changes in natural environmental factors to be involved.

Natural environmental factors cover natural resources and natural environment.

(1) Natural resources

Natural resources can be divided into three categories: A) Limited and non-renewable resources, such as petroleum and minerals; B) Limited and renewable resources, such as forest; C) Other natural resources, like air and water. With the growth of world economy, people's demand for resources also rises spirally and its growth has surpassed the bearing capacity of the natural system of the earth. Energy shortage will become more intensified and development of the replaceable limited resources will bring new chances to enterprises at large.

(2) Natural environment

Natural environment is a prerequisite for human existence and the worsening environment has constituted a serious menace to human existence. The public has a keen concern about environmental issues and demands those enterprises that affect the environment and resources in production and business operation change their business mode and technology. To improve the environment, the government has to adopt intervention measures and demands relevant enterprises develop and utilize environmentally friendly products and facilities, which will also bring new opportunities to enterprises.

(3) International organizations and governments of all countries have strengthened intervention in environmental protection.

The worsening geo-bio-environment has also aroused close attention of some countries and international organizations.

In 1992 the UN held a conference attended by representatives from 183 countries in Rio de Janeiro, Brazil, in which *Agenda 21* was published and the idea of coordinated development between economy and ecology was put forward. Sustainable development has become a strategic issue of global concern.

(4) Green barrier has become a new marketing environment.

With enhanced awareness of environmental protection, all the countries introduced relevant standards for environmental inspection of imported commodities successively, which served as a new non-tariff barrier. Many of the garments cannot be exported from China because of residual contaminants found in the environmental inspection. After accession to WTO, western countries carry out much more stringent environmental inspection of the garments exported from our country. For example, the indicators of the EU for inspection of our garment exports have increased from 6 to 21.

Currently, the environmental protection certification standard practiced internationally is the general-purpose standard— ISO 14000 for establishment, implementation and examination of the environmental management system promulgated by International Standardization Organization (ISO) in 1996. To achieve ISO 14000 certification is just like getting a green pass. To break out

Chapter 3 Analysis of Marketplace and Marketing Environment

trade barrier and enter international market successfully, it is imperative to pass ISO 14000 certification.

3.4 Analysis of Micro-Marketing Environment

The micro-environmental factors for marketing activities mainly refer to various forces that produce a direct effect upon the process and results of marketing activities and these factors correlate with the supply chain of business operation directly and include the enterprise itself, marketing channel institutions, buyer's market, competitors and general public confronted with by an enterprise.

3.4.1 Enterprises

Marketing activities and departments in an enterprise constitute the first micro-factor of corporate marketing environment.

A corporate organization set up with business flow as the focus must take marketing as the outpost and all the functional elements that provide services for customers must cooperate closely, pull together and offer efficient services to customers.

3.4.2 Marketing Channel Institutions

On the supply chain that provides services for customers outside an enterprise exists a series of interactive institutions, which are in different division links respectively and shoulder different tasks in converting resources to production mix to be consumed by consumers. They cooperate with each other and play their role jointly for satisfaction of needs and realization of consumption. Therefore these institutions constitute the intermediary environmental factors in marketing activities.

Suppliers are enterprises and organizations that provide enterprises with raw materials, parts, energy, funds and intelligence. An enterprise has to give consideration to the supply capability of these enterprises and organizations in designing the size and level of marketing service and their bargaining power as sellers.

An intermediary is an intermediary agency engaging in resale of commodities. In many cases product distribution in marketing activities is undertaken by an intermediary. From the angle of labor division system an intermediary is in the links of commodity circulation and a major micro-environment in marketing activities as it exerts a profound effect upon consumer convenience, efficiency and cost of production distribution.

3.4.3 Buyer's Market

The size of buyer's market, consumption behavior, general condition of the market and its change trend directly affect the sales volume and cost of an enterprise. The market is one of the most important micro-environmental factors in marketing environment. From the buyer's angle we can divide the market into three types: consumer market, producer market and government market.

3.4.4 Competitors

Market economy is competition economy. Based on the substitution degree of products competitors of enterprises can be divided into four types: brand competitors, industrial competitors, demand competitors and consumption competitors. The analysis of competitors will be detailed in the following sector.

3.4.5 General Public

General public refers to social organizations that influence corporate marketing activities, which include mass media public, government public, citizen action public and locality public.

The media public includes various mass media, which can exert negative or positive effects upon the spread of information about enterprises and their products. The government public relates to relevant government departments that administer and standardize business activities of enterprises, such as industrial and commercial administration and taxation authorities. The citizen action public includes various organizations for protection of consumers' rights and environmental protection organizations. The locality public covers enterprises, communities, residents, masses of people and local administrative officials.

These micro-environmental elements will produce varying effects upon the successful carrying out of marketing activities and an enterprise should give consideration to these environmental details in designing the marketing program, especially the action program.

Chapter 3 Analysis of Marketplace and Marketing Environment

3.5 Summary

市场是指某种商品或某类商品需求的总和。市场营销环境由宏观和微观两部分所构成：宏观环境是指直接影响企业市场营销活动的各种社会约束力量，包括人口环境、经济环境、政治与法律环境、社会文化环境、科学技术环境和自然环境；微观环境指对企业营销活动过程和结果有直接影响的各种力量，这些要素与企业经营的供应链直接发生关联，包括企业本身、市场营销渠道机构、购买者市场、竞争者和公众。

Key Terms

Marketplace   Macro-Marketing Environment   Micro-Marketing Environment   Cultural Factors   Economic Factors   Population Factors   Political and Legal Factors   Sci-tech Factors   Competitors   Marketing Channel Institution   Buyer's Market   General Public

【案例】 美的：帮出来的好汉

2000年11月8日，对美的空调事业部总经理方洪波来说，是个很高兴的日子。这天，美的空调2001年工商恳谈会在顺德召开，来自全国各地以及日本、香港等国家和地区的300多名供应厂商聚在一起，共同探讨在新经济条件下，谋求下一步战略合作和长远发展的问题。据有关数据显示，2000年销售年度，美的空调销售165万套，实现销售收入60亿元，同比增长40%，占全国空调市场13%左右的市场份额。对此，总经理方洪波说，取得这样的成绩，除了严格按照市场策略行事外，美的还有四大优势：一是规模和品牌优势；二是技术优势；三是美的集团多元化发展的辐射力；四是渠道优势。美的目前的渠道建设是两块，一块是和上游供应商之间的战略伙伴关系，二是和销售商之间的合作关系。目前美的已与很多供应商之间达成了战略伙伴关系合作协议。美的空调自1996年开始创造性地提出与供应商建立永久性的战略合作伙伴关系以来，三年多的生产实践证明，与供应商之间的良好协作关系是企业优化资源配置，强化成本和品质管理工作的基础，是全面参与市场竞争和提高核心竞争力的必然选择。在企业发展规划中，他们明确提出：制造系统的工作要密切围绕品质和成本两大主题，以战略性合作伙伴关系为纽带，积极探索制造模式的创新和生产组织体系的发展，最大限度地发挥资源配置和规模效应，今年美的集团的空调销售量能达到165万的好成绩，与上游供应商的支持是密不可分的，今年很多企业在旺季都因供应链不顺畅而导致产品断货，但美的空调却从来未出现过。同样，针对下游的经销商来说，美的又成了他们的供应商，所以，与下游经销商也是战略伙伴关系。美的与上游供应商和下游经销商之间的战略伙伴关系是"同心、同步、同超越"的。所谓"同心"，指的是真正稳定的上下游关系，意味着要建立长期的战略合作关系，意味着上下游各企业对各自发展目标、经营理念、市场前景的认同和理解。只有上下游各级企业同心才能谋求发展，只有上下游各级企业同心才能实现共荣。"同步"的意思是：美的是个大命运共同体，美的的发展离不开上下游企业的发展，上下游企业的发展不能离开美的空调长期的市场策略。"同超越"则是指：美的空调是创新领导者，创新的本质在于不断的自我否定，不断的自我超越；经历了多年的发展，无论是上下游企业，都会不可避免地遇到进一步发展的瓶颈，因此上下游各企业都应该抛弃旧有的思想习惯，改变旧有的行为方式，共同突破发展的瓶颈，共同实现新一轮的快速增长。

(资料来源：曹刚，李桂陵，王德发等. 国内外市场营销案例. 武汉：武汉大学出版社，2003.)

【案例分析】

在企业的市场营销活动中，通常会遇到各种因素的影响，这些因素会给企业带来市场机会，也会造成环境威胁。企业应及时采取适当的对策，使其经营管理与市场营销环境的发展变化相适应。企业市场营销环境包括微观环境和宏观环境，其中，微观环境是指对企业服务其顾客的能力构成直接影响的力量，如市场营销渠道企业，上游的供应商和下游的经销商。在长期的企业活动中，似乎是形成了一种思维定势：企业将供应商作为竞争对手，尽可能地减弱其讨价还价的能力，以便使企业获得更大的利益。但这样做你可能暂时成功了，作为竞争对手的供应商可能维持不下去了，不与你合作了，甚至破产了，对于企业来说，需要寻找新的供应商，建立新的关系，花费新的人力、物力、财力，也是得不偿失。事实上，将供应商作为竞争对手的寄生关系下，企业的许多策略由于市场诸多因素的影响达不到预期的效果。长虹囤积彩管事件就是典型的例子。企业不如掉过头来将供应商作为自己的合作伙伴，以此作为基础带动自己的营销活动。美的集团的成功就说明这种共生关系的重要性。

当前，各行各业的企业都应该从美的集团的成功中，反思一下自己的策略。

【思考题】

1. 企业为什么要与供应商搞好关系？
2. 企业与供应商之间存在哪些关系？
3. 在共生关系下，企业可以采取哪些方式与供应商合作？
4. 企业进行市场营销活动应该研究哪些微观环境？
5. 企业应如何分析供应商？

Chapter 4

Analysis of Market Behavior

Focus on:

1. Classification of the competitor.
2. Features of consumers' buying behaviors.
3. Definition and features of the organizational market.

4.1 Analysis of Competitors

4.1.1 Competition Types of Marketplace

The factors that affect competition situation and competitor's behavior in the marketplace comprise the following: number of competitors, homogeneity and heterogeneity of products, size of enterprises and so on. Based on these factors the marketplace can be divided into different types:

1. Perfect Competition

The industry of perfect competition is composed of many enterprises that turn out the same products. The products made by the enterprises are without any difference and can be replaced fully. The price of the competitors will be the same. In real economy perfect competition doesn't exist at all.

2. Monopolistic Competition

In the industry of monopolistic competition the products supplied by the sellers are not homogeneous and differ more or less. But these products with some difference are replaceable to some extent. Product difference entitles an enterprise to some monopoly right to exclude its competitors, but at the same time the substitutive nature of these products with difference will result in some competition in the industry of monopolistic competition. The competitors set up a market barrier by providing the specific segmentation market with characteristic products and services to maintain their market position and price.

3. Oligopoly

Oligopoly can be divided into pure oligopoly and differentiated oligopoly. In the industry of pure oligopoly several enterprises produce the same type of product (such as petroleum and iron and steel) and the main way to gain competitive advantages (almost the only way) is to reduce cost, which is often achieved by increasing production. The industry of differentiated oligopoly is composed of several enterprises that turn out products with partial difference (such as cars and cameras). Each enterprise carries out the differentiation strategy in product quality, features and service and seeks a leading position in some aspect.

4. Perfect Monopoly

In the industry of perfect monopoly there is only one enterprise with one type or category of product without any (or few) substitute(such as power or gas company). Perfect monopoly is controlled by three factors: some product calls for large-scale investment with remarkable scale-economy efficiency; patent right of monopoly with no access by others; one enterprise has controlled the source of basic raw materials for some product.

4.1.2 Classification of Competitors and Their Behavior Features

To identify competitors is a major job. Lucky knows Kodak and Fuji are its rivals. Changhong knows TCL, Chuangwei and Konka are its main rivals.

Superficially, to identify competitors is a very simple job. But due to the complexity, level and variability of demand, rapid development and evolution of technology and industrial change, enterprises in the market are confronted with a complicated competitive environment. Who are the rival enterprises? Who are the current rival enterprises? Who are the potential rival enterprises? Who are the immediate rival enterprises? Who are the indirect rival enterprises? It is not easy to answer these questions.

Only when an enterprise makes a profound analysis of its competitive environment and rivals and knows the features and nature of different rivals well can it win in competition.

Competitors can be classified into the following types in light of the substitution degree of products:

1. Brand Competitors

Brand competitors refer to those enterprises in the same industry that provide the same customers with similar products or services at the similar price. They are the immediate rival enterprises. For example, in the auto industry, manufactures that produce cars of the same grade

Chapter 4 Analysis of Market Behavior

regard their rivals as brand competitors. Audi, Honda, Toyota and Buick are the brand competitors of medium-grade cars.

As the products of brand competitors feature high mutual substitution, competition is fierce. To foster customer's brand loyalty through brand strategy is a major means to scramble for consumers.

2. Industrial Competitors

An industry is a congregation of enterprises that supply one type or category of products, such as pharmaceutical industry and auto industry. Enterprises regard the enterprises that offer the same type or category of products as competitors in the broad sense of term, known as industrial competitors.

In the same industry different enterprises produce or offer products of varying grades, types and varieties, but these enterprises also compete with each other. As consumers may make selections among products of varying grades, types and varieties, the products are mutually substitutive to some extent. For example, all the car makers are the industrial competitors of Shanghai Volkswagen.

3. Demand Competitors

We call the enterprises that satisfy and address the same demand of consumers as demand competitors. Enterprises in the different industries can deliver the same interest through different types of products and address the same demand of consumers. Therefore competition can be carried out across the industry.

These products or services in the different industries that meet the same demand are mutually substitutive. For example, if a consumer wants to go on an outing, he or she can select train, airplane, bicycle, motor-bike or other means of transportation in addition to his or her private car. When air ticket's price rises, customers traveling by train may be increased. So Shanghai Volkswagen should not ignore suppliers of other means of transportation and should pay more attention to the introduction of new ones.

4. Consumption Competitors

Enterprises regard the enterprises that offer different products with the same target consumers as consumption competitors. For example, the same consumer may spend money on either traveling or purchase of real estates or cars. Enterprises with the same target consumers have to compete in consumption expenditure structure and its change will influence the position of competitors.

4.2 Analysis of Consumer Market Purchasing Behavior

4.2.1 Characteristics of Consumer Market Purchasing Behavior

The consumer market is also known as the consumer goods market, which is the market that sales consumers goods and services to individuals and families. On the consumer market, the purpose of consumers purchasing products and services is to meet the final consumption in itself, rather than to reap profits as capital goods. Consumer needs are primitive requirements of human society, and the market requirements of manufacturers, intermediaries as well as the government are derived from it. The consumer market fundamentally determines requirements of other markets, which makes it the main object of modern market research.

Marketing researches consumer market, with its core task is to research on purchasing behaviors of consumers.

In order to meet demands of market consumption, enterprises must analyze and recognize the requirements of consumers and the characteristics of consumer market are mainly described as the following:

1. Diversity of Purchasers

Individuals and families are the basic purchasing unit of consumer goods market, because consumption is needed when people want to survive and develop. Transaction of consumer products exists in places where there are people. The purchasers on consumer goods market are distributed across all places and on all levels. Hence, the consumer market is extremely diverse.

2. Diversity of Needs

The diversity in this respect is multifold. Because of differences in age, sex, occupation, income, educational level, belief system and hobbies, huge disparities exist in their needs of consumer goods and purchasing behaviors. Ordinarily, the rule of change of consumer needs switches from low-level to high-level; from being simple to complex; from pursuit of quantity to quality; from materialistic fulfillment to spiritual fulfillment and from catering for general needs to customized needs.

3. Importance and Repetitiveness of Purchasing Behaviors

Owing to limitation of family storing conditions and financial constraint as well as the characteristics of consumer goods, consumers will only purchase the amount of daily consumer

Chapter 4　Analysis of Market Behavior

goods that suffices the needs for individual and families during a specified period of time. Normally it is low. Coupled with daily characteristics of consumption, consumers, therefore, are required to purchase regularly and repetitively.

4. Non-Professionalism of Purchasers

The majority of consumers lack professional knowledge of commodities; they barely study the performance, characteristics, usage, maintenance and repair of consumer products, unleashing intense emotion and malleability in purchasing consumer goods. They are easily influenced by advertisement, packaging, brand reputation, services, unique characteristics of commodities, discount, general atmosphere inside stores, persuasive efforts made by shop assistants and other factors that may contribute impulse buying. With the improvement of general population, people's consuming curiosity and purchasing behavior have become more emphasizing on emotional needs and pursuit of spiritual enjoyment.

5. Flexibility of Needs

Because consumers are influenced by politics, economy, society, psychological factors and enterprise' efforts to promote products, their consumption needs and purchasing power may increase or decrease during a particular period of time, which is the flexibility of consumption needs. The flexibility of consumers for different types of products varies. Generally, if the needs of daily essentials decrease, its corresponding flexibility of market is rather limited. Hence, the flexibility of non-essential consumer goods in our daily life is huge. Therefore, its corresponding flexibility of market is huge, i.e. the needs of non-essential consumer products are largely affected by price fluctuation and changes of income.

4.2.2　Factors Affecting Purchasing Behavior of Consumers

1. Social Cultural Factors

Social cultural factors include cultural, sub-cultural and social hierarchic factors that influence consumer behaviors and are the most comprehensive and profound factors on consumers.

(1) Culture

It refers to the sum of belief, value and habit that is intended to guide consumer behaviors after being learnt and acquired in the society. Understanding each type of cultural factors in specific social environment and its influence on consumer behaviors will help to boost the ability of marketing and sales personnel to analyze purchasing decisions of consumers and adaptability of consumers to promotional campaigns.

(2) Subculture

It refers to the smaller group that shares common value system and similar living experience and environment in each culture, including Ethnic group, such as Han race and other minority ethnic groups in our nation; these different racial groups have their respective racial habits, lifestyles and hobbies. Religious group: Different religious groups have their respective respect, taboo and cultural preference. Racial Group, such as white, yellow and black: These different racial groups have their unique lifestyles and hobbies. Geographical regional group: Ordinarily, consumers in different geographical regions have their own lifestyles, traditions and hobbies on account of factors of climate, geography and history.

The differences in sub-cultural group will collectively influence purchasing decision and behaviors of consumers.

(3) Social Hierarchy

It refers to the division of population into different levels of categories. The members of each level share similar value system, hobbies and behaviors. Because of their difference in financial conditions, value system and lifestyle in various levels, they have different preferences of enterprises, commodities, brands and so on.

2. Financial Factors

Financial factors that affect consumer behaviors may include commodity price, consumer income, effectiveness of commodity, etc.

(1) Price of commodities

This is the most important and direct factor that affects consumers' purchasing behaviors and there are three influences, namely, the price of commodity itself, the expected price of consumers, the price of other relevant consumer goods.

(2) Income of consumers

Income is an essential factor shaping purchasing behaviors of consumers. Different income level determines different levels and inclinations of needs. In developed western nations where the general income of consumers is high, it is characterized with diverse value systems, customized and diversified consumption. It is difficult to find a dominant value standard and increasingly difficult to draw up the trend of consumers. Conversely, in countries where the general income level of consumers is low, price plays a key role in consumer's decision-making process and consumption demonstration effects are rather evident.

(3) Effectiveness of commodities

The consumer purchasing behavior is a reasonable behavior and consumers will always

Chapter 4   Analysis of Market Behavior

reasonably arrange their expenses as allowed by their income to maximally meet their needs.

Economics complies with the 'principle of maximum marginal utility' in elaborating and analyzing the above mentioned rule. Marginal utility is decreasing and the influence of decreasing principle of marginal utility on purchasing behaviors exists in any market. When the price of any commodity falls, new needs will be created. Meanwhile, modification of products may stimulate new needs. Hence, enterprises are required to adopt multiple effective measures, such as lowering cost, selling price, improving product functions, increasing the usage of products, boosting product quality and modifying the exterior and furnishing of products so as to maximize marginal utility acquired by consumers in purchasing products of this enterprise to promote product sales of this enterprise.

3. Psychological Factors

The influence of psychological factor influences each and every single aspect of purchasing activities of consumers. This mainly analyzes motive, awareness, learning, faith and attitude as well as other factors that influence purchasing behaviors of consumers.

(1) Motive

Motive is an internal driving force behind bodily activity, maintaining existing activities and propelling activities towards a particular goal. Motive is the direct cause of behavior; it drives one to adopt certain actions, and pointing out the direction of activity. Researching motive is a prerequisite for researching human behavior.

Regarding needs and motives of human race, Abraham Maslow raises the theory of hierarchy of human needs. Their importance is ranked in the order of physical needs, security needs, social needs, respect needs, and self-fulfillment needs. The needs are ranked in increasing order; as the needs on lower level are met, one may try to fulfill needs on the next higher level. The hierarchy of needs proposed by Maslow is illustrated as in Figure 4.1.

The theory of Maslow's need and motive helps people to understand purchasing motive and behavior of consumers.

(2) Sense and Perception

The knowledge of consumers about the outside world starts from sense. Consumers feel the color, size, shape, sound and smell of commodities through sensory organs so that they may perceive the unique properties of a particular commodity.

As the sense deepens, information detected by each sense is connected in the brain to analyze, helping people to form a comprehensive overview of the product or scenario, which is the perception.

Perception is characterized with option, expressed in selective attention, understanding and memory.

The option of attention perception can engage the attention of consumers towards products or brands, understanding and memorizing tasks of marketing people.

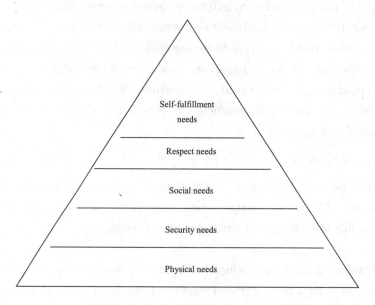

Figure 4.1　Maslow's Hierarchy of Needs

(3) Learning

Consumers gradually acquire knowledge, accumulate experience and adjust their purchasing behaviors based on experience in purchasing and utilizing commodities. The cognition of an individual is carried out through driving force, stimulant, trigger, mutual influence and interaction of response and reinforcement.

(4) Faith and Attitude

Faith refers to correctness of sticking closely to a certain opinion and deploying personal inclination of one's own behaviors, like when consumers believe that certain branded fridges are more energy-efficient than other brands. Marketing people should be concerned of faith formed in the brain towards its products and services, i.e. the image of product and image of this enterprise.

Attitude refers to relatively lasting and consistent psychological preparation or character inclination for people, events and things based on past experience. Once consumers have formed their fixed attitude towards a particular product or brand, they will be disposed to make repetitive purchasing decisions based on attitude and they are reluctant to compare and make judgment. The attitude held by consumers will influence the reception of information and purchasing

Chapter 4　Analysis of Market Behavior

decision-making process.

4. Personal Factors

The decision-making process of purchasers may be influenced by personal outward characteristics, especially the influence of the stage of life cycle one is in, economic environment, lifestyle, personality and self concept.

4.2.3　Consumer Purchasing Behavior Mode

There are enormous differences in consumer purchasing behavior due to different products purchased or brands. Besides, the extent of involvement differs due to different previous experience, interest and self-confidence.

According to different products purchased and the extent to which consumers are involved in shopping, consumer purchasing behaviors can be categorized into four types (see Figure 4.2)

		Extent of involvement	
		High	Low
Brand differences	Large	Complex purchasing behaviors	Purchasing behaviors of seeking for diversity
	Small	Reducing uncoordinated purchasing behaviors	Habitual purchasing behaviors

Figure 4.2　Types of Consumer Purchasing Behavior

1. Complex Purchasing Behaviors

Complex purchasing behaviors refer to the time when consumers are purchasing expensive, infrequently used and unfamiliar products, they will invest considerable energy and time in it, such as computers, automobiles and commercial houses.

2. Habitual Purchasing Behaviors

Habitual purchasing behaviors refer to the time when consumers are purchasing commodities that are cheap and rather similar between different brands, their involvement is pretty minimal. It will lead to development of purchasing habits, such as soy sauce and beer.

Regarding similar products, consumers have not conducted comprehensive research on brand information, nor have they made any assessment of brand characteristics. They are not concerned of which brand they want to purchase. Instead, they just passively receive information while watching TV or reading printed advertisements.

3. Reducing Uncoordinated Purchasing Behaviors

Reducing uncoordinated purchasing behaviors refer to the fact that consumers are not very much involved in purchasing products. However, once the purchasing process is done, it may generate feelings of regret and remorse and will manage to eliminate this sense of compromised coordination. For instance, some products are pricey, but the tremendous differences among brands are hard to discern. The process of purchasing is fast and simple, but after the purchase, they may easily feel the products they have bought are flawed or other similar products have more advantages.

4. Purchasing Behaviors of Seeking for Diversity

Purchasing behaviors of seeking for diversity refer to the situation when consumers are purchasing some inexpensive products that differ greatly among different brands; they may randomly and frequently change brands. For instance, products like biscuits are diverse in range and huge differences exist between different brands and price is low. Consumers usually make their purchasing decisions without giving adequate evaluation until one reaches cashier's counter.

4.2.4 Process of Consumers' Purchasing Decision-Making

Complex purchasing behaviors will ordinarily go through the full process of consumer decision-making (see Figure 4.3), which includes five steps: (1) requiring confirmation; (2) information searching; (3) selective plan assessment; (4) purchasing decision; (5) after-purchasing behavior. These five steps represent the entire process of consumers from purchasing need to final purchasing. Apparently, purchasing process has already started before actual purchasing takes place and will continue to exert potential influence after purchasing is done.

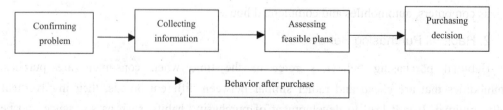

Figure 4.3 Process of Consumers' Purchasing Decision-Making

Chapter 4 Analysis of Market Behavior

4.3 Purchasing Behavior Analysis of Organizational Market

4.3.1 Concept and Types of Organizational Market

The organizational market is the market formed by organizations for purchasers in companies – a relative terms of consumer market. For buyers, the consumer market refers to the personal market and the organizational market refers to the market of legal representatives with the features of high volume, close relationship between supply and demand, and procurement professionals, etc. The organization market includes market of producers, intermediaries and the government.

(1) Producers' market refers to companies and individuals that purchase products or services to manufacture other products or services that will be, in turn, sold or leased to others in order to reap profits. The market of producers includes industry, agriculture, forestry, fishing industry, mining industry, construction, transportation, communication, public affairs, finance, insurance and service industries.

(2) Intermediaries' market is also known as resellers' market, which refers to companies and individuals, including wholesalers and retailers that purchase products to be resold or leased in order to reap profits.

(3) Government market refers to each level of government departments that purchase or rent products for the executive governmental organizations. Government is a special non-profit organization. Government has a solid grip or a considerable grip on the national income via taxation and finance, forming a hugely potential government sourcing market.

4.3.2 Analysis of Producers' Market Purchase Behavior

1. Features of Producers' Market Purchase Behavior

Producers' market is to sell products and services for enterprises, companies, hotels and other types of economic organizations. Various types of enterprises to purchase products and services are not intended to meet the organization's own consumption, but as the means of production, through the production process in order to profit. The main features of producers' market are as follows:

(1) Purchasers fewer, larger and more focused

Manufacturing enterprises, which are various types of production organizations, are the basic purchasing unit of producers' market. The number of them is much less than that of individuals and families. Due to production concentration and economy scales, the manufacturing enterprises want to reach a certain production lot, the purchase amount must be significant at one time.

(2) Derived demands

Derived demands or pulled demands, namely, producers' demands for production means are fundamentally caused by consumers' demands for consumable. For example, consumers' demands for domestic cars derive automobile plants' demands for steel. Derived demands require enterprises not only to understand the demand for direct service object, but also to understand the associated demands of the consumer market trends.

(3) Inelastic demands

Production means primarily depends on the demand for goods mix, production scale, process and technology factors, such as less affected by changes in prices. Their demand will not increase significantly because of low price, and will not result in a significant reduction in short-term demands in particular. In general, during purchasing, the producer often has a high requirement in product specifications, quality, function, delivery, service and technical guidance. By contrast, the unit price is usually not a major factor in purchasing decisions, which make the elasticity of demand not sufficient.

(4) Specialized purchase

Various types of economic organizations have the plan and strict requirements in the product quality, specifications, functions, etc. For technical advice, installation and maintenance, spare parts supply, delivery and credit conditions, they have higher requirements, and are not susceptible to advertising publicity and other promotional measures, and have a stronger reason to buy.

(5) The long-term purchaser-seller relationship

Purchasers and sellers on the producers' market tend to establish long-term business contacts, interdependence. The seller is often to participate in the decision-making in all stages of customer's purchase decision, to help customers solve some of the problem in the purchasing process and provide comprehensive pre-sales consulting, questions and answers and sale, after-sale service, and sometimes to help customers find products to meet their demands. Industry market supply-side must through effective customer service establish long-term business contacts, in order to maintain his stability of market share and corporate clients.

2. Major Factors in Affecting Purchase of Producers

Purchase for the means of production is one of the important decisions to an enterprise, which is subjected to the four major factors as follows (see Figure 4.4).

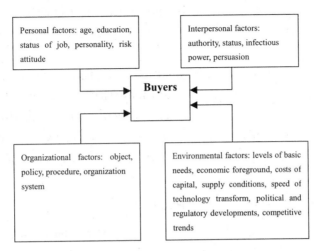

Figure 4.4 Major Factors in Affecting Purchase of Producers

(1) Environmental factors

Environmental factors point to all the external factors that affect marketing activities of an enterprise, which mainly include polity, law, economy, culture, technology, competition and the natural environment, etc. Buyers of producers' market are subjected to the time and expected economic impact of environmental factors greatly, such as the economic outlook, market demand, technological developments, market competition, and political law, etc.

(2) Organizational factors

Organizational factors point to a variety of internal factors of producers, including business goals, policies, business processes, organizational structure and system, etc. These factors affect the producer's buying decision on the interests of the organization, operation and development strategies and so on. Suppliers and marketing personnel who's in charge of the means of production, should understand and capitalize on these organizational factors, change trends, the possible impacted direction and extent of corporate buying, meanwhile, take appropriate measures to accelerate the making process of the producer's buying decision.

(3) Interpersonal factors

Interpersonal factors refer to the relationship between the personnel within the enterprise. Producer purchases are specifically implemented by the enterprise procurement center, the procurement center is made up of users, influencers, buyers, decision-makers, and information controllers and these five members are jointly involved in the purchase decision-making process, due to their position in the enterprise, terms of reference, sense of fun, convincing, and their inter-relationship between the different pairs have different, sometimes subtle, effects on purchasing decisions. Mastering these sensitive interpersonal factors is conducive to clear the purchase process and its role in population dynamics.

(4) Personal factors

Personal factors refer to individuals' motives, perception, preferences and buying styles, which are involved in production purchasing decisions. These factors are also constrained by the participants' age, income, education, personality, vocational identity, and risk attitudes. Purchase for the means of production initiated by an enterprise is essentially a specific buying behavior conducted by members of the procurement center, under the constraints of various factors both within and outside the enterprise.

3. Producers' Purchasing Behavior Patterns

Purchasers of production means don't make only one purchasing decision, but a series of decisions. The complexity of the decision-making depends on the complexity of the purchasing situation. As for purchase of production means, there are basically three types:

Direct repurchase: This refers to the simplest purchase, namely, the producers, according to routine situation, repurchase similar products. Procurement departments within an enterprise usually place the goods catalog according to past orders to the original supplier, sometimes they will make minor adjustments with consideration that various suppliers can meet their needs and the level of quality of service and supply units.

Amendments to repurchase: This refers to that the producer's purchasing department changes its procurement of certain industrial products specifications, prices and other conditions, and suppliers in order to better complete the procurement task. Such purchasing situation is more complicated, and therefore the number of people involved in the purchase decision-making process is more. This situation provides market opportunities to suppliers of "outside supplier firms" not included in the original list, while gives threat to the "listed supply enterprises".

Newly purchase: This refers to that the producer purchases a product for the first time. It often occurs on the occasion when the enterprises increases new projects or update their equipment. The higher cost of newly purchase is, the greater the risk is. Therefore, the number of people involved in the purchase decision-making and market information to be mastered must be large. Such purchase needs the most complex decision-making, and the time is the longest. Newly purchases are both opportunities and challenges for the providers.

In the case of direct repurchase, industrial purchasers make purchasing decisions least, which are essentially practice-oriented decision-making; while in the case of newly purchase, industrial purchasers make decisions most, usually including the following major decisions:

Chapter 4 Analysis of Market Behavior

product specifications, prices, delivery terms and time, conditions of service, payment terms, quantity, acceptable suppliers and selected providers. In general, the industrial purchasers need to negotiate with suppliers on the above issues, and make purchase choice according to results of the negotiations.

4. Process of Purchase Decision-Making

The purchase decision-making process of producers' market purchaser is somewhat similar to that of consumer, but differs to some extent. The process is classified into eight stages (see Table 4.1):

Table 4.1 Process of Producer Purchase Decision-Making

Stage	Types of Purchase		
	New Purchase	Modified repurchase	Direct repurchase
1. Concern confirmation	Yes	Possible	No
2. General demand confirmation	Yes	Possible	No
3. Product specs confirmation	Yes	Yes	Yes
4. Quotation search	Yes	Possible	No
5. Quotation collection	Yes	Possible	No
6. Quotation selection	Yes	Possible	No
7. Formal order	Yes	Possible	No
8. Application evaluation	Yes	Yes	Yes

(1) Concern confirmation

Members of an enterprise consider it is necessary to purchase some products. This marks the beginning of purchase decision.

(2) General demand confirmation

After concern confirmation, the category, features and amount of products demanded should be confirmed generally. For standard products, this is simple; while for complicated ones, purchasers should discuss and confirm the category, features and amount with engineering technicians and users.

(3) Product specification confirmation

After the general demand confirmation, specification, model and other technical parameters of the products should be specified in detail.

(4) Quotation search

Then the purchasers begin to search proper suppliers according to the demanded specifications. Later they will make an initial selection among suppliers. Thus suppliers should make their enterprises on the directory and establish a good reputation on the basis of popularity expansion.

(5) Quotation collection

Purchasers propose requirements for suppliers that have been selected out preliminarily, acquire information and suggestion from them, and ask them to send samples as soon as possible or product instructions, catalogue, etc. Detailed data are needed for complicated and expensive products.

(6) Quotation selection

Purchasers then compare and analyze suppliers after receiving relevant data from them. The following factors will be taken into account: production capability, delivery performance, enterprise credibility, product quality, price and specifications, financial status, service quality, maintenance ability, method of settlement, location, etc.

(7) Formal order

After selecting out the supplier, the user can make an order and contract with supplier on product specifications, amount, delivery, warranty and method of settlement.

(8) Application evaluation

After product arrival, the purchase department should contact the user department to know the application status of newly bought product and check and evaluate the performance of the contract signed with supplier so as to provide proof for purchase in future.

Of course, these eight stages are not necessarily to be carried out by all clients, because specific steps should be decided according to the category and decision of the purchase.

4.3.3 Analysis of Reseller and Government Purchase

1. Analysis of Reseller Purchase

(1) Features

A reseller market refers to a market of products and services resold by retailers and wholesalers. It is an important part of the organizational market with retailers and wholesalers as the main body. It has the following features compared with producer market and consumer market:

- Derived demands: Demands of resellers are triggered by those of consumers, thus products are restricted by consumers' demands in view of the category, color, specs, amount, price and delivery date, etc.

Chapter 4 Analysis of Market Behavior

- Strong selectiveness: Resellers pay particular attention to the reasonable combination during selecting products. They prefer to complete categories and plentiful colors so as to cater for consumers' diverse demands and improve their own benefits.
- Large demand elasticity: For resale's, resellers are sensitive to the cost, namely the price of reseller market, whose change will cause fluctuation of the demand.
- Bulk purchase and periodic ordering: With fixed purchase channels, resellers are always making bulk purchase and periodic ordering.

(2) Reseller purchase decision

As the social functions work, the resellers buy products first at a lower price and then sell them at a higher price to obtain the sales profit. Purchase decision plays a role in the strategy, because factors like category, specs, price, amount and time directly affect the profitability. Details are as below:

- Selection of product combination: The product combination not only acts as the feature of marketing, but also the main factor to attract customers. Besides, it effects and even decides the supplier combination, customer combination and marketing combination to a larger extent. Therefore, a reasonable and artful combination of products is the basic and most important strategy for resellers.

  Four combinations are generally adopted by resellers:
  - Exclusive sales: refers to that the reseller only sells products of one supplier, e.g. a household appliances store sells only Haier products. This mode is applicable to boutiques and franchise stores which deal with patent commodities, and those with technical skills and also special products.
  - Deep combination: refers to that the reseller sells the similar products of different specs, models, patterns and colors from numerous suppliers, e.g. a household appliances store sells air conditioners of various specs and models from Haier, Kelon and Chunlan.
  - Wide combination: refers to that the reseller sells different products of numerous suppliers, with wide scope but never beyond that of a reseller.
  - Comprehensive combination: refers to that the reseller sells diversified products of different types and specs from many suppliers, e.g. department stores, supermarkets and warehouse-style stores which cover products of plentiful colors, specs and all qualities.

- Supplier selection: Compared with consumers, the purchase of resellers enjoys stronger planning and sense. It is very important to select suppliers. Main factors cover the brand, popularity, quality, specs, production capability, delivery time and conditions together with cooperative willingness.

Producers always consider the demands of final consumers during design, development and production, but also take into account that of the resellers.

- Time and amount of purchase: As stated above, the derived demands of resellers are dependent on consumer market. Therefore, resellers are particularly concerned about the time and amount of purchase. They always hope to catch the market demand in time and meanwhile minimize the stock and improve the turnover velocity. Delivery time is more significant for seasonal, fashionable and fresh goods.
- Purchase terms: The terms of purchase are directly related to the benefit of resellers. Risks from market also compel resellers to get more favorable terms, such as discount, promotion allowance, store advertisement fee discount, freight reduction, credit security, and terms of payment, replacement of defective products, parts supply, price reduction guaranty, complaint assistance and after-sale service.

Under the condition of market economy, the resellers at the middle stream of commodity distribution connect the producers and final consumers and finally realize the value of commodity. Producers need to distribute their products through resellers, while the resellers are always trying to gain the best purchase terms for maximum benefits. Therefore, they face a fierce competition.

2. Analysis of Government Purchase

(1) Features

The government market emerges for sales of daily products and services demanded by government departments who are the main body.

As a significant part of the society, governments of all countries control most of the national income through tax collection and fiscal budget. For effective functions, they have a huge expenditure, thus shapes a special and large consumer market. Features are introduced as below.

- Demand restricted by policies: Economic policies have a strong impact on the consumption of governments, namely consumption demand will decrease in case of a reduced fiscal expenditure, and conversely it will rise.
- Strong planning of demand: All expenditure should be listed into the fiscal budget. Thus the demand is limited by the budget and the purchase planning should experience process like budget and approval.
- Various purchase modes: The mode of government purchase is more complicated than that of consumer market or reseller market. For ordinary office supplies, government purchasers usually choose suppliers first and then order and reorder at a regular time; for expensive bulk commodity such as planes and cars, a public bidding will be carried

Chapter 4 Analysis of Market Behavior

out; welfare commodity are always subject to the promotion of merchandisers.
- Demand supervised by public: The expenditure of governments comes from state finance which is accumulated by the tax. Thus the public enjoys the right to supervise the purchase actions of governments in different forms, and requires the governments to be efficient, just and honest and fulfill functions by minimum expenditure.
- Multiplicity of targets: During purchase, government purchasers not only consider the price but also other political, military and social targets. E.g. the purchase of national defense supplies and arms is connected with the political and diplomatic relations between two or multi countries; government purchase may be designed as support for some regions and some fields.

(2) Main modes

For effectively maintaining the social security, public interests and infrastructures, governments purchase goods of various types and huge amount, which is paid close attention to by the public. Thus the purchase mode is special.
- Public bidding: Government departments purchase goods and services through public bidding. Potential suppliers fill in the tender document within regulated duration, and specify names, category, specs, amount, delivery time, price and payment term of goods and then send the disclosed document to the purchase department concerned which then will open the tender at the stated time and contact one supplier with lowest price and qualified conditions.

  Through this mode, governments have no need to negotiate with sellers and can gain the maximum benefit through the competition among renderers. This is popular for all government purchase.
- Negotiation: The purchase department negotiates with one or several suppliers and then chooses only one qualified supplier.

  Generally speaking, this mode is applicable to purchase with complicated planning, tremendous risk and small competition.
- Regular buying: This is applicable to office supplies, consumables and welfare goods required by government departments for daily functions, because the category, specifications, price and payment terms are relatively fixed. Purchase departments always choose suppliers they are familiar with and keep stable cooperation relations with.

4.4 Summary

竞争是市场经济的基本特性，其基本概念反映在行业及行业结构、行业集中度、进入和退出障碍、竞争战略和战略集团、竞争目标和顾客价值分析等方面；识别竞争者的行为特点可根据不同层次、反应模式、在同一目标市场中的地位和其特性进行分类。

根据市场购买者和购买动机，市场分为两大类：消费者市场和组织市场。消费者市场是向个人和家庭销售消费品和服务的市场，具有广泛性、差异性、经常性和重复性、非专业性和伸缩性等特点。消费者购买行为受社会文化因素、经济因素、心理因素和个人因素的影响。在消费者购买行为模式中，购买者角色包括：发起者、影响者、决定者、购买者和使用者。消费者行为类型可分为四种：复杂的、习惯的、减少不协调感的和寻求多样性的。典型的消费者购买决策要经历确认问题、收集信息、评估可行方案、购买决策和购物行为五个阶段。组织市场指工商企业为从事生产、销售等业务活动以及政府部门和非营利组织为履行职责而购买产品和服务所构成的市场，具体包括生产者市场、中间市场和政府市场。组织市场具有购买者少、购买数量大、供需双方关系密切、购买者的地理位置相对集中、派生需求、需求弹性小、需求波动大、专业人员采购、影响购买的人多、销售访问多、直接采购、互惠购买和租赁的特点。生产者市场购买决策过程由确认问题、说明一般需要、确定产品价格、寻求报价、征求报价、选择报价、正式订购和评估使用结果所构成。中间商市场购买决策主要有选择购买的商品的编配组合、选择供应商、选择购买的时间和数量以及选择购买条件等项目。政府市场的主要购买方式有公开招标竞购、议价合约选购和例行选购。

Key Terms

Competitor Analysis   Competitor Classification   Competitor Behavior Features   Consumer Market Purchasing Behavior   Purchasing Behavior Analysis of Organizational Market   Producers' Marketing Purchase Behavior   Reseller and Government Purchase

【案例】小商品也能赚大钱

尼西奇公司在过去是一个生产雨衣、游泳帽、防雨篷等橡胶制品小商品的综合性企业。当时由于经济不稳，订货不足，曾濒临倒闭。作为尼西奇公司董事长的多川博，清楚地认识到如果不生产一种需求量大的产品，公司就站不住脚。他从日本政府的人口普查资料获悉，日本每年大约出生250万个婴儿，这个数字给了他一个不小的启示：如果每个婴儿每年只用两块尿垫，那么总需求就有500万块，除此以外，潜在市场需求也很大。他从这一数字中找到了做生意的思路，决定企业转产，专门生产经营尿垫。而生产尿垫，在当时，是大企业不屑干、小企业不愿干的买卖。商品不在大小，只要市场有需要，小商品同样能成为大宗货，做成大生意。正是基于这样的考虑，尼西奇公司做出了专门生产尿垫的经营决策，并集中力量创名牌产品。经过几十年的努力，终于使尼西奇公司尿垫在日本与丰田汽车、东芝彩电、夏普音响一样有名。

目前，日本婴儿所使用的尿垫，每三条中有两条是他们生产的。不仅如此，尼西奇公司生产的尿垫还远销西欧、非洲、美洲70多个国家和地区。近几年来，销售额每年持续递增20%，年销售额高达70亿美元，从而成为世界上最大的尿垫生产厂商。公司也连年被日本政府授予"出口有功企业"称号，并被誉为"尿布大王"。

(资料来源：曹刚，李桂陵，王德发等．国内外市场营销案例．武汉：武汉大学出版社，2003.)

【案例分析】

尼西奇公司生产的尿垫在日本与丰田汽车、东芝彩电、夏普音响一样有名，公司连年被日本政府授予"出口有功企业"称号，原因并不在于生产尿垫需要尖端的技术。作为一个拥有一定实力的综合性企业，生产尿垫并不难。尼西奇公司给予我们的启示在于：它从日本政府发布的人口普查资料中找到了做生意的思路，这是难能可贵的事情。联想到我们一些公司的经理、企业的厂长，敏感性却不强，有些生意赚头很大，却视而不见，甚至有些麻木不仁。俗话说："处处留心皆学问。"此话印证了尼西奇公司成功的经营之道。

【思考题】

1. 尼西奇公司的成功说明了什么？
2. 信息对企业的经营决策起什么样的作用？
3. 如何分析消费者行为？
4. 小商品如何能赚大钱？

Chapter 5

Market Segmentation, Targeting and Positioning

Focus on:

1. Levels, patterns and process of the market segmentation.
2. Foundations to segment the consumer market and the industrial market.
3. Effective market segmentation.
4. Evaluation and selection of the segments.
5. Choice and diffusion of the market positioning strategy.

A company cannot serve everyone in broad markets such as soft drinks (for consumers) and computers (for businesses), because the customers are too numerous and diverse in their buying requirements. This is why successful marketers look for specific market segments that they can serve more effectively. Instead of scattering their marketing efforts (a "shotgun" approach), they will be able to focus on the buyers whom they have the greatest chance of satisfying (a "rifle" approach). The most targeted marketing strategies are built around meeting each customer's unique requirements. Such mass customization strategies are particularly well suited to Internet marketing, where leaders such as Dell can maintain an interactive dialogue with customers and create a unique bundle of goods and services specifically for their individual needs and wants.

Target marketing requires marketers to take three major steps: (1) Identify and profile distinct groups of buyers who might require separate products or marketing mixes (market segmentation); (2) select one or more market segments to enter (market targeting); and (3) establish and communicate the products' key distinctive benefits in the market (market positioning).

5.1 Market Segmentation

Markets consist of buyers, and buyers differ in one or more ways. They may differ in their wants, resources, locations, buying attitudes, and buying practices. Through market segmentation,

Chapter 5 Market Segmentation, Targeting and Positioning

companies can divide large, heterogeneous markets into smaller segments that may be reached more efficiently and effectively with products and services that match their unique needs.

A marketer can rarely satisfy everyone in a market. Not everyone likes the same soft drink, automobile, college, and movie. Therefore, marketers start with market segmentation. They identify and profile distinct groups of buyers who might prefer or require various products and marketing mixes. Market segments can be identified by examining demographic, psychographic, and behavioral differences among buyers. The firm then decides which segments present the greatest opportunity, namely, whose needs the firm can meet in a superior fashion.

For each chosen target market, the firm develops a market offering. The offering is positioned in the minds of the target buyers as delivering some central benefit(s). For example, Volvo develops its cars for the target market of buyers for whom automobile safety is a major concern. Volvo, therefore, positions its car as the safest a customer can buy.

Traditionally, a "market" was a physical place where buyers and sellers gathered to exchange goods. Now marketers view the sellers as the industry and the buyers as the market. The sellers send goods and services and communications (ads, direct mail, e-mail messages) to the market; in return they receive money and information (attitudes, sales data).

A global industry is one in which the strategic positions of competitors in major geographic or national markets are fundamentally affected by their overall global positions. Global firms–both large and small–plan, operate, and coordinate their activities and exchanges on a worldwide basis.

Today we can distinguish between a marketplace and a market-space. The marketplace is physical, as when one goes shopping in a store; market-space is digital, as when one goes shopping on the Internet. E-commerce-business transactions conducted on-line–have many advantages for both consumers and businesses, including convenience, savings, selection, personalization, and information. For example, on-line shopping is so convenient that 30 percent of the orders generated by the Web site of REI, a recreational equipment retailer, is logged from 10 P.M. to 7 A.M., sparing REI the expense of keeping its stores open late or hiring customer service representatives. However, the e-commerce market-space is also bringing pressure from consumers for lower prices and is threatening intermediaries such as travel agents, stockbrokers, insurance agents, and traditional retailers. To succeed in the on-line market-space, marketers will need to reorganize and redefine themselves.

The meta-market, a concept proposed by Mohan Sawhney, describes a cluster of complementary products and services that are closely related in the minds of consumers but are spread across a diverse set of industries. The automobile meta-market consists of automobile manufacturers, new and used car dealers, financing companies, insurance companies, mechanics, spare parts dealers, service shops, auto magazines, classified auto ads in newspapers, and auto sites on the Internet. Car buyers can get involved in many parts of this meta-market. This has created an opportunity for meta-intermediaries to assist buyers to move seamlessly through these groups. One example is Edmund's (www.edmunds.com), a Web site where buyers can find prices for different cars and click to other sites to search for dealers, financing, and accessories. Meta-intermediaries can serve various meta-markets, such as the home ownership market, the parenting and baby care market, and the wedding market.

5.1.1　Using Market Segmentation

Market segmentation aims to increase a company's precision marketing. In contrast, sellers that use mass marketing engage in the mass production, distribution, and promotion of one product for all buyers. Henry Ford epitomized this strategy when he offered the Model T Ford "in any color, as long as it is black." Coca-Cola also used mass marketing when it sold only one kind of Coke in a 6.5-ounce bottle.

The argument for the mass marketing is that it creates the largest potential market, which leads to the lowest costs, and in turn to lower prices or higher margins. However, many critics point to the increasing splintering of the market, making the mass marketing more difficult. According to Regis McKenna,

"[Consumers] have more ways to shop: at giant malls, specialty shops, and superstores; through mail-order catalogs, home shopping networks, and virtual stores on the Internet. And they are bombarded with messages pitched through a growing number of channels: broadcast and narrow-cast television, radio, on-line computer networks, the Internet, telephone services such as fax and telemarketing, and niche magazines and other print media."

This proliferation of media and distribution channels is making it difficult to practice "one size fits all" marketing. Some observers even claim that the mass marketing is dying. Therefore, to stay focused rather than scattering their marketing resources, more marketers are using market segmentation. In this approach that falls midway between mass marketing and individual marketing, each segment's buyers are assumed to be quite similar in wants and needs, yet no two buyers are really alike. To use this technique, a company must understand both the levels and the patterns of market segmentation.

Chapter 5 Market Segmentation, Targeting and Positioning

5.1.2 Levels of Market Segmentation

Regardless of whether they serve the consumer market or the business market-offering either goods or services-companies can apply segmentation at one of four levels: segments, niches, local areas, and individuals.

1. Segment Marketing

A market segment consists of a large identifiable group within a market, with similar wants, purchasing power, geographical location, buying attitudes, or buying habits. For example, an automaker may identify four broad segments in the car market: buyers who are primarily seeking (1) basic transportation, (2) high performance, (3) luxury, or (4) safety.

Because the needs, preferences, and behavior of segment members are similar but not identical, Anderson and Narus urge marketers to present flexible market offerings instead of one standard offering to all members of a segment. A flexible market offering consists of the product and service elements that all segment members' value, plus options (for an additional charge) that some segment members' value. For example, Delta Airlines offers all economy passengers a seat, food, and soft drinks, but it charges extra for alcoholic beverages and earphones.

Segment marketing allows a firm to create a more fine-tuned product or service offering and price it appropriately for the target audience. The choice of distribution channels and communications channels becomes much easier, and the firm may find it face fewer competitors in certain segments.

2. Niche Marketing

A niche is a more narrowly defined group, typically a small market whose needs are not being well served. Marketers usually identify niches by dividing a segment into subsegments or by defining a group seeking a distinctive mix of benefits. For example, a tobacco company might identify two subsegments of heavy smokers: those who are trying to stop smoking, and those who don't care.

In an attractive niche, customers have a distinct set of needs; they will pay a premium to the firm that best satisfies their needs; the niche is not likely to attract other competitors; the nicher gains certain economies through specialization; and the niche has size, profit, and growth potential. Whereas segments are fairly large and normally attract several competitors, niches are fairly small and may attract only one or two rivals. Still, giants such as IBM can and do lose pieces of their market to nichers: Dalgic labeled this confrontation "guerrillas against gorillas."

Some larger firms have therefore turned to niche marketing. Ramada Franchises Enterprises, for example, offers lodgings in several niches: Ramada Limited for economy travelers; Ramada Inn as a mid-price, full-service hotel; Ramada Plaza for the upper-mid-price niche; Ramada Hotels for good quality, three-star service; and Ramada Renaissance hotels, offering excellent, four-star service. Many German midsize companies are also profiting through smart niching: Tetra Food supplies 80 percent of the food for tropical fish; Hohner holds 85 percent of the world harmonica market; and Becher has 50 percent of the world's oversized umbrella market. These firms are succeeding in their chosen niches because they are dedicated to their customers, offer superior services, and innovate continuously.

Now the low cost of marketing on the Internet is making it more profitable for firms-including small businesses-to serve even seemingly minuscule niches. In fact, 15 percent of all commercial Web sites with fewer than 10 employees take in more than $100,000, and 2 percent ring up more than $1 million. The recipe for Internet niching success: choose a hard-to-find product that customers don't need to see and touch. Consider Steve Warrington's successful on-line venture selling ostriches and every product derived from them (www.ostrichesonline.com). Launched for next to nothing on the Web, Warrington's business generates annual sales of $4 million-plus. Visitors to the site can buy ostrich meat, feathers, leather jackets, videos, eggshells, and skin-care products derived from ostrich body oil.

3. Local Marketing

Target marketing is leading to some marketing programs that are tailored to the needs and wants of local customer groups (trading areas, neighborhoods, even individual stores). Citibank, for instance, adjusts its banking services in each branch depending on neighborhood demographics; Kraft helps supermarket chains identify the cheese assortment and shelf positioning that will optimize cheese sales in low-, middle-, and high-income stores and in different ethnic neighborhoods.

Those favoring local marketing see national advertising as wasteful because it fails to address local needs. On the other hand, opponents argue that local marketing drives up manufacturing and marketing costs by reducing economies of scale. Moreover, logistical problems become magnified when companies try to meet varying local requirements, and a brand's overall image might be diluted if the product and message differ in different localities.

4. Individual Marketing

The ultimate level of segmentation leads to "segments of one", "customized marketing", or "one-to-one marketing". For centuries, consumers were served as individuals: The tailor made

Chapter 5 Market Segmentation, Targeting and Positioning

the suit and the cobbler designed shoes for the individual. Much business-to-business marketing today is customized, in which a manufacturer will customize the offer, logistics, communications, and financial terms for each major account. Now technologies such as computers, databases, robotic production, intranets and extranets, e-mail, and fax communication are permitting companies to return to customized marketing, also called "mass customization". Mass customization is the ability to prepare individually designed products and communications on a mass basis to meet each customer's requirements.

Although individual customers are taking more initiative in designing and buying products, marketers still need to influence the process in a variety of ways. They need toll-free phone numbers and e-mail addresses to enable buyers to reach them with questions, suggestions, and complaints; they must involve customers more in the product-specification process; and they need a Web site with complete, updated information about the company's products, service guarantees, and locations.

5.1.3 Patterns of Market Segmentation

Market segments can be built up in many ways. One common method is to identify preference segments. Suppose ice cream buyers are asked how much they value sweetness and creaminess as two product attributes. Three different patterns can emerge:

1. Homogeneous Preferences

Figure 5.1 shows a market in which all of the consumers have roughly the same preference, so there are no natural segments. We predict that existing brands would be similar and cluster around the middle of the scale in both sweetness and creaminess.

2. Diffused Preferences

At the other extreme, consumer preferences may be scattered throughout the space (see Figure 5.1), indicating great variance in consumer preferences. One brand might position in the center to appeal to the most people; if several brands are in the market, they are likely to position throughout the space and show real differences to reflect consumer-preference differences.

3. Clustered Preferences

The market might reveal distinct preference clusters, called natural market segments (see Figure 5.1). The first firm in this market might position in the center to appeal to all groups, choose the largest market segment (concentrated marketing), or develop several brands for different segments. If the first firm has only one brand, competitors would enter and introduce brands in the other segments.

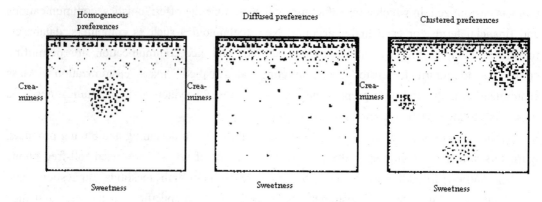

Figure 5.1   Basic Market-Preference Patterns

Smart marketers examine such segmentation patterns carefully to better understand the various positions they might take in a market-and the competitive implications.

5.1.4   Market-Segmentation Procedure

Marketers use a three-step procedure for identifying market segments:

1. Survey Stage

The researcher conducts exploratory interviews and focus groups to gain insight into customer motivations, attitudes, and behavior. Then the researcher prepares a questionnaire and collects data on attributes and their importance ratings, brand awareness and brand ratings, product-usage patterns, attitudes toward the product category, and respondents' demographics, geographics, psychographics, and media-graphics.

2. Analysis Stage

The researcher applies factor analysis to the data to remove highly correlated variables, and then uses cluster analysis to create a specified number of maximally different segments.

3. Profiling Stage

Each cluster is profiled in terms of its distinguishing attitudes, behavior, demographics, psychographics, and media patterns, and then each segment is given a name based on its dominant characteristic. In a study of the leisure market, Andreasen and Belk found six segments: passive homebody, active sports enthusiast, inner-directed self-sufficient, culture patron, active

Chapter 5 Market Segmentation, Targeting and Positioning

homebody, and socially active. They found that performing arts organizations could sell the most tickets by targeting culture patrons as well as socially active people.

Companies can uncover new segments by researching the hierarchy of attributes that customers consider when choosing a brand. For instance, car buyers who first decide on price are price dominant; those who first decide on car type (e.g., passenger, sport-utility) are type dominant; those who first decide on brand are brand dominant. With these segments, customers may have distinct demographics, psychographics, and media-graphics to be analyzed and addressed through marketing programs.

5.1.5 Bases for Segmenting Consumer Market

In segmenting the consumer market, marketers can apply geographic, demographic, and psychographic variables related to consumer characteristics as well as behavioral variables related to consumer responses. Once the segments are formed, the marketer sees whether different characteristics are associated with each consumer response segment. For example, the researcher might examine whether car buyers who want "quality" versus "low price" differ in their geographic, demographic, and psychographic makeup. This will determine whether the segments are useful for marketing purposes.

1. Geographic Segmentation

Geographic segmentation calls for dividing the market into different geographical units such as nations, states, regions, counties, cities, or neighborhoods. The company can operate in one or a few geographic areas or operate in all but pay attention to local variations. Some marketers even segment down to a specific zip code. Consider Blockbuster, which has databases to track the video preferences of its 85 million members and buys additional demographic data about each store's local area. As a result of this segmentation, it stocks its San Francisco stores with more gay-oriented videos, reflecting the city's large gay population, while it stocks Chicago stores with more family-oriented videos. Blockbuster can even distinguish between patterns of East Dallas and South Dallas customers.

2. Demographic Segmentation

In demographic segmentation, the market is divided into groups on the basis of age and the other variables. One reason is that the most popular consumer segmentation method depending on consumer wants, preferences, and usage rates are often associated with demographic variables. Another reason is that demographic variables are easier to measure. Even when the target market is described in non-demographic terms (say, a personality type), the link to the demographic characteristics is needed in order to estimate the size of the target market and the media that should be used to reach it efficiently.

Many demographic variables may be used to segment consumer market as below: age and life-cycle stage; gender; income; generation; social class.

3. Psychographic Segmentation

In psychographic segmentation, buyers are divided into different groups on the basis of lifestyle or personality and values. People within the same demographic group can exhibit very different psychographic profiles.

Psychographic variables include (1) Lifestyle. People exhibit many more lifestyles than are suggested by the seven social classes, and the goods they consume express their lifestyles; (2) Personality. Marketers can endow their products with brand personalities that correspond to consumer personalities; (3) Values. Core values are the belief systems that underlie consumer attitudes and behaviors. Core values go much deeper than behavior or attitude, and determine, at a basic level, people's choices and desires over the long term. Marketers who use this segmentation variable believe that by appealing to people's inner selves, it is possible to influence purchase behavior.

4. Behavioral Segmentation

In behavioral segmentation, buyers are divided into groups on the basis of their knowledge of, attitude toward, use of, or response to a product. Many marketers believe that behavioral variables-occasions, benefits, user status, usage rate, loyalty status, buyer-readiness stage, and attitude-are the best starting points for constructing market segments.

5. Multi-Attribute Segmentation (Geo-Clustering)

Marketers are increasingly combining several variables in an effort to identify smaller, better defined target groups. Thus, a bank may not only identify a group of wealthy retired adults, but may distinguish several segments depending on current income, assets, savings, and risk preferences within that group.

One of the most promising developments in multi-attribute segmentation is geo-clustering, which yields richer descriptions of consumers and neighborhoods than do traditional demographics. Geo-clustering can help a firm answer such questions as follows: Which clusters (neighborhoods or zip codes) contain our most valuable customers? How deeply have we already penetrated these segments? Which markets provide the best opportunities for growth?

Chapter 5　Market Segmentation, Targeting and Positioning

5.1.6　Bases for Segmenting Business Market

The business market can be segmented with some variables that are employed in consumer market segmentation, such as geography, benefits sought, and usage rate. Yet business marketers can also use several other variables.

The major segmentation variables for segmenting the business market as below: (1) Demographic: including industry, company size and location; (2) Operating variables: including technology, user or nonuser status and customer capabilities; (3) Purchasing approaches: including purchasing-function organization, power structure, nature of existing relationships, general purchase policies and purchasing criteria; (4) Situational factors: including urgency, specific application, and size of order; (5) Personal characteristics: including buyer-seller similarity, attitudes toward risk and loyalty toward the supplier.

A company should first decide which industries it wants to serve. Then, within a chosen target industry, the company can further segment by company size, possibly setting up separate operations for selling to large and small customers.

5.1.7　Effective Segmentation

Even after applying segmentation variables to a consumer or business market, marketers must realize that not all segmentations are useful. For example, table salt buyers can be divided into blond and brunette customers, but hair color is not relevant to the purchase of salt. Furthermore, if all salt buyers buy the same amount of salt each month, believe all salt is the same, and would pay only one price for salt, this market would be minimally able to be segmented from a marketing perspective.

To be useful, market segments must be

1. Measurable

The size, purchasing power, and characteristics of the segments can be measured.

2. Substantial

The segments are large and profitable enough to serve. A segment should be the largest possible homogeneous group worth going after with a tailored marketing program.

3. Accessible

The segments can be effectively reached and served.

4. Differentiable

The segments are conceptually distinguishable and respond differently to different marketing mixes. If two segments respond identically to a particular offer, they do not constitute separate segments.

5. Actionable

Effective programs can be formulated for attracting and serving the segments.

5.2 Market Targeting

Once the firm has identified its market-segment opportunities, it is ready to initiate market targeting. Here, marketers evaluate each segment to determine how many and which ones to target and enter.

5.2.1 Evaluating Market Segments

In evaluating different market segments, the firm must consider two factors: (1) the segment's overall attractiveness, and (2) the company's objectives and resources. First, the firm must ask whether a potential segment has the characteristics that make it generally attractive, such as size, growth, profitability, scale economies, and low risk.

Second, the firm must consider whether investing in the segment makes sense in the firm's given objectives and resources. Some attractive segments can be dismissed because they do not mesh with the company's long-run objectives; some should be dismissed if the company lacks one or more of the competences needed to offer superior value.

5.2.2 Selecting and Entering Market Segments

Having evaluated different segments, the company can consider five patterns of target market selection, as shown in Figure 5.2.

Chapter 5 Market Segmentation, Targeting and Positioning

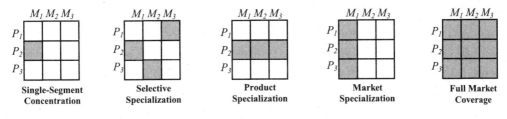

Figure 5.2 Five Patterns of Target Market Selection

1. Single-Segment Concentration

Many companies concentrate on a single segment: Volkswagen, for example, concentrates on the small-car market, while Porsche concentrates on the sports car market. Through concentrated marketing, the firm gains a thorough understanding of the segment's needs and achieves a strong market presence. Furthermore, the firm enjoys operating economies by specializing its production, distribution, and promotion; if it attains segment leadership, it can earn a high return on its investment.

However, concentrated marketing involves higher than normal risks if the segment turns sour because of changes in buying patterns or new competition. For these reasons, many companies prefer to operate in more than one segment.

2. Selective Specialization

Here the firm selects a number of segments, each objectively attractive and appropriate. There may be little or no synergy among the segments, but each segment disperses the firm's risk.

3. Product Specialization

Another approach is to specialize in making a certain product for several segments. An example would be a microscope manufacturer that sells microscopes to university laboratories, government laboratories, and commercial laboratories. The firm makes different microscopes for different customer groups but does not manufacture other instruments that laboratories might use. Through a product specialization strategy, the firm builds a strong reputation in the specific product area. The downside risk is that the product may be supplanted by an entirely new technology.

4. Market Specialization

With market specialization, the firm concentrates on serving many needs of a particular customer group. An example would be a firm that sells an assortment of products only to university laboratories, including microscopes, oscilloscopes, and chemical flasks. The firm gains a strong reputation in serving this customer group and becomes a channel for further products that the customer group can use. However, the downside risk is that the customer group may have its budgets cut.

5. Full Market Coverage

Here a firm attempts to serve all customer groups with all of the products they might need. Only very large firms can undertake a full market coverage strategy. Examples include IBM (computer market), General Motors (vehicle market), and Coca-Cola (drink market). Large firms can cover a whole market in two broad ways: through undifferentiated marketing or differentiated marketing.

In undifferentiated marketing, the firm ignores market-segment differences and goes after the whole market with one market offer. Focusing on a basic buyer need, it designs a product and a marketing program that will appeal to the broadest number of buyers. To reach the market, the firm uses mass distribution backed by mass advertising to create a superior product image in people's minds. The narrow product line keeps down costs of research and development, production, inventory, transportation, marketing research, advertising, and product management; the undifferentiated advertising program keeps down advertising costs. Presumably, the company can turn its lower costs into lower prices to win the price-sensitive segment of the market.

In differentiated marketing, the firm operates in several market segments and designs different programs for each segment. General Motors does this with its various vehicle brands and models; Intel does this with chips and programs for the consumer, business, small business, networking, digital imaging, and video markets. Differentiated marketing typically creates more total sales than undifferentiated marketing does. However, the need for different products and marketing programs also increases the firm's costs for product modification, manufacturing, administration, inventory, and promotion.

Because differentiated marketing leads to both higher sales and higher costs, we cannot generalize this strategy's profitability. Still, companies should be cautious about over-segmenting their market. If this happens, they may want to use counter-segmentation to broaden their customer base. Smith Kline Beecham introduced Aquafresh toothpaste to attract three benefit segments simultaneously: those seeking fresh breath, whiter teeth, and cavity protection. Next, the company moved deeper into counter-segmentation by launching flavored toothpastes for children, toothpastes for people with sensitive teeth, and other toothpaste products.

5.2.3 Targeting Multiple Segments and Super-Segments

Very often, companies start out by marketing to one segment, then expanding to others. For example, Paging Network Inc. – known as PageNet – is a small developer of paging systems, and was the first to offer voice mail on pagers. To compete with Southwestern Bell and other Bell companies, it sets its prices about 20 percent below rivals' prices. Initially, PageNet used geographic segmentation to identify attractive markets in Ohio and Texas where local competitors were vulnerable to its aggressive pricing. Next, the firm developed a profile of users for paging services so it could target salespeople, messengers, and service people. PageNet also used lifestyle segmentation to target additional consumer groups, such as parents who leave their children with a sitter. Finally, PageNet began distributing its pagers through Kmart, Wal-Mart, and Home Depot, offering attractive discounts in return for the right to keep the monthly service charge revenues on any pagers sold.

In targeting more than one segment, a company should examine segment interrelationships on the cost, performance, and technology side. A company that is carrying fixed costs, such as a sales force or store outlets, can generally add products to absorb and share some of these costs. Smart companies know that economies of scope can be just as important as economies of scale. Moreover, companies should look beyond isolated segments to target a super-segment, a set of segments that share some exploitable similarity. For example, many symphony orchestras target people with broad cultural interests, rather than only those who regularly attend concerts.

Still, a company's invasion plans can be thwarted when it confronts blocked markets. This problem calls for mega-marketing, the strategic coordination of economic, psychological, political, and public-relations skills to gain the cooperation of a number of parties in order to enter or operate in a given market. Pepsi used mega-marketing to enter India after Coca-Cola left the market. First, it worked with a local business group to gain government approval for its entry over the objections of domestic soft-drink companies and anti-multinational legislators. Pepsi also offered to help India export enough agricultural products to more than cover the cost of importing soft-drink concentrate and promised economic development for some rural areas. By winning the support of these and other interest groups, Pepsi was finally able to crack the Indian market.

5.2.4 Ethical Choice of Market Targets

Market targeting sometimes generates public controversy. The public is concerned when marketers take unfair advantage of vulnerable groups (such as children) or disadvantaged groups (such as inner-city poor people), or promote potentially harmful products. For example, the cereal industry has been criticized for marketing to children. Critics worry that high-powered appeals presented through the mouths of lovable animated characters will overwhelm children's defenses and lead them to eat too much sugared cereal or poorly balanced breakfasts.

Thus, in the choice of market targets, the issue is not who is targeted, but rather how and for what purpose. Socially responsible marketing calls for targeting and positioning that serve not only the company's interests but also the interests of those targeted.

5.3 Market Positioning

Beyond deciding which segments of the market it will target, the company must decide what position it wants to occupy in those segments. A product's position is the way the product is defined by consumers on important attributes-the place the product occupies in consumers' minds relative to competing products. Positioning involves implanting the brand's unique benefits and differentiation in customers' minds. The end result of positioning is the successful creation of a market-focused value proposition, a cogent reason why the target market should buy the product.

Consumers are overloaded with information about products and services. They cannot reevaluate products every time they make a buying decision. To simplify the buying process, consumers organize products, services, and companies into categories and "position" them in their minds. A product's position is the complex set of perceptions, impressions and feelings that consumers have for the product compared with competing products.

Consumers position products with or without the help of marketers. But marketers do not want to leave their products' positions to chance. They must plan positions that will give their products the greatest advantage in selected target markets, and they must design marketing mixes to create these planned positions.

Chapter 5　Market Segmentation, Targeting and Positioning

5.3.1 Choosing a Positioning Strategy

Some firms find it easy to choose their positioning strategy. For example, a firm well known for quality in certain segments will go for this position in a new segment if there are enough buyers seeking quality. But in many cases, two or more firms will go after the same position. Then each will have to find other ways to set itself apart. Each firm must differentiate its offer by building a unique bundle of benefits that appeal to a substantial group within the segment.

The positioning task consists of three steps: identifying a set of possible competitive advantages upon which to build a position, choosing the right competitive advantages, and selecting an overall positioning strategy. The company must then effectively communicate and deliver the chosen position to the market.

1. Identifying Possible Competitive Advantages

To build profitable relationships with target customers, marketers must understand customer needs better than competitors do and deliver more value. To the extent that a company can position itself as providing superior value, it gains competitive advantages. But solid positions cannot be built on empty promises. If a company positions its product as offering the best quality and service, it must then deliver the promised quality and service. Thus, positioning begins with actually differentiating the company's marketing offer so that it will give consumers superior value.

To find points of differentiation, marketers must think through the customer's entire experience with the company's product or service. An alert company can find ways to differentiate itself at every customer contact point. In what specific ways can a company differentiate itself or its market offer? It can differentiate along the lines of product, service, channels, people, or image.

Product differentiation takes place along a continuum. At one extreme we find physical products that allow little variation: chicken, steel, aspirin. Yet even here some meaningful differentiation is possible. At the other extreme are products that can be highly differentiated, such as automobiles, clothing, and furniture. Such products can be differentiated on features, performance, or style and design.

Beyond differentiating its physical product, a firm can also differentiate the services that accompany the product. Some companies gain services differentiation through speedy, convenient, or careful delivery.

Installation can also differentiate one company from another, as can repair services. Many automobile buyers will gladly pay a little more and travel a little farther to buy a car from a dealer that provides top-notch repair services. Some companies differentiate their offers by providing customer training services or consulting services-data, information systems, and advising services that buyers need.

Firms that practice channel differentiation gain competitive advantages in the way they design their channel's coverage, expertise, and performance.

Companies can gain a strong competitive advantage through people differentiation-hiring and training better people than their competitors do. Disney people are known to be friendly and upbeat. Singapore Airlines enjoys an excellent reputation largely because of the grace of its flight attendants.

Even when competing offers look the same, buyers may perceive a difference based on company or brand image differentiation. A company or brand image should convey the product's distinctive benefits and positioning. Developing a strong and distinctive image calls for creativity and hard work.

2. Choosing the Right Competitive Advantages

Suppose a company is fortunate enough to discover several potential competitive advantages. It now must choose the ones on which it will build its positioning strategy. It must decide how many differences to promote and which ones.

(1) How many differences to promote? Many marketers think that companies should aggressively promote only one benefit to the target market. Ad man Rosser Reeves, for example, said a company should develop a unique selling proposition (USP) for each brand and stick to it. Each brand should pick an attribute and tout itself as "number one" on that attribute. Buyers tend to remember number one better, especially in an over-communicated society.

Other marketers think that companies should position themselves on more than one differentiator. This may be necessary if two or more firms are claiming to be best on the same attribute. Today, in a time when the mass market is fragmenting into many small segments, companies are trying to broaden their positioning strategies to appeal to more segments.

(2) Which differences to promote? All products can be differentiated to some extent. But not all brand differences are meaningful or worthwhile. A difference is worth establishing to the extent that it satisfies the following criteria:

Important: the difference delivers a highly valued benefit to a sufficient number of buyers.

Distinctive: the difference is delivered in a distinctive way.

Superior: the difference is superior to other ways of obtaining the benefit.

Preemptive: the difference cannot be copied easily by competitors.

Chapter 5 Market Segmentation, Targeting and Positioning

Affordable: the buyer can afford to pay for the difference.

Profitable: the company will find it profitable to introduce the difference.

3. Selecting an Overall Positioning Strategy

Consumers typically choose products and services that give them the greatest value. Thus, marketers want to position their brands on the key benefits that they offer relative to competing brands. The full positioning of a brand is called the brand's value position-the full mix of benefits upon which the brand is positioned. It is the answer to the customer's question "Why should I buy your brand?"

Five possible value propositions can be selected upon which a company might position its products: more for more, more for the same, the same for less, less for much less, and more for less.

More for more: "More for more" positioning involves providing the most upscale product or service and charging a higher price to cover the higher costs.

More for the same: Companies can attack a competitor's more-for-more positioning by introducing a brand offering comparable quality but at a lower price.

The same for less: Companies can offer many of the same brands but at deep discounts based on their superior purchasing power and low-cost operations. Possibly they can develop imitative but lower-priced brands in an effort to lure customers away from the market leader.

Less for much less: "Less for much less" positioning involves meeting consumers' lower performance or quality requirements at much lower price.

More for less: "More for less" positioning involves providing the best product or service but charging a quite low price.

5.3.2 Communicating the Company's Positioning

Once the company has developed a clear positioning strategy, it must communicate that positioning effectively through all facets of the marketing mix and every point of contact with customers. Suppose a service company chooses the "best-in-quality" strategy. A good example is Ritz Carlton hotels, which signals high quality by training its employees to answer calls within three rings, to answer with a genuine "smile" in their voices, and to be extremely knowledgeable about all hotel information.

On the other hand, companies risk confusing the target audience if their marketing tactics run counter to their positioning. For example, a well-known frozen-food brand lost its prestige image by putting its products on sale too often. A smart company carefully coordinates its marketing-mix activities and its offers to support its positioning. New products may be the lifeblood of a growing firm, but they must be clearly differentiated and properly positioned to be competitive.

5.4 Summary

  目标营销策略涉及三方面的活动：市场细分、目标市场的选择和市场定位。市场细分的层次包括：细分、补缺、本地化和个别化。市场细分的过程包括调查、分析和成型三个阶段。消费者市场细分的变量包括地理细分、人文细分、心理细分和行为细分，企业市场细分除了应用这些变量之外，还有经营变量、购买方法、环境因素及个人特质等。有效的市场细分必须考察可衡量性、足量性、可接近性、差异性和行动可能性。

  评估细分市场需要考察其吸引力以及是否与公司的目标和资源相一致。在目标市场的选择上，公司可以集中力量在单一市场、选择多个市场、产品专门化、市场专门化或完全市场覆盖。营销者在选择目标市场时必须考虑社会责任问题。

  公司在选择定位战略时必须识别可能的竞争优势并选择正确的竞争优势。定位战略一旦形成，公司必须强有力地传播所选择的定位。

Key Terms

Market Segmentation Choice of Target Market Market Location Segment Marketing Niche Marketing Local Marketing Individual Marketing Homogeneous Preference Diffused Preference Clustered Preference Geographic Segmentation Demographic Segmentation Psychographic Segmentation Behavioral Segmentation Multi-Attribute Segmentation Single-Segment Concentration Selective Specialization Product Specialization Market Specialization Full Market Coverage Multiple Segments Super-segment Competitive Advantage

【案例】 乔安娜的晚装租赁业务

  英国伦敦的时装设计师乔安娜·多尼格，是一位很能发现经营目标的有心人。有一次她的朋友因为要出席皇家宴会而没有合适的晚装，紧张得如热锅上的蚂蚁。这事令她醒悟到，女士们遇到这一困境是很有普遍性的，这是英国社会现象的一种规律。英国是个很注重表面礼仪的社会，各种社交活动很多，人们参加社交活动时，对穿着非常讲究。但大多数人收入并不十分多，买不起华贵的服装，如果付较少的钱，就能在一夜中穿上名贵的时装出席高贵的活动，这确是光彩又省钱的事，这成为许多人的共同心愿。

  乔安娜有了这一想法后，做了大量的调查，找了不少妇女征询，证实了上述分析和预测是准确的。于是，她确定了开展晚装租赁业务的经营目标。她筹集了一笔资金，买回各种款式的欧美名师设计的晚礼服，价值每套数百美元到数千美元不等。她租出一夜的租金为每套 75 美元至 300 美元，另加收 200 美元的保证金。

果然不出所料，她的租赁生意十分兴旺，不少客人是由朋友介绍来的。也就是说，那些女士们毫不介意告诉别人，自己的晚装是租回来的。人们并不认为不光彩，反而觉得合算及明智呢！

乔安娜的这项业务越做越大，在伦敦开了两间店后，还越洋到美国纽约去开分店。现在，她除了经营晚装，还将业务扩展到配饰、手袋、首饰以及肥胖者、孕妇用的晚装，乃至男士用的服装等一应俱全。她已由一个设计师成为一名富豪了。

(资料来源：改编自赵光忠等著. 领导决策力 18 法则. 北京：中华工商联合出版社，2006.)

【案例分析】

在欧美社会，人们经常举行大大小小的舞会、宴会、庆祝会、生日会。宾客讲究仪表雍容，女士们穿的晚礼服更是款式时髦，艳丽高贵。但是，不管多么华丽名贵，若连续在这类场合穿着同一款三次，人们就会窃窃私语，穿者自然会感到失体丢脸。因此，无论多好的晚礼服，也只能显赫一两次。这样，不但使普通收入的人们忧愁，连有钱的人们亦操心。这些市场消费现象被乔安娜看准了，她"见微知著"确定了一个经营目标，也准确无误地实现了她的决策目标。

【思考题】

1. 乔安娜是如何选择其目标市场并进行定位的？
2. 该案例带给你哪些启示？

Part III   Marketing Elements

Chapter 6

Marketing Strategies

Focus on:

1. Connotation and composition of the marketing strategy.

2. How to determine the firm's business or business portfolio by using the Grand Strategy Model.

3. Respective features of the overall growth investment strategy, the sustainable market-expansion strategy, the alternative growth strategy, and the shifted-out control strategy.

4. Analyze the roles of the forward integration strategy, the backward integration strategy and the horizontal integration strategy in the firm's operational activities.

6.1   Generalities

6.1.1   Connotation of the Marketing Strategy

Strategies usually mean the pathway to reach the target. Philip Kotler points out that when an organization has ascertained its targets, it knows what it is doing and where it will go. The problem lies in which pathway is the best to go there and thus it needs an overall plan to implement its plan, and this is the strategy, he adds.

The marketing strategy means a whole action plan with a long period made by the enterprise for the marketing activities so as to survive and develop in the dynamic sharpened competitive market. It is laid down upon the analysis of the conditions inside and outside the enterprise. It is

Chapter 6 Marketing Strategies

aimed at adapting to the fluctuating marketing environment by expanding the horizon, seizing the market opportunities and avoiding the marketing myopia in the angle of the enterprise's strategy.

6.1.2 Functions of the Marketing Strategy

The marketing strategy has the following functions in the marketing activities:

It is the overall guiding ideology and elementary tool to coordinate all sorts of activities such as fund raising, resource allocation, production, selling process, etc. in the enterprise. It is favorable to integrating the ideas of the employees and to making effective use of all kinds of resources like human resources, finance, material resources, and the invisible assets of the enterprise so as to carry out all the plans as quickly as possible.

The marketing strategy can make it possible for the decision makers to take a broad and long view to the issues existing in the operation in order to overcome the difficulties both in the favorable and the unfavorable conditions. The considerations in advance can help the enterprise react rationally to the actual situation and keep the various aims coherent. The establishment of the strategic plan may also consolidate longitudinal and transversal information communication among different departments and levels in the enterprise so as to minimize the potential conflicts. This will promote the implementation of each target that accords with the whole benefits of the enterprise.

The marketing strategy urges the managers to carefully observe and analyze the market tendency and to foresee the orientation in the future. In this way, the action plan will be clearer, which greatly reduces the blindness in the operation of the enterprise.

The marketing strategy may alleviate or even eliminate the damage caused by the unexpected market fluctuation or events and then avoid the grave chaos correspondently.

To sum up, by formulating the marketing strategy, the enterprise can greatly strengthen the motivation, the predictability, the integrality, the orderliness, and the effectiveness of the marketing activities in order to sharpen the competitiveness and reaction capacities of the enterprise. Therefore, in the contemporary era, effective marketing strategies have been becoming the bottleneck for the firm to survive and develop either in the open marketplace at home or in the fierce competitive international market.

6.1.3 Difference Between the Marketing Strategy and the Overall Strategy

The marketing strategy is quite different from the overall strategy. The former is established upon the following bases: in the fixed business fields, the marketing department has worked out the marketing plans for various products in comprehensively considering multiple factors, combining the relative resource situation, and assessing the market chances of the business growth for all kinds of products in the light of the tasks, aims, growth tactics and product input portfolio decided in the firm's strategy while the latter aims at explicating the whole business field, development orientation and pathways, and the anticipated goals and resource arrangement. The former only concerns the product direction and choice and it is the important components of the whole strategy and the latter cares for the orientation of the whole market where the firm faces and it is the focus of the firm's operation.

6.2 Business Determination Adapt to the Marketing Strategy

To establish the marketing strategy, it is essential to determine the business of a firm. Many approaches can be used in deciding what and how to be marketed in the firm, for example, analysis model of five forces as competitors, suppliers, buyers, substitutes, and latent rivals and that of value chains put forward by Michael Porter; BCG model, IE model, the Grand Strategy model and so on . Here we mainly introduce the Grand Strategy model.

6.2.1 Grand Strategy Model

The Grand Strategy model was adapted from *Policy Formulation and Administration* by Roland Christensen, Norman Berg, and Malcolm. It can be used to formulate the strategy of a firm or to decide the business, too. It is based on two evaluative dimensions; namely, competitive position and market growth, on which four quadrants are formed and the business of a firm can be determined in each quadrant (see Figure 6.1).

Chapter 6 Marketing Strategies

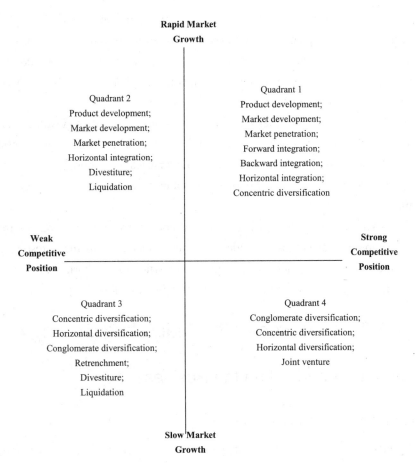

Source: Adapted from Roland Christensen, Norman Berg, and Malcolm Salter, *Policy Formulation and Administration*, Homewood, IL:Richard D. Irwin, 1976:16-18.

Figure 6.1   The Grand Strategy Matrix

6.2.2 Determination of the Business by the Grand Strategy Approach

When a firm locates itself in Quadrant 1, its competitive position is strong and the market of its business grows rapid, so it is wise for the firm to develop the product and the market. Several approaches can be used to expand its business, for example, the forward integration, the backward integration and the concentric diversification and so on.

Quadrant 2 shows us that the market grows fast, but the competitive position of the firm is relatively weak, therefore the firm located in Quadrant 2 should analyze the reason why it operates ineffectively and how it improves its competitiveness quickly. To be strongly competitive, it is obliged to abandon certain business so as to concentrate its funds and resources on the main product or service; or the horizontal integration tactics may be adopted to acquire other businesses to make it become stronger. Then, correspondent approaches such as the product development, the market penetration can be used.

In Quadrant 3, one can find that the firm is in weak competitive position and the market where its business lies grows slowly. The reasonable way for the firm to go is to shift quickly from its current business into the other field. Diversification approaches as concentric or horizontal or conglomerate one are alternatives. Otherwise, divestiture or liquidation for its present business is also feasible.

Quadrant 4 tells us that the firm lies in strong competitive position, but its market grows slowly. To develop new businesses is its ideal selection, since it holds many resources or cashes. So, diversification approaches such as concentric diversification or horizontal diversification or conglomerate diversification and even joint venture are its best tactics to pursue.

6.3 Varieties of the Marketing Strategy

6.3.1 Strategy Readjusting the Business

1. Overall Growth Investment Strategy

The overall growth investment strategy refers to an active investment from the firm to support and develop the business. It is mainly suitable for the star-like business. Its main contents are introduced hereinafter:

(1) It focuses on the input of the marketing costs so as to maintain and enlarge the market share and consolidate the leading position of the firm in the market.

(2) It focuses on the input of the production costs so as to enlarge the production capacities and its investment rate into equipments may be superior to the average level in the industry.

(3) It focuses on the input of the scientific research funds, keeps innovating, strives to shape good image of the firm by applying the high R&D funds, intensive promotion, good quality and high price. Differentiation strategy is its remarkable feature.

(4) It focuses on the input of the management costs in a certain business and assigns the backbone forces in production and sale departments to manage this business.

Chapter 6 Marketing Strategies

2. Sustainable Market-Expansion Strategy

This strategy is aimed at sustaining, consolidating and expanding the market position of some businesses. It adapts to the cash-dog-like business. Its main contents include the following points:

(1) It emphasizes the market competition, inputs suitable promotion costs, uses all kinds of tools so as to solidify the existent market position, to maximize the profits and to maintain the current market share.

(2) It also controls the investment of equipments in order to keep the existent production capacities.

(3) Founded on the market segmentation, it improves appropriately the product by investment for the sake of satisfying the demands in the different target market to strengthen the response abilities to the market.

With the above measures, it strives to prolong the life span of the business in the market, maintain the relative advantages of the firm and obtain more profits so as to provide the funds for the other businesses.

3. Alternative Growth Strategy

This strategy means that the firm focuses on investing some businesses with bright future and eliminating those that are in weak competition position by analysis. It is suitable for the problem-like business. Some of the business may be further invested, others less invested or retreated from the market. A further investigation and analysis should be made by the enterprise. It is detailed thereinafter.

(1) It emphasizes the market investigation and forecasting of the market growth rate of each business and the investment effects of the firm.

(2) It will intensify the investment of the business with continuous market growth rate rising and with good returns of investment and expand the market to raise the market share by way of augmenting the investment and promotion, bettering the quality, and pricing reasonably.

(3) It controls the investment to the business with the drop of the market growth rate and with the worse effectiveness and makes it retreat from the market.

(4) It pays much attention to the management of the business, assigns the able persons who dares to take risks to direct the implementation of this strategy. If necessary, experts will be invited to form a temporary decision consultation department to give advice.

4. Shifted-Out Control Strategy

The shifted-out control strategy means that the firm gradually reduces the investment of some businesses and withdraws from the market. It adapts to the dog-like business. It contains the following points:

(1) Cut down the investment into this business and squeeze more profits from it as soon as possible.

(2) Strives to reduce the expenditure in compressing the production volume and varieties, target markets, sale network and channels.

(3) The declining unprofitable business will be made over, auctioned, severed, and abandoned, or finally retreated thoroughly from the market.

The above-said four strategies can have the cash-cow-like business acquire abundant funds that will be offered to the star-like and partial potential problem-like businesses so that the market share of problem-like business should be raised and that it will be developed into the star-like business that may be transformed into the cash-cow-like and not the dog-like business in keeping and enlarging its market share. They can impel the structure of the existent business into rationality, namely, more cash-cow-like and star-like businesses, partial problem-like ones and fewer dog-like ones.

6.3.2 Growth Planning Strategy

The growth planning strategy says that the existent business will be developed in the current market to reach the aim of expanding the business. It primarily contains the market penetration strategy, the market development strategy and the product development strategy.

1. Market Penetration Strategy

The market penetration strategy refers to the expansion of the market share, the increase of the sale volume in the current market by giving publicity to the existent product. The concrete methods to enlarge the market share and increase the sale volume are mainly introduced here.

(1) Encourage the existent customers to buy more and raise the use frequency of the product.

By way of disseminating and piloting, one may increase the use frequency of the current product, the quantities of product purchase so as to realize the goal of using more and buying more. For example, giving publicity of brushing teeth in the morning and evening does benefits both to leading the consumer to form a healthy habit and to doubling the use of toothpaste and brushes. This publicity can promote the selling of the toothpaste and brushes. Naturally, while it is favorable to the present firm, it is also helpful to the other firms in the industry, which may get their support and form a stronger propaganda team. But this method is only used selectively and

Chapter 6 Marketing Strategies

can't be abused.

(2) Strive for the customers from the rivals.

One should pay close attention to the market trends, seize the opportunities to enter into the market, surpass the rivals so as to expand the market share of the firm. For instance, the "Golden Fish" produced by No. 2 Chemical Works in Beijing dominates the market of "White Cat" in Shanghai by using this method.

(3) Strive for the potential customers who haven't bought the product.

By investigation and research, marketers should analyze the reason that the customer hasn't bought the product yet. And then specific marketing measures ought to be adopted to urge the potential customer to be transformed into the actual one as quickly as possible. Usually, the reasons may be economic, or psychological, or lack of the knowledge about the product, etc. Only in the investigation and analysis can one catch the crux of the issue and take correspondent countermeasures to win over these customers. This method is a bit difficult, but effective in avoiding the competition.

2. Market Development Strategy

The market development strategy says that the firm keeps expanding outward upon the existent market in the search for the new market in utilizing the current product and increasing the market development and promotion costs so as to broaden the business. The means to develop the market includes the following types:

(1) Increase new target markets in the initial selling districts.

Through extensive publicity, new target customers are piloted to buy and use the firm's product.

(2) Increase new sale channels.

The single channel where exclusive sales are controlled by the commercial department is changed into numerous selling means as direct selling, conjoint selling by industrial and commercial departments and bloc selling, etc. By flexible approaches, the business is expanded.

(3) Increase new sale areas.

It is a valid way to increase new sale areas, amplify the product market and agitate a new selling wave, for example, make the products to be sold on the domestic market enter into the international market, those for sale abroad into the domestic market, those at the mature stage on the city and town market into the rural areas.

3. Product Development Strategy

This strategy aims at having the existent products enter into the current market with a new look through improving them by increasing the product development charges, strengthen the competition and enlarge the business. The approaches are presented hereinafter.

(1) Add new traits.

Improvement on the initial products is made based on the demands of the customers for the function, appearance, and color, etc. so as to embody their own properties and to agitate the potential demands of the customers. For example, the washing machine branded "Tiny Quiz Kid" produced by Haier Group has been the favorite of common and single family because of its peculiarity.

(2) Add new levels.

The product line with high, medium and low levels at the customer's demands should be added for the purpose of catering for various consumers. For instance, on the furniture market, the furniture both ordinary and luxury is displayed.

(3) Increase new successors.

As science and technology are going forward, new products are emerging one after another. Take the washing machine for example, various washing machines keep appearing on the market from simplex to full-automation to those with heating-up installations to those with drying-up equipments and so on, which has brought much convenience to the consumer.

6.3.3 Integration Development Strategy

The integration development strategy, based upon the existent business, moves forwards and backwards along the line by acquiring, alliance, participation and holdings in order to form an integration of production, provision and sales and extend the current business. It usually contains backward, forward and horizontal integrations.

The backward integration moves upward upon the current business, namely controlling the raw materials, parts and components and the other provision systems and carrying out the integration of provision and production, such as automotive spare parts held by the car production factory, chemical works integrating its raw material suppliers, etc. It not only enlarges the existing business, but also ensures the supply and quality of the raw material and parts.

The forward integration moves downward on the current business, that's to say, realizing the integration of production and selling by acquiring, merger and alliance, etc. Or on the basis of raw material production, the firm goes toward the finished product so as to form production-provision-sale integration.

The horizontal integration elementarily acquires mergers or unites the other enterprises in the same industry for the purpose of managing the business integrated. Big enterprises or branded

Chapter 6 Marketing Strategies

products often integrate the sites, equipments, personnel and funds of the other firms horizontally in order to expand their own businesses; medium and small enterprises utilize the technology and popularity of the other firms by the horizontal integration strategy to upgrade their own professional quality and the fame of their products.

6.3.4 Diversification Development Strategy

The diversification development strategy means that the enterprise uses the existent resources and advantages to invest into other businesses in the different industry by capital operation. According to the different resources used, the diversification development strategy can be divided into technology, market and complex relationship diversifications.

The technology relationship diversification is founded on the existing business, utilizes the product line, technology, equipments, experience and special skills to increase the types of products, and extend toward the edge of the industry. For example, the medical company handles the healthy foods besides medicines, and the factory producing television sets also manufactures computers and so on. This kind of strategy can make a full play of the initial technology advantages with less investment, fewer risks, quicker returns and be easier to succeed.

The market relationship diversification aims at developing the concerned business of the other industry at the demands of the customers on the current target market. For instance, in the airport, train station or bus station, shops, hotels, restaurants and financial organizations are set up to serve the travelers. The target customers for this strategy are relatively centered, and the existing and the new businesses may co-exist and inter-enhance.

The complex relationship diversification refers to taking the advantage of talents, funds of the firm or investing into the new business unrelated to the initial business of the enterprise at the demands of conjoint operation.

To sum up, the diversification development strategy is favorable to decentralizing the risks, transferring to the emerging industry with bright future and driving the old business to move forward and then agitating the development of the whole enterprise.

However, the diversification development strategy also has some risks. The firm must pay attention to the aspects hereinafter. On the one hand, the conditions inside and outside the firm to carry out the diversification strategy should be enough. The internal conditions include the following: the firm has surplus resources that are not fully used; the firm has the capacities of expanding its business; the decision makers of the firm have the pioneering spirits while the outer ones contain the following: the social demands bring new chances, which require the firm to broaden its business to cater for the change; new technology provides new bases for developing new business; the fluctuation of the competitive situation asks the firm to respond to the change quickly. On the other hand, the firm ought to make a full investigation of the market, and fix its investment aims, orientation after a feasible analysis, well balance the "degree" of developing the diversification so as to avoid the mistakes and risks because of the blind investment and expansion.

6.4　Summary

　　战略决定着一个组织的发展方向。营销战略指企业为了在激烈的市场竞争中求得生存，在分析企业所面临的内外部环境以及自身优劣势的条件下建立的指导企业市场活动的一定时期内的行动方案。营销战略的建立离不开对企业业务组合的分析与研究，目前营销学界常采用迈克尔·波特五力分析模型或价值链分析模型分析行业内部或企业的竞争态势，从而研究企业业务在行业中的竞争地位，利用波士顿矩阵或大战略矩阵可以分析并确定企业业务或业务组合。不论采用什么样的方法，营销战略的建立都必须首先确定企业的业务或业务组合。

　　市场营销战略主要包括业务调整战略、成长规划战略、一体化发展战略和多样化发展战略。随着企业的发展，企业必须根据自身发展阶段选择不同的战略来指导自己的营销活动。

Key Terms

Marketing Strategy　　Strategy Readjusting Business　　Growth Planning Strategy　　Market Development Strategy　　Product Development Strategy　　Integration Development Strategy　　Diversification Development Strategy　　Grand Strategy Model

> **【案例】　R 保健食品市场营销战略案例**
>
> 　　所有的人都能看到获取胜利所采用的战术，但没有人认识到这个胜利是战略展开的结果。
> 　　R 公司是一家民营生物技术开发企业，凭借其独特的原料和专利技术，五年前上马了保健食品生产线，经过充分论证并经国家卫生部批准，该公司生产的具有调节血脂功效的保健食品——Q 产品上市销售。
> 　　Q 产品问世五年来，电视广告也做了，列车冠名也有了，宣传画册也印了，专卖店也开了，但就是"只听雷声响，不见雨点下"，销售业绩裹足不前。再加上最近政府出台了有关保健食品广告管理和直销企业管理等方面的政策，更让 R 公司雪上加霜。面对严峻形势，小 Z 与同事们翻阅大量资料，进行了深入的调查，结合 R 公司营销现状进行了再次的调查研究。

一、调脂市场概况

1. 调脂市场是个"金矿"

随着国家经济飞速发展,中国人的饮食结构也发生了巨大的变化,动物性食物消费迅速上升,植物性食物消费却呈下降趋势。这种饮食结构变化的直接结果就是血脂异常(俗称高血脂),其发病率快速攀升。据有关专家估算,中国30岁以上的成年人中,血脂异常的比例在25%左右,估计中国的高血脂症患者就高达一亿人左右。假设每个高血脂症患者年服用100元的调脂产品,调脂市场的规模就达到每年100亿,这无疑称得上是一个商机无限的"金矿"。

2. 高血脂与相关疾病的关系

A. 高血脂与心脑血管疾病的关系:调查显示,中国人的死亡原因中,心脑血管疾病位居各种死因之首。而这些心脑血管疾病患者,大多数死于高血脂导致的动脉硬化。因此,高血脂被称为"头号杀手"。

B. 高血脂与糖尿病的关系:高血脂可以加重糖尿病,糖尿病患者调节血脂可以减少糖尿病的死亡率和致残率。糖尿病合并高血脂更易致脑中风、冠心病、肢体坏死、眼底病变、胃肠病变、神经衰弱等。这些糖尿病的远期并发症是造成糖尿病残疾和早死的主要原因。

3. 调脂市场没有领导品牌

国家批准的调节血脂类保健产品达千余种。另外,还有众多的"营养品"和OTC药品也在调脂市场活跃。在诱惑力强大的调脂市场中,迄今为止尚没有领导品牌。

4. 调脂市场的两大特点

A. 非渴求性。据统计,中国的血脂异常(俗称高血脂)人群中,知道自己有高血脂的只有25%;高血脂人群中,了解高血脂危害的只有20%左右;即使比较了解高血脂的患者,采取措施的也非常少。

B. 非显效性。血脂异常是一种富贵病,是一种生活习惯病,是长期不健康的生活方式缓慢积累起来的,所以调节血脂也是个长期持续作用的过程,不会在短期内采取措施便有明显效果。

二、Q产品营销诊断

(一)问题

1. 产品

Q产品是纯天然的绿色食品,但无论是外形还是内容物均设计得类似药品,在国家明令必须在包装上标明"本产品不能代替药物"的要求下,Q产品在消费者面前便成了"四不像"。

2. 价格

产品包装数量过多导致单瓶价格过高,人为抬高了消费门槛。

3. 传播

各种平面宣传资料、广播广告、电视广告要么连篇介绍Q产品的十几种保健功能,要么就调节血脂功能大而全地阐述原料天然、工艺先进、成分多元、功效确切等特色。

4. 市场定位

最根本的问题是"Q产品到底是什么"的问题。产品的市场定位是什么尚没有一个明确的回答。

(二)诊断

小Z了解了R公司的营销现状后，明确了以下认识。

1. 认识市场定位

A. 市场定位是全部营销工作的统帅，是方向。市场定位不准确，具体战术运作就会出现盲目行为，造成人财物和时间的浪费。

B. 最好的竞争是没有竞争，市场定位是最大限度避免竞争的有力武器。并且，准确而独特的市场定位也会使产品以较小的代价赢得目标消费者。

C. 市场定位就是要产品在目标消费者头脑中留下的印象。简单地说，就是要告诉目标消费者"产品是什么"，而且这种回答必须足够确切，足够与众不同。

2. 认识Q产品的市场定位

A. Q产品诚然具有许多功能和特色，包括原料天然、工艺先进、成分多元、功效确切(提高免疫力、延缓衰老、抵抗疲劳等)。但是让一个产品承载一个以上的功能或特色去面对消费者，想让消费者对产品或企业有一个全面的了解，用意无疑是好的，但效果并不能如人意，特别是在上市初期，超过一个的特色会因为信息量大反而大大减少人们的兴趣和记忆，会淡化产品的特色。

B. 国家卫生部批准Q产品的保健功能为调节血脂，营销工作应围绕此功能做文章。至于产品的其他功能，可以通过产品的系列化来实现。例如"提高免疫力"功能，可以通过研究"提高免疫力"的有关专业知识，由另一个产品来承载"提高免疫力"的功能，加上技术、研发的努力，也能为企业带来持续增长的业务和利润来源。

C. 就调节血脂来讲，消费者关心的是结果(功效、与同类产品的差异等)，而对过程的关注是居于其次的(如原料、工艺、成分、企业情况等)。因此，必须改变以前"大而全"的信息传播模式。

3. Q产品的机会

目前市场上众多的调脂产品，大多数定位并不明确，这也是造成调脂市场尚没有领导品牌的重要原因之一，同时也给了Q产品以机会。

4. 明确Q产品市场定位的方法

人们剥洋葱时，是从外层到里层直至核心，一层比一层精小。明确Q产品的市场定位也可以用"剥洋葱法"来进行分析。

三、Q产品的目标市场

在分析Q产品的市场定位之前，小Z首先对Q产品的目标市场进行了分析。

第一步，分析调脂市场的两大特点可以得到以下结论。

1. 即使是治疗高血脂的产品(药品)，营销难度也是非常大的；作为调节血脂的保健食品(保健食品强调预防)，针对健康人群打"预防"牌难度更大。
2. 如果选择健康人群作为目标市场去打"预防"牌，势必要承担市场教育者的角色，那样会耗时耗资很大，并且有可能为他人做嫁衣，由"先锋"成为"先烈"。一句话，会出力不讨好。

因此，在目前的情况下，可以初步确立Q产品的目标市场为：高血脂症患者[与非处方药(OTC)争夺市场]。因为只有被诊断为高血脂症的患者才较清楚明白高血脂的危害和调脂特点。

第二步，对高血脂症患者，可以划分为两个细分群体。

一是30～55岁的中年人，这类人群正值人生的黄金阶段，提高家庭经济收入是其第一要务，健康往往被忽略，是"用健康换金钱"的群体。

二是55岁以上的人群，基本是退休人员，这类人群健康意识非常强，健康是其最为关注的问题，是"用金钱换健康"的群体。

本着先易后难的原则，可以进一步确立Q产品的目标市场为：

第一阶段：老年高血脂症患者。

第二阶段：中、老年高血脂症患者。

第三步，考虑到城乡消费者购买能力方面的差别，可以更进一步确立Q产品的目标市场为：

第一阶段：城市老年高血脂症患者。

第二阶段：城市中、老年高血脂症患者。

第四步，考虑到消费者调脂意识差异，最后可以确定Q产品的目标市场为：

第一阶段：城市老年高血脂症患者。

第二阶段：城市中、老年高血脂症患者。

第三阶段：城市中、老年心脑血管病患者和糖尿病患者。

四、Q产品的市场定位

小Z对Q产品的市场定位，分"五步走"进行了分析。

第一步，Q产品是调节血脂的食品。这里强化"食品"的概念，就是要告诉目标消费群，Q产品是食品，而不是药品，食品没有毒副作用(产品在设计上也应独树一帜，避免与药品雷同)。

第二步，Q产品是调节血脂的保健食品。Q产品不是一般食品，是保健食品，是食品中的精品。但是仅如此定位是不够的，因为调节血脂的保健食品太多，这样不能给消费者选择Q产品的充分理由。

第三步，Q产品是调节血脂的绿色保健食品。在众多调节血脂的保健食品中，Q产品同时有绿色食品认证，这样就把Q产品跟非绿色食品区分开来，给了消费者选择Q产品的更有说服力的理由。但如此定位显然还是不够的，由于同时拥有"双证"并不能深层次阐明Q产品的特色，还是不能给消费者选择Q产品的充分理由。

第四步，Q产品是能够全面调脂的绿色保健食品。Q产品的一个明显特色是"在降低胆固醇、甘油三酯的同时，不降低对人体有益的高密度脂蛋白胆固醇。"《中华心血管病杂志》编委会血脂异常防治对策专题组，把高血脂症分为四类：一是高血胆固醇症，二是高血甘油三酯症，三是混合型高血脂症(胆固醇和甘油三酯都高)，四是低高密度脂蛋白胆固醇血症。从医学知识讲，高血脂症患者在"降"血脂的同时也极易降低对人体有益的高密度脂蛋白胆固醇。很多调节血脂的产品都对前三类高血脂症有效，但同时能调节高密度脂蛋白胆固醇的不多。Q产品要告诉目标消费者"Q产品能够全面调节血脂"。这里，强调"调节血脂"，而不用大家习惯了的"降低血脂"。

第五步，考虑到当前和较长时期内，Q产品的目标消费群是老年人，而老年人体质相对较差，吸收是其非常关切的问题。如果Q产品能够比竞争产品在吸收方面更有特色，将会大大吸引目标群体的注意力。从消费者角度讲，吸收好也意味着降低了他们的消费支出；从企业角度讲，也使较高的价格更有说服力。分析Q产品成分特色，以下三点可以支撑"充分吸收"的概念。

一是Q产品属于植物油，比动物油易于被人体充分吸收(鱼油是目前调脂类保健食品中的很大一块)；二是Q产品中的不饱和脂肪酸比例接近母乳，易于被人体充分吸收；三是Q产品中的维生素E具有很强的抗氧化作用，有效防止不饱和脂肪酸被氧化，使其能够被人体充分吸收。

综上所述，Q产品的市场定位为：

充分吸收 全面调脂 的 绿色 保健 食品
⑤　　　　④　　　　　③　②　　①

至此，小Z完成了Q产品的市场定位工作。这期间，小Z也对调脂市场和Q产品有了相当深刻的认识。

在业内，认为调节血脂就是将"粘稠"的血液调节到"清晰"的水平。小Z完成了Q产品的市场定位，其实是将R公司的营销工作从此前的"粘稠"的状态调节到了目前的"清晰"状态。

小Z和同事们知道，解决了Q产品的市场定位问题，只是万里长征走完了第一步，接下来还有更为艰巨的任务要去完成，但经过这一段时间的共同努力，每个人都信心十足。愿Q产品能够在被营销界称为"不可多得的富矿"的调脂市场有所作为，为血脂异常的人们送去福音。

(资料来源：周文虎. R保健食品市场营销战略案例. [2008-7-9]. www.emkt.com.cn.)

【案例分析】

从本案例中，我们可以看到营销战略的确定在公司产品开发和市场拓展中的地位和作用,同时,也可以看到营销战略与战术的区别之所在。案例告诉我们,R 公司是一家民营生物技术开发企业,凭借其独特的原料和专利技术,五年前上马了保健食品生产线,经过充分论证并经国家卫生部批准,该公司生产的具有调节血脂功效的保健食品——Q 产品上市销售了。这样,确立了 R 公司的市场营销战略。

Q 产品问世五年来,电视广告也做了,列车冠名也有了,宣传画册也印了,专卖店也开了,但就是"只听雷声响,不见雨点下",销售业绩裹足不前。以上所述的 R 公司针对具体的营销战略而采取的战术措施效果并不理想。再加上最近政府出台了有关保健食品广告管理和直销企业管理等方面的政策,更让 R 公司雪上加霜。

R 公司的问题到底出在哪里?面对严峻形势,小 Z 与同事们翻阅大量资料,进行了深入的调查,结合 R 公司营销现状进行了再次的调查研究并对问题进行了诊断,发现 R 公司虽然制定了战略,但过于粗放,目标市场与市场定位缺乏精细度,结果导致营销战术措施无法带来预期效果。

【思考题】
1. 你认为案例中小 Z 在发现 Q 产品营销存在问题后,所采取的解决问题的一系列措施是否得当?为什么?
2. 以该案例为基础,讨论营销战略与营销战术之间的关系。

Chapter 7

Marketing Competitive Strategies

Focus on:

1. Five forces influencing the market competition.
2. Basic competitive strategies and the conditions in implementing them.
3. Classification of the rivals and choice of the market competitive strategy.

7.1　Five Basic Competitive Forces

The best way to avoid head-on competition is to find new or better ways to satisfy customers' needs and provide value. The search for a breakthrough opportunity or some sort of competitive advantage requires an understanding not only of customers, but also of competitors. Competitor analysis is an organized approach for evaluating the strengths and weaknesses of current or potential competitors' marketing strategies. The idea of competitor analysis relies on a comparison of the strengths and weaknesses of the company's current target market and marketing mix with those that other companies are currently using, or are likely to use, in response to the company's strategy.

One relatively recent approach to undertaking a competitor analysis is to use Porter's 'five forces' framework. In summary, this model suggests that there are five forces influencing competition in an industry:

(1) The threat of new entrants;
(2) The threat of substitute products or services;
(3) The bargaining power of buyers;
(4) The bargaining power of suppliers;
(5) The competitive rivalry among current members of the industry.

A discussion of each factor is listed in the following.

Chapter 7 Marketing Competitive Strategies

7.1.1 Threat of New Entrants

New entrants bring more competition to an industry. They might provide new approaches to satisfy customers' needs and wrest market share from the market leader or other companies in the industry. The emergence of new entrants always leads to price cutting and reduced industry profitability. According to Porter's theory, there are six major barriers to entry, the presence or absence of which determines the extent of threat of new industry entrants.

1. Economies of Scale

Economies of scale refer to the decline in per-unit product costs as the absolute volume of production per period increases. If existing firms in an industry achieve significant economies of scale, it is difficult for new entrants to enter or be competitive. The reason is that new entrants might have higher product costs than existing firms because of the limited sales volumes. Therefore, existing firms are able to set lower prices or obtain higher profitability than new entrants.

2. Product Differentiation

Product differentiation is the extent of a product's perceived uniqueness. Unique product attributes, excellent customer services or effective marketing communications can provide differentiated product or service image in the eyes of consumers which results in brand loyalty. Product differentiation and brand loyalty raise the barrier for new entrants who are required to make substantial investment in R&D or advertising.

3. Switching Costs

Switching costs are caused by the need to change suppliers and products. These might include the cost of searching for or assessing a new supplier, retraining and so on. High switching costs may form an insurmountable obstacle to prevent new entrants from gaining target customers and market share.

4. Capital Requirement

The enormous capital requirements in an industry prevent firms with limited resources from entering or achieving success. Capital is not only required for manufacturing equipments, but also for assisting R&D, promotion, advertising, sales, after-sales service, distribution channel exploring and inventories. Several industries such as chemicals and mineral extraction which require giant investment present formidable entry barriers.

5. Government Policies

Nearly in every country, the government will restrict competitor entering in some industries. For instance, because of the economic crisis, many countries such as the United Sates, EU and Japan increase barriers to prevent products which are made in China from entering to protect their national industries. Thus, it is hard or impossible to enter some industries which are protected by the government.

6. Distribution Channels

The access to distribution channels can be a barrier to entry. If channels are full or unavailable, the cost of entry is substantially increased because a new entrant must invest time and money to establish new channels or to gain access to existing ones. This is true in some countries such as Japan and some developing countries.

7.1.2 Threat of Substitute Products or Services

Substitute products or services also influence competition in an industry. Companies might be offering quite different products or services to meet the same needs, but the companies are competitors if customers view them as offering close substitutes. For example, breakfast cereals, more traditional snack food such as chips and muesli bars, fruit and ice-creams, all compete in the same generic market concerned with snack food. The availability of substitute products prevents the market leader from charging high prices to customers. If the price is unaffordable to customers, they will switch to substitute products or services to satisfy their needs.

Identifying a broad set of potential competitors assists marketing managers to understand different ways in which customers are currently meeting needs and sometimes identifies new opportunities. There are two questions that existing companies in an industry should ask: What are substitute products or services that might compete with us? How these substitutes threaten the industry?

7.1.3 Bargaining Power of Buyers

Apart from identifying threats of new entrants and substitutes, the marketing management also needs to consider influence exerted by buyers in the industry. For buyers, if possible, they would like to pay the lowest price to purchase products or services that they need. Therefore, buyers can drive down profitability in the supplier industry if they have gained leverage over

Chapter 7 Marketing Competitive Strategies

suppliers.

Buyers will try hard or be able to bargain for lower prices when

(1) Buyers purchase a large quantity of products from supplier companies;

(2) Suppliers' products or services represent a significant portion of buyer's costs;

(3) Suppliers' products or services are viewed as undifferentiated and there are many substitutes are available to satisfy buyers' needs at reasonable prices;

(4) Buyers' switching costs for other products or services are low;

(5) Buyers are willing and able to achieve backward integration;

(6) Buyers are able to obtain enough information of products or services that they want to purchase.

7.1.4 Bargaining Power of Suppliers

Bargaining power of suppliers exerts influence on the industry either. If suppliers have enough bargaining power, they will raise prices as high as possible to gain significant profitability.

Suppliers are able to gain leverage over the industry when

(1) Suppliers are large and relatively few in number in an industry;

(2) Suppliers' products or services are highly differentiated and there is no substitute or only a few substitutes are available;

(3) Suppliers' products or services are important inputs to user companies;

(4) Users need to pay high switching costs for changing another supplier;

(5) Suppliers are willing and able to achieve forward integration.

7.1.5 Competitive Rivalry Among Current Members of the Industry

Competitive rivalry among current competitors of the industry refers to all competitive activities taken by companies in the industry to improve their marketing performances and gain advantage over each other. Price competition, advertising battles, product development, new product introduction, distribution channel exploration and other marketing activities are examples of rivalry between current competitors. To some extent, rivalry among competitors is helpful to the sound development of the industry. It forces companies to control their product costs, improve customer service, and strive to develop new products or create more attributes of current products or services. On the other hand, rivalry also has negative effect on the industry for driving down market prices and profitability.

The rivalry among current competitors can be intense if

(1) There are great many competitors existing in the industry;

(2) The industry is mature and firms try hard to gain market share;

(3) Firms are under pressure to keep production at full capacity to achieve economies of scale and decrease fixed costs or inventory costs. Therefore, companies with excessive production capacity will find every means to sell their products or services;

(4) Products or services provided by current members in the industry are lacking of differentiation which encourages buyers shop for the best prices;

(5) Buyers' switching costs for substitutes are low;

(6) Expenses of leaving the industry are high.

In summary, competitor analysis gives firms a useful model to analyze competitive environment in the industry. It helps companies identify not only threats of current and potential competitors, but also influences of suppliers and buyers.

The five forces analysis focuses on identifying threats of current and potential competitors. Rivals offering similar products are usually easy to identify. However, if a strategy involves a product concept that is really new and different, there may not be a current competitor with a similar product. In such a case, the closest competitor may be a company that is currently satisfying similar needs with a different product. Although such companies may not appear to be close competitors, they are likely to fight back, perhaps with a directly competitive product, if another company starts to take away their customers.

Even if no specific competitors can be identified, marketing managers must consider how long it might take for potential competitors to appear, and what they might do. Assuming that there will not be competition in the future, or discounting how aggressive competition may become, are common mistakes. Successful strategies will always attract the interest of others who are eager to share in the profits. Sometimes, a creative imitator finds a way to provide customers with superior value leading to erosion of the pioneer company's sales before it is even aware of what is happening.

Finding a sustainable competitive advantage requires special attention to competitors' strengths and weaknesses. For example, it is very difficult to dislodge a competitor who is already a market leader, by simply attacking with a similar strategy. An established leader can usually defend its position by quickly copying the best parts of what a new competitor is attempting to do. On the other hand, an established competitor may not be able to defend itself quickly if it is attacked where it is weak.

In a competitor analysis, competitor barriers, the conditions that may make it difficult or

Chapter 7 Marketing Competitive Strategies

even impossible for a company to compete in a market must also be considered. Such barriers may limit the company's plans or, alternatively, block competitors' responses to an innovative strategy.

A marketing manager should actively seek information about current or potential competitors. Although most companies try to keep the specifics or their plans secret, much public information may be available. For instance, many companies routinely monitor competitors through local newspapers. Other sources of competitor information include trade publications, alert sales representatives, intermediaries and other industry experts. The internet is fast becoming a powerful way to obtain information about competitors.

7.2 Basic Competitive Strategies

After analyzing competitive environment in the industry, the company now must design competitive strategies to achieve competitive advantages. According to Michael Porter's competition theory, there are three basic competitive strategies that companies can follow to gain their competitive advantages and win the competition.

7.2.1 Overall Cost Leadership

A company which implements overall cost leadership strategy works hard to be a cost leader by controlling overall costs of production, R&D, sales, service and advertising. Low costs let the price lower than competitors' and win the competitive advantage in the fierce competition.

There are several advantages of achieving cost leadership which are stated in the following.

1. Forming Entry Barrier

Low manufacturing costs can form a higher entry barrier for potential or new entrants in an industry. It is difficult for a company which lacks of scale economies and advanced manufacturing technologies to enter the industry.

2. Reinforcing Bargaining Power

The company which achieves low costs is able to cover increasing expenses, bargain with suppliers and reduce influences caused by changing inputs. Meanwhile, low costs let the company gain more leverage over buyers.

3. Decreasing Threat of Substitutes

In the competition, low-cost company always attracts customers by offering low-price products or services. Low costs make the company in the advantageously competitive position by decreasing or alleviating threat of substitutes.

4. Maintaining Leader Position

Low-cost company is able to offer products or services at very low prices to customers and still make profits in the price war. However, its competitors with higher overall costs have no profit if they sell products or services at the same price. Therefore, low-cost company can expand market share and maintain absolutely competitive advantage by achieving cost leadership.

All in all, overall cost leadership makes the firm rivaling with competitors effectively in an industry and gaining profit higher than the average level.

There are two factors that the company should consider before strategy implementation. One is what resources and techniques are needed. In order to achieve the cost leadership, the company must keep investing resources needed by strategy implementation, improving research and development capability, reinforcing marketing techniques and enhancing internal managerial level. Another factor that the company must take into account is what is necessarily required in the implementation. For instance, in order to gain cost leadership, the company should strictly control its overall costs, design sound organizational structure and perfect incentive management system.

The company which has achieved overall cost leadership sometimes may be still in disadvantageous position if the following circumstances occur.

First, if a competitor develops new manufacturing technologies to make products at even lower costs, it can gain a new low-cost advantage. The company which was the low-cost leader will be in the disadvantageous position because it has lost its competitive advantage.

Second, a company which has achieved competitive advantages will face difficulty if its competitors copy its successful strategies and provide similar products or services with same costs.

Third, paying too much attention in pursuing low cost may lead to bad product or service quality which results in customers' complain. The company then will lose the competitive advantage.

7.2.2 Differentiation

The company which adopts differentiation strategy concentrates on creating highly

Chapter 7 Marketing Competitive Strategies

differentiated products or services to satisfy special customer needs. Therefore, product or service differentiation becomes the source of competitive advantage. Here, cost control is still important even though it is not the main issue that the company must consider.

By creating differentiation advantage, the company is able to compete with others and gain above-average profits in the industry.

There are several advantages of achieving differentiation advantage which are stated in the following.

1. Forming Entry Barrier

Unique products or services can form an entry barrier to prevent potential or new competitors from entering because customers would have high loyalty to differentiated offerings. Potential or new competitors must spend lots of time and money to attract customers and overcome the uniqueness of products or services in competition.

2. Decreasing Customer's Price Sensitivity

Because of customer loyalty which is caused by differentiation, most customers would be less price-sensitive if the price of a unique product or service is changed. Therefore, its manufacturer can defend itself from price competition and charge a premium price to obtain significant financial returns.

3. Reinforcing Bargaining Power

Product differentiation can bring high gross margin, decrease overall costs and reinforce bargaining power of suppliers. At the same time, the company can also gain leverage over loyal customers which are less price-sensitive and do not bargain hard for lower prices.

4. Preventing Threat of Substitutes

Highly differentiated products or services gain customer trust and help the company be more competitive while competing with substitutes.

The successful implementation of differentiation strategy requires special managerial skills and unique organizational structure. For instance, the company must completely enhance capabilities of product quality improvement, brand image creation, advanced technology maintenance and well-designed distribution channels establishment. Furthermore, it needs management staffs are quite capable of working on research & development and marketing. Meanwhile, the successful differentiation demands an organizational structure which can coordinate every functional department. The motivation and managerial system which can stimulate employees' creativity are also necessary. Corporate culture is another issue that should be taken into account. The culture that encourages creativity and innovation is especially important to high technology corporations.

There are two types of risk that the company might face in differentiation strategy implementation process. One is that the company may not be able to provide unique products or services to customers. And the other which always happens is that the company can not keep differentiation if competitors copy or attack its strategy.

In order to be differentiation, the firm might face four threats.

First, the firm is unable to gain profits if costs of product differentiation are so high that most of buyers cannot afford it. If competitors charge very low price, buyers are not willing to pay high price for the differentiated product even though the firm keeps its costs low.

Second, buyers may not view the product or service as unique, if competitors provide products with similar attributes.

Third, buyers do not need unique attributes of the product or service. For example, because of the continual product quality improvement, customers are more and more price-sensitive to the household electronic appliance such as television and DVD. Therefore, product differentiation becomes not that important to customers.

Fourth, buyers switch to competitors who offer more highly differentiated products or services.

7.2.3 Focus

While applying focus strategy, a company focuses on serving a narrowly defined market and provides special products or services to a specific buyer group or in a certain area. Focus is different from other two basic strategies. Cost leadership and differentiation can be applied in the whole industry. However, focus targets on a specific market with intensive manufacturing activities. It requires the firm providing more effective services than its competitors.

A company can use product differentiation or cost leadership to develop focus strategy once it has chosen its target market. In other words, a company which adopts focus strategy is basically a kind of cost leader or differentiated product provider. A small-sized focus firm cannot achieve differentiation and cost leadership at the same time. If a focus company wants to achieve cost leadership, it can establish low cost advantage on complex products or special products. On the other hand, if a focus company wants to achieve differentiation, it can apply differentiation strategy in its narrowly defined market other than other segmented markets. By doing so, a focus company is able to provide better products and services because it has better understanding of its market and customers.

Chapter 7 Marketing Competitive Strategies

Just as other two competitive strategies, focus defends rivalries in the industry and helps the company gain above-average profits. It can be used to defend threat of substitutes and attack the weakest point of competitors. Focus strategy also has limitation on market share occupation because the focus company only gains competitive advantage and high market share in its narrowly defined market which accounts for a small portion of the whole market. Therefore, a company must make the balance between product profitability and sales volumes, product differentiation and overall cost while it is selecting the strategy.

The key point of focus strategy implementation is strategic objective selection. The general principal is that a company must select the objective which is not the main objective of competitors and unlikely be attacked by substitutes. Before objective selection, a company should ascertain following aspects.

First, buyer groups have different needs for products or services.

Second, no competitor uses focus strategy in the target market.

Third, its target market is attractive in market volume, growth speed, profitability, and competition intensity.

Last, the company cannot pursuit larger target market because of its limited resources.

There are two risks that the focus company might face.

First, competitors with wider target markets might adopt focus strategy as well and find sub-segmented market in a focus company's target market.

Second, because of technology advancement, emergence of substitutes, value conception update and preference change of consumers, focus advantage will lose when customer needs for products or services between target market and overall market become nearly same.

7.3 Competitor Ranking and Marketing Competitive Strategy

Market occupation of a firm determines its competitive position and competitive strategies in the target market. According to the competitive position in the market, competitors can be ranked as market leader, market challenger, market follower and market niche.

7.3.1 Market Leaders

Most industries have a market leader which occupies the largest market share. There are some well-known market leaders such as Kodak (photographic film), Procter & Gamble (laundry detergent), Coca-Cola (soft drinks) and Nike (athletic footwear).

The leader is the pioneer in the competition. Its competitive behavior has wide effect on other companies in the market. Competitors focus on the leader as a company to challenge, imitate or avoid. For instance, Changhong is the leader of color television industry. In 1996, every company in the industry cut price after Changhong decreased its products' price. The market leader not only exerts influence on price setting, but also on product and technology innovation, new product introduction, distribution channel and promotion.

The leader faces challenges in the market. Other firms and even some small companies in the industry may challenge its authority. Generally speaking, the market leader has large market share and enjoys the economy of scale, therefore, it is hard to attack the leader through price strategies. However, it might be defeated by product, technology and distribution innovation of other firms in the industry. For example, Pepsi challenges Coca-Cola through product position and new product introduction, Nokia and Ericsson's digital phones challenge Motorola's analog models. All in all, there are three actions that can be taken by the market leader to remain the number one position: expand total demand, protect current market share and expand market share further.

1. Expanding Total Demand

In order to remain the leader position, the market leader can explore and expand the total market demand to gain the most. Normally, the leader must adopt market penetration and market development strategies to find new users, new uses and more usage of its products.

The so-called market penetration refers to increase the sale volumes of current products by implementing vigorous marketing activities. For example, the leader can persuade current users to use the product more often to increase the sales volumes. Market development refers to sell current products to new markets. It is can be divided into geographic expansion (sell products to other counties and areas) and new market development (find new uses of current products). Those two strategies aim to find new users, new uses and expand usage.

(1) Finding new users

Every product has the potentiality to attract buyers. People who do not buy the product may not realize its existence or regard the price as high. Moreover, people may refuse to buy the product since it lacks of some attributes. The company can find new users by solving those problems listed above. For instance, the women perfume maker might find new perfume users by convincing women who do not use perfume to try it (market penetration); persuade men to use perfume (new market development); or sell perfume to other countries (geographic expansion).

(2) Developing new uses

The leading firm can expand markets by discovering and developing new uses for the

Chapter 7 Marketing Competitive Strategies

product. Nylon, an important product of Dupon is a typical example. Nylon was originally used to make parachute. Then it became the main material of stockings and clothing making. In most people's eyes, nylon is in the mature stage of the product life cycle. However, through the continuous new use development of Dupon and other international companies, nylon is used in automobile manufacturing industry to make tire and cushion. It is important that companies must pay attention to how consumers use the product. This is applicable to industry of industrial and consumption product as well. Studies have shown that, ideas of most new industrial products are not originated from research & development lab of organizations but put forward by customers. Therefore, it is important to systematically collect consumer demands which help new product development.

(3) Encouraging new usage

Market leaders can encourage more usage by convincing customer to use the product more often or to use more per occasion. For instance, if people use cameras more often and consume more films, the sales volumes of Kodak will be increased undoubtedly. And it is possible to enhance sales if the company suggests consumers that it is better to use shampoo twice per time instead of once.

2. Protecting Market Share

Besides trying to expand total market size, the market leader also needs to protect its current market share against competition. There are several strategies that can be used to protect current market share.

(1) Innovation

The best defense for the market leader who wants to protect its current market share is continuous innovation. The leader refuses to content with the way things are and must lead the industry in continuous innovation for products, customer services, distribution channels and manufacturing technology.

(2) Building barrier

The market leader must keep alert to competitors. It should not provide any opportunities to competitors. The product's price must be reasonable and remain consistent with the value that customers see in the brand. The leader needs to satisfy different demands in the market by using the same brand and trademark to produce a large number of products in different sizes, models and prices.

(3) Front confrontation

If a firm is attacked by its competitors, it must beat back without delay. Promotion and low price strategies can be used to beat competitors and the leader should plug holes so that competitors do jump in.

In summary, the market leader can defend competition by reinforcing market position of current products, improving its weaknesses or establishing some less important businesses, initiating attack to beat competitors, exploring new business, or focusing on main business area and giving up businesses which cannot gain enough profits.

3. Expanding Market Share

Market leaders also can strengthen its leading position by increasing their market share. Expanding market share is important for companies to remain the leading position and gain profits.

(1) Introducing new product

New product introduction is a widely used method to increase market share. According to studies concerning the effect of marketing strategy on profit, a company's market share rises with the increasing sales of the new product. Therefore, product innovation is an effective strategy that can be applied in the market which begins to form or has already formed. Computer and semi-conductor industries always keep updating their products to meet market demands for better performance, function and appearance. Other industries like food-processing and household supplies also need to make regular product innovation to encourage more purchases.

(2) Improving product quality

Improving the quality of products or services also increases market share. For some organizations, they are going to improve product or service quality gradually. It is necessary not only to improve the quality of luxury products, but also the end products which actually gain the most sales.

(3) Increasing market exploration expenses

Increasing marketing expenses such as advertising and promotion can help the market leader gain more market share. Promotion expense enhancement contributes most to market share gaining for organizations which produce consumption and production materials. While, for companies which produce raw materials, it is not that useful. Advertisement expense contributes a lot to expand market share for consumption material production organizations, but less helpful for companies which produce raw material and production material.

7.3.2 Market Challengers

1. Strategic Objective and Competitor Assessment

Large firms that are second, third in an industry with eager to wrest more market share are

Chapter 7 Marketing Competitive Strategies

called market challengers. There are some famous market challengers such as Fuji (photographic film), Colgate (commodity) and Pepsi (soft drinks). Just as market leaders, the followers' strategic objectives are to increase market shares as well. Therefore, they must challenge their leaders.

As a market challenger, it must determine its strategic objective first. Most strategic objective of challengers is market share growth which can lead to large profit rise. Second, the market challenger needs to find out all that can be its competitors. Basically, a challenger can choose companies to attack which are listed in the following.

(1) Market leaders

The market challenger can attack the market leader, a high-risk but potentially high-gain strategy. If the market leader is not the real leader in the market and cannot serve the market well, the attacking strategy is more helpful. The challenger must understand customer needs and find out what they are not satisfied with. There will be a strategic target market left for the market challenger, if a customer need is not satisfied or not completely satisfied.

(2) Firms as its own size

The challenger can attack firms as its own size. These firms may be underfinanced and bad-managed and cannot serve customers well; the challenger can attack them successfully. As the challenger, it must do the research about customer satisfaction at all times and find out potential innovation opportunity.

(3) Smaller regional or local firms

The challenger can attack smaller regional or local firms to gain more market share. Many large firms grew to their present size not by challenging large competitors, but by gobbling up small local or regional competitors.

Remember, the important point is: the challenger must choose its competitors carefully and have a clearly defined objective. If the competitor going to attack is a market leader, the objective is to wrest more market share. When the challenger goes after a small regional company, the objective is to put that company out of business.

2. Special Marketing Strategies

There are some special marketing strategies that can be chosen to attack competitors.

(1) Discount and allowance

The challenger can provide discounts and allowances for channel members and end customers to gain more market share. There are three conditions that should be met when using the strategy: first, the buyer must consider the product or service provided by the challenger are as good as the market leader's; second, the buyer is price-sensitive and willing to switch the supplier; third, the market leader never cut its price at any conditions.

(2) Low price product

If there are a large number of customers who are price-sensitive, the challenger can provide product at very low price to attack its competitors. This is a strategy that only can be used for a short period of time, and if the product is not good enough, the competitive advantage gained by the low price strategy cannot last long. Therefore, the challenger must improve product quality gradually in order to challenge the leader in the long run.

(3) Famous branding

The challenger can take efforts to provide a product of famous brand and charge a premium price to wrest more market share.

(4) Product expansion and innovation

The challenger can follow the market leader to create different kinds of new products. The likelihood of success of the strategy is depending on whether the forecast of new product market is reasonable. Moreover, the responses of the market leader and other companies as its own size are also important.

(5) Low cost management

Low cost management is the strategy combining price strategy, cost management and technological research together. The challenger can obtain lower production costs than its competitors by utilizing effective material purchasing, low labor costs and advanced production equipments. By applying low cost management, the company can set offensive price to gain market share since its product costs are lower than competitors'.

(6) Service improvement

The challenger can find some new or better way to service customers.

(7) Distribution innovation

The challenger can develop a new distribution channel to increase market share.

(8) Intensive promotion

Some challengers may attack the market leader by utilizing intensive advertisement and promotion which are designed better than their competitors'.

3. Attack Strategies

After selecting competitors and determining objective, the challenger needs to consider what strategy can be used to attack its competitors. There is an important point: The challenger must take advantage of its strengths at right time and in the right place to attain the objective, instead of launching a full attack. There are two strategies can be chosen.

Chapter 7 Marketing Competitive Strategies

(1) Frontal attack

The attack that the challenger launched to beat competitors head-on with all strengths in hands is called a frontal attack. It attacks the competitor's strengths rather than its weaknesses. The outcome depends on who has the greater strength. In a fully frontal attack, the challenger may attack the competitor's product, advertising and price efforts.

In order to make a fully frontal attack successfully, the challenger must have more strengths than its competitor. If the market challenger has fewer resources than the competitor, a frontal attack makes little sense and even leads to great loss.

Price war is also used in the frontal attack. The challenger may provide the product with the same quality and features as the leader's product at lower price. Price competition works well if the leader does not attack back by price cutting and the challenger can make customers believe that the product it provides is not only cheaper, but also as good as the leader's.

(2) Indirect attack

The challenger can make an indirect attack on the competitor's weaknesses. It makes sense if the challenger has less resource than its competitors.

First, the challenger can launch the indirect attack in the area where the competitor does not have much market share.

Second, the challenger can find the market which is not serviced by the competitor and try to satisfy it. It leads firms to provide the fully service to satisfy diverse needs in the whole industry and avoids fierce competition between companies in the same segmented market.

To sum up, the challenger needs to choose the right competitor first. It can attack the market leader, firms as its own size, and smaller competitors. It is high-risky but potentially high-gain to attack the leader. Its goal is to take over market leadership. Alternatively, the challenger can attack firms as its own size to expand market share. Moreover, the challenger may attack a small company to put it out of business.

The challenger can launch a frontal or an indirect attack. It may launch a fully frontal attack on a small competitor's product, price and promotion efforts or only attack one element of a competitor's marketing mix. If the challenger has more resource, a frontal attack works well. By analyzing the competitor's weaknesses or on gaps in the competitor's market coverage, the challenger can launch a direct attack.

7.3.3 Market Followers

A firm that is second, third, or lower in the industry which follows after the market leader is called a market challenger. The follower pays close attention to the development of the market leader, and keeps accordance with the leader's product development and other marketing mixes as price, distribution channel and promotion. It develops unique marketing strategy without arising competitor's retaliation. The follower holds the stable market share and obtains high profit return. The top manager of the firm focuses on profit gaining rather than market share enhancement.

The follower always follows the market leader closely. It learns valuable experiences from the leader by observing. The follower is not an explorer or a first-user of new technology, but an active learner and improver. It can copy or improve on the leader's products and programs, usually with much less investment and risk.

There are many market followers existing in industries of computer, watch, cosmetics and food, especially in developing countries. By implementing the following strategy, the follower grows gradually into a strong market challenger to attack the market leader.

Not all the followers want to challenge the market leader. Challenges may lead to fierce market competition. The leader probably has more staying power in an all-out battle. Therefore, it is better to follow rather than challenge the leader if the challenger does not have break-through and advantages in product innovation or marketing channel.

A market follower must know how to hold current customers and win new ones. It must try its best to bring actual profits to its target market – location, services, financing. Furthermore, in order to avoid the attack launched by the market challenger, the follower must keep its manufacturing costs low and its product quality and services high. It must also enter new markets as they open up. The follower does not only passively copy everything of the leader. It should find the way to win customers without causing retaliation. There are several marketing strategies can be chosen by the follower.

There are three types of follower: the follower, the distant follower and the selective follower. And there are three kinds of strategies according to the type of follower.

First, the follower copies the product, brand name and package of the market leader and modifies a little. For instance, the follower can adopt the product, brand name and package similar as the leader, and set the price lower.

Second, the distant follower makes product, price, brand, package and price are different from the leader.

Third, the selective follower copies some parts of strategies from the leader according to its requirement as its foundation of strategy drawing.

Even though the market follower holds smaller market share than the leader, it still makes profit and probably earns a lot. Studies have shown that, by implementing right marketing strategies, the target return rate of the firm which follows the market leader can exceed the

Chapter 7 Marketing Competitive Strategies

average profit level in the industry.

1. Competition-Oriented Pricing

The competition-oriented pricing strategy is especially applicable to the distant follower. The competitive pricing helps the firm follows the market leader closely and avoids frontal conflict with the leader.

2. Market Development

The market development strategy is applicable to the distant follower. It can decrease interference from the competitor on marketing plan. The follower grows by competing with small companies in the industry.

3. Market Segmentation

It is applicable to the selective follower. Selecting the market which is not chosen by the market leader avoids direct conflict. If the follower carries on research and develops new products which meet customers' needs in some segmented markets, it becomes the challenger which can challenge the leader indirectly.

7.3.4 Market Niches

A market niche specializes in market, customer, product, service and marketing mix lines. For instance, the niche sells product in specific market area and provides special product or service for specific customers.

Most industries include some small firms that specialize in serving market niches. Instead of purchasing the whole market, or even large segments, these firms target sub-segments. Niches are often small organizations with limited resources. But smaller divisions of large companies also may pursue niche strategies.

1. Market Niche Selection

Firms or divisions of large companies that implementing niche strategy must try to find one or more market niches that are safe and profitable. Generally speaking, an ideal market niche has key features as the following:

(1) The niche is big enough to be profitable and has growth potential.
(2) It is of little interest to major competitors.
(3) The firm has enough skills and resources to serve it effectively.
(4) The firm is able to build the customer goodwill to defend itself against major

competitors as the niche grows and becomes more attractive.

The major risk of niche strategy is that the market niche may dry up or it might attract larger competitors. That is why many companies choose multiple niches instead of a single niche. Therefore, a firm can develop two or more niches to increase its chances for survival according to key features of an ideal market niche listed above.

2. Niche Specialization

The key point of the niche strategy is specialization. A market niche-seeker must be specialized in the market, customer, product or marketing mix line. There are some types of niches that are classified by specialization.

(1) End user niche. The niche-seeker can specialize in serving one type of end user. For example, a law firm specializes in the criminal, civil, or business law markets.

(2) Customer-size group niche. The niche-seeker can specialize in serving small, middle or large-size customers who are neglected by the major companies.

(3) Specific customer niche. The niche-seeker can focus on one or a few specific customers. For instance, many firms sell entire products to a single company.

(4) Geographic market niche. Some niche-seekers specialize by geographic market. They sell products or services only in a certain locality, region or area.

(5) Product or product line niche. The niche-seeker only holds one product or product line.

(6) Service niche. The niche-seeker offers one or several services not available from other companies.

(7) Distribution niche. The niche-seeker only services one marketing channel.

(8) Quality-price niche. The niche-seeker operates at the low or high end of the market.

7.4　Summary

根据美国学者波特的研究，企业在行业竞争中会面临来自五个方面的力量的威胁，包括现有企业间的竞争、入侵者威胁、替代品威胁、买方讨价还价能力和卖方讨价还价能力。这些作用力决定着该行业的利润和竞争状况。

通过对行业竞争环境的分析，企业可以选择总成本领先、差别化和重点集中作为基本战略。总成本领先战略是指企业通过加强内部成本控制，尽可能地降低成本，成为行业中的成本领先者的战略。通过成本优势，企业可以在竞争中获得竞争优势。差别化战略是指提供与众不同的产品或服务，满足顾客的特殊需求，形成竞争优势的战略。重点集中战略是指把经营战略的重点放在一个特定的目标市场上，为特定的地区或购买者集团提供特殊的产品或服务。

Chapter 7 Marketing Competitive Strategies

根据竞争者在同一目标市场中的地位进行分类,可以划分为市场领导者、市场挑战者、市场追随者和市场补缺者。处于不同市场地位的竞争者需要根据其竞争状况选择相应的市场营销战略。

Key Terms

Competitor Advantage   Competitor Analysis   Competitive Marketing Strategy   Market Leader   Market Challenger   Market Follower   Market Nicher

【案例】 沃尔玛的竞争战略

沃尔玛的战略标志是:天天低价,商品的选择范围宽广,较大比例的名牌商品,使顾客感到友善而温馨的商店环境,较低的营业成本,对新的地理含义上的市场进行训练有素的扩张,创新性的市场营销以及优良的售后服务保证。在每一家沃尔玛商店的外面都用大字母传递着这样的信息:"永远的低价,永远!"沃尔玛还向它的顾客灌输这样一种观念:"竞争者在当地做出任何广告,我们都将对之产生反应!"沃尔玛的主要商品系列包括:家庭用品、电器用品、体育用品、用于草坪和花园的器具、健身与健美器材和设备、家庭时尚用品、油漆、涂料、床上用品和浴室用品、五金商品、家用修理设备、玩具和游戏软件以及杂货类商品。在1994年,沃尔玛商店的规模从40 000平方英尺到180 000平方英尺不等,平均的规模为84 000平方英尺。每个商店的结构是大体一致的,商店的光线明亮,气氛欢快,空气新鲜,而且商店里的通道宽阔,并有吸引人的最流行的商品陈列。商店的员工友善并乐于助人,他们的目标就是要使每一个逛商店的顾客都感到愉悦满意。在1993年,沃尔玛宣布了更换100个标准快餐店的计划,代替它们的是麦当劳的特许经营分店。

节约成本的意识贯穿于沃尔玛经营的方方面面——从商店的建设,到供应商给沃尔玛提供低价的仓储商品,再经由高速的分销系统给每个商店配送商品,从而使沃尔玛保持着成本领先优势。而沃尔玛节约的成本又以更低的零售价格的形式转移给了商店的顾客。

一、竞争环境

折扣零售业是一个竞争激烈的行业。沃尔玛的两个最近的竞争者是凯马特和西尔斯,三家公司都有着相似的战略,并有相似的成长过程,但是在整个20世纪80年代,沃尔玛的增长速度远比凯马特和西尔斯要快。在1989年,西尔斯由于增长太慢而落后了,沃尔玛升到了行业老大的地位。沃尔玛由此开始推行天天低价的战略,并将各种名牌商品冠以其自身的商标推向市场。此后几乎所有的折扣商都采用了某种形式的大大低价的战略。

折扣零售商竞争的中心主要围绕定价、商店位置、商店布局、商品组合、商店规模、购物环境以及商店形象。在前10家最大的折扣零售商中,沃尔玛是唯一一家将其大部分商店设立于乡村市场的。将沃尔玛与凯马特和塔吉特做比较的家庭调查表明,沃尔玛具有很强的竞争优势。《折扣商店新闻》的资料揭示:当被要求对沃尔玛和凯马特及塔吉特做比较时,各个家庭比较一致的意见是沃尔玛更好或至少一样的好。例如,在有沃尔玛的地方,

59%的家庭认为沃尔玛比凯马特和塔吉特更好，33%的家庭认为一样好，只有4%的家庭认为沃尔玛比凯马特和塔吉特更差……当被问到沃尔玛为什么更好时，在他们所在的地区开设有沃尔玛的商店的被访问者中，55%的人认为是沃尔玛更低或更优的价格……多样化的商品或广泛的选择范围和优质的产品质量是被顾客引用的另外几个主要原因。30%的人认为是产品的丰富多样，18%的人认为是产品的高质量。沃尔玛的声誉传到了还没有开商店的地区，从而降低了它进入新的地理区域的推广成本。在各种媒体中，有着关于萨姆·沃尔顿和沃尔玛的市场营销的超凡能力或超凡技术的大量报告，这使得公司在顾客心目中树立了极佳的形象和品牌认知度。

在实施战略方面，沃尔玛将其重点置于与供应商和员工结成稳固的工作关系，对商品陈列和市场营销的任何一个小细节都给予关注，充分利用每一个节约成本的机会，并且造就一种追求高业绩的精神。对于大公司的成长和成功来讲，经常有这样一些阻碍因素：管理层次过多，缺乏内部交流，以及不愿或不能做出改变。而这些因素在沃尔玛的商店中是找不到的。

二、天天低价的战略主题

虽然沃尔玛并没有发明天天低价战略，但在"执行"这个要领上，它比任何一家别的折扣商店都做得更好。在市场中，沃尔玛有这样的声誉：它每天均是最低价格的日用品零售商。在沃尔玛开设有商店的区域，对顾客的调查表明，55%的家庭认为沃尔玛的价格比其竞争者更低或更优；而在沃尔玛没有开设商店的区域，也有33%的家庭持有同样的观点。沃尔玛采用多种方式向顾客宣传它的低价战略，如在商店的前面，在广告中，在商店内的各种标志上，以及在包装袋的广告语中，随处可见"我们的售价更低"！

三、广告

沃尔玛比它的竞争者更少依赖于广告公司，在第一个月只发布1次或2次，通过使其环保包装的产品更醒目，沃尔玛也得到了免费的媒体报道。公司还经常允许各种慈善机构使用其停车场进行各种募集资金的活动。

四、分销

这些年来，沃尔玛的管理层已经把公司的中心分销系统变成了一个有竞争力的武器。大卫·格拉斯说："我们的分销设备是我们成功的关键之一。如果我们比竞争对手做得更好一点的话，那就是我们的分销设备。"由于它在乡村的商店布局，沃尔玛在分销效率方面在早期就已经走在竞争对手的前面。因为其他的折扣零售商依赖于生产厂家或分销商将货物直接运送到它们在大城市区域内的商店。沃尔玛发现，它在20世纪70年代的快速增长充分利用了供应商的能力——使用其独立的运货公司给沃尔玛不断增加的乡村商店进行频繁而及时的货物运送。在1980年，沃尔玛开始建立地区分销中心，并且通过自己的运输车队从这些中心给各家商店分送货物。当新的、边远的商店从现有的分销中心不能得到可靠而经济的服务时，沃尔玛就设立新的分销中心。在1994年，公司拥有22家分销中心，覆盖了2150万平方英尺的面积。这些分销中心总共雇用了1600名员工，他们每年要以准确率达99%的装运顺序，处理850 000卡车的商品。沃尔玛的分销中心采用了大量的自动化系统。最初的运输装置系统采用单体运送的方式，这样就有一个顺序选择问题。纸板盒通过运输装置运送到处理中心，在那里，操作员将纸板盒放入分类系统。激光扫描机识别商品的条形码，并且指示分类机对纸盒进行分类，其处理速度为每分钟超过120个纸板盒。然后，纸板盒被分送到不同的运输出口。1988年的研究数据表明：沃尔玛相对西尔斯和凯马特的分销成本优势是很明显的。沃尔玛具有向它几乎所有的商店当天分销的能力；而凯马特要每4～5天分销一次，塔吉特每3～4天分销一次。

五、最新技术的使用

沃尔玛积极地应用最新技术成果，以提高生产率和降低成本。公司的技术目标就是要向员工提供这样的工具：通过对这些工具的应用，可以使他们更有效地工作，更好地做出决策。技术的使用并不仅仅是代替现有员工的一个手段，沃尔玛应用技术的方法就是积极地尝试、试验，开始使用最新的设备、零售技巧和计算机软件。而这些技术即使不是优先于所有的其他折扣零售商，也要优于它们中的大多数。

在1974年，公司开始在其分销系统中心和各家商店运用计算机基于一定的标准进行库存控制。在1981年，沃尔玛开始在销售点使用扫描机，并且承诺到1983年，在其整个连锁店系统都用上条形码扫描系统。这一变动导致其顾客服务速度提高了25%到30%。在1984年，沃尔玛开发了一套计算机辅助市场营销系统。这套系统可以在每一家商店按照自身的市场环境和销售类型制定出相应的产品组合。在1985年到1987年之间，沃尔玛安装了国内最大的私人卫星通信网络。该网络的应用使得总部、分销中心和各个商店之间可以实现双向的声音和数据传输，从本顿维尔的公司办公室到各分销中心和各家商店之间可以实现单向的图形传输。这套系统比先前使用的电话网络系统还要安全，可视系统通常被公司的管理人员用于与公司的全体职员进行即时的直接通话。

在1989年，沃尔玛与大约1700个供应商建立了直接的卫星联系，而后者供应着沃尔玛所售商品的近80%，这种联系使得沃尔玛可以使用电子订货，并迅速地进行数据交换。沃尔玛也利用了卫星系统的能力，即通过开发一套信用卡的授权程序，平均5秒钟就可以完成一宗授权的买卖，从而相对于原来的手工处理系统来说，顾客使用信用卡结账的速度可以提高25%。公司有标准的数据处理系统和信息系统。沃尔玛不仅开发了计算机系统针对公司经营的每一个方面为公司的管理层提供详细的数据，而且在世界上同类规模的公司中，沃尔玛被认为是成本最低、数据处理效率最高的公司之一。沃尔玛在其遍布各个地域的众多商店中，对于最新零售技术的快速采纳，又使它拥有了相对于大多数其他折扣商的技术优势。

六、建筑政策

沃尔玛的管理层努力地工作着，在他们的新商店、商店改造及商店的附属装置的资本支出上尽量节约。对于商店的陈列、附属装置的设计以及有效展示所需要的窗户这样一些问题，公司诚恳地向供应商们征求意见和建议。沃尔玛的商店设计为：有着开放式窗口的管理人员办公室——装修起来比较经济，有着大面积展示空间的特点——重新整理和翻新均比较容易。沃尔玛所雇用的建筑公司可以利用计算机建模技术，一周之内就可以设计出几家建筑风格完全一样的新商店。此外，商店的设计还要达到建筑周期短，建筑费用低且维修和改造的成本也应较低的要求。所有的商店在 7 年之内至少进行一次翻新和重新装修。由于新的道路、高等级公路和新商业中心的设立，如果某一家商店已经跟不上时代了，那么旧的商店就要被放弃，并在合适的位置开设一家新的商店。例如在 1994 年，沃尔玛以一年 100 家的速度扩张或迁建商店。

为了在设施上保持低成本，沃尔玛的分销中心和公司的办公场所花费的建筑费用均较少，且装修简单。高层经理们的办公室十分质朴且毫不做作。在沃尔玛所有商店中的照明、供热和空调控制系统均通过计算机与本顿维尔的总部相连，这样就可以使得节约成本的能量控制措施可以集中加以控制，并且它还使得商店的管理者可以腾出时间来，从容地控制公共开支。沃尔玛实行商品大量生产和室内批量展示的做法，这样不仅省钱省时，而且在不到 30 天的时间内就可以推出一次新的展示概念。

七、与供应商的关系

由于有着巨大的购买力做支持，通常人认为沃尔玛有着强有力的与供应商讨价还价的能力。公司的采购部门严格而功利，采购代理商们也尽其所能去获得最低的价格，并且他们从不接受供应商的宴请。一家主要供应商的市场营销副总裁告诉《财富》杂志："他们是一群对工作极为关心的人，他们对其购买力的有效利用要强于美国国内的任何其他人。所有的祷告仪式都是口头的方式。他们最优先考虑的事情是，确保每一个人在任何时候任何情况下都知道谁在主持局面。这就是沃尔玛。他们说话很温和，但他们有着水虎鱼(piranha，产于南美洲的一种淡水鱼，会攻击并吞食动物)的心，当你去他们那里的时候，如果不做一个通盘考虑，你就会把自己当成一个笨蛋被涮一通。"

虽然沃尔玛在争取绝对的低价的谈判中表现强硬，沃尔玛仍会努力与供应商做到相互尊重，并结成互惠的长期伙伴关系。供应商被邀请到沃尔玛的分销中心参观，亲临现场看到事情是怎样运转的，并且也了解到沃尔玛在获得更高的效率方面所碰到的各种难题。供应商们也会被鼓励就他们与沃尔玛关系中的任何难题发表意见，并且积极地参与沃尔玛的未来发展计划。例如，在 1987 年，在萨姆·沃尔顿要求宝洁公司的经理们观看沃尔玛的一群经理就他们与宝洁公司的不和谐关系的讲座后，宝洁公司在沃尔玛的总部附近派驻了一组人员，让他们持续地与沃尔玛的人员一起工作。这一合作项目的首要目标包括对宝洁公司供应的大多数商品采用可回收利用的包装材料，以与沃尔玛的政策相一致，而这一政策就是沃尔玛对外宣称的它们所销售的产品都是环保产品。另一个涉及的问题就是将两家公司的计算机相连接，从而为宝洁公司供应给沃尔玛的大多数商品建立起一个及时订货和传送系统。当沃尔玛库存到了订货点时，计算机就通过卫星向最近的宝洁工厂发出订单，然后这些工厂将其商品运送到沃尔玛的分销中心，或者直接运送到商店。宝洁公司和沃尔玛公司都认为自动订货系统是一个双赢的处理方案。因为通过更好的协调，宝洁公司能够有

Chapter 7 Marketing Competitive Strategies

效地做出生产计划，进行直线分销，并降低其成本，最后宝洁公司又可将节约的一部分成本让利给沃尔玛。

沃尔玛寻找着这样的供应商：在他们所生产的产品领域居主导地位的供应商(这样他们可以提供高品牌认知度的产品)；能与沃尔玛一块成长的，有着丰富产品系列的供应商(他们提供的产品可以使得沃尔玛的顾客既有丰富的选择性，又可以使他们准备选择的产品有着某种程度的有限的排他性)；有长期的研究开发计划，从而使得沃尔玛的零售货架上总是能够摆上新的和更好的产品的供应商；还有那些对他们所供应的产品有能力提高生产和分销效率的供应商。正如一家供应商所评论的："沃尔玛总是希望分销商们跟上他们的步伐。"几家供应商将沃尔玛与他们做交易的方式描述为：他们不断地向我们提出挑战。我们能做到这点吗？如果我们尝试着那样去做结果会怎样？他们不断地寻找着对自身加以改进的方法。他们把困难看成是机会，而不是抱怨。他们开会时十分投入……所有的问题都摆在桌面上。

无论你的产品多么好，如果他们没有告诉你它们在货架上的表现，则它们在沃尔玛的商店中表现并不怎么样。他们正在寻找着精力充沛的、富有创造力的包装人员，这些人员将承担起销售人员的责任。他们了解他们的商店、他们的产品以及他们的市场，并且他们有出奇的能力，能够预测他们的顾客需要什么。他们关于产品的建议对我们很有价值。他们信守承诺并且期望着同样的回报。如果我们拉了一次促销的后腿，促销的广告就会被取消，但他们会继续订货。这就是他们做生意的方式。

(资料来源：完美人生. 沃尔玛的竞争战略. [2009-01-24]. http://www.docin.com/p-7024429.html.)

【案例分析】

"天天低价"是沃尔玛的竞争战略。从案例中我们得知沃尔玛竞争战略的成功实施受益于其与战略相匹配的诸多措施，例如商品的选择范围宽广，较大比例的名牌商品，使顾客感到友善而温馨的商店环境，较低的营业成本，对新的地理含义上的市场进行训练有素的扩张，创新性的市场营销以及优良的售后服务保证。同时，节约成本的意识贯穿于沃尔玛经营的方方面面，使其低价战略的成功实施成为可能，例如从商店的建设，到供应商给沃尔玛提供低价的仓储商品，再经由高速的分销系统给每个商店配送商品，每个环节都使沃尔玛保持着成本领先优势；而沃尔玛节约的成本又以更低的零售价格的形式转移给了商店的顾客。为了达到节约成本和提高效率的目的，沃尔玛还非常重视最新技术的采用、搜集供应商的建议等，这些措施有效地保证了"天天低价"战略的实现。

【思考题】

1. 分析沃尔玛"天天低价"战略主题的有效性。
2. 讨论沃尔玛的竞争战略的风险。

Chapter 8

Marketing Engineering

Focus on:

1. Connotation and composition of the marketing engineering.
2. Origin and evolution of the marketing engineering.
3. Merits and drawbacks of the conceptual model, graphical model and mathematical model in the marketing engineering.
4. Roles of the cluster analysis, factor analysis, decision tree analysis, hierarchy processing analysis and conjoint analysis in the marketing engineering.

8.1 Origin and Development of the Marketing Engineering

The marketing engineering is a systematic one, which can raise the correctness of the decision making and the benefits of the marketing input by way of integrating marketing knowledge, its data, issues, decision-making models, management systems, information and case banks, etc. so as to help the marketing decision-maker realize the streamlining, quantification, science, and normalization of the decision. Its origin and development have seen the following stages:

(1) Application of the mathematic models in the marketing, which is represented by the book "Quantitative Technologies in Analyzing the Marketing" written by R. Frank, etc.;

(2) Management information systems (1965). They are mainly embodied in the "Design of the Marketing Neurological Centre for the Enterprise" written by Philip Kotler;

(3) Decision-making calculation (1970). ADBUDG systems by John Little and CALLPLAN ones by Lodish are the typical of it;

(4) Econometric models (1975);

(5) Marketing decision support systems (1980). STRATPORT by Srinivasan and BEII by Gary L. Lilien are typical;

(6) Marketing expert systems (1987). INFER by Arvind Rangaswamy and ADVISORY by

Gary L. Lilien are well established;

(7) Application of artificial neural network (1991);

(8) Data digging.

Since the beginning of the 21th century, the experts and scholars in the United States, European and Australia have made a deep and extensive investigation and study in the marketplace. The result proves that the marketing engineering, as decision-supporting tools, is playing an important role in marketing decision making. However, a relatively perfect decision method system is still to be improved, for the marketing engineering approaches remain in the decision model stage that can only make an analysis of some decision tasks and can't simulate the operation of the whole marketing system. Although this situation of the marketing engineering needs improving, it has laid a foundation in the respect that marketing really becomes a science. In China, the research about the marketing engineering is now lying in the start stage. The actual research outcomes are limited except the introduction of the foreign study results.

8.2 Connotation and Elements of the Marketing Engineering

As what Gary L. Lilien says, the marketing engineering means analyzing, planning and implementing the marketing tactics and strategies with the interactive computer decision models based on customers and being a systematic process applying the marketing data and knowledge to the marketing practice in planning and designing the structural decision support and the marketing management support system. Inferred from the definition said, to construct the marketing decision model and methods is the key of the marketing engineering. And its main parts include marketing theoretic bases, marketing mathematic models and their solving, and marketing practice. The relationship among them is shown as in Figure 8.1.

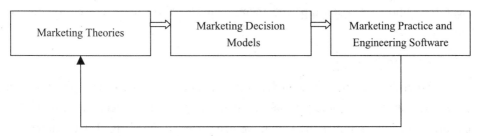

Figure 8.1 Relationship Among Various Elements of the Marketing Engineering

8.2.1 Theoretic Bases of Marketing Engineering

The marketing theories are the foundation of the marketing engineering and analyzing the actual marketing issues. Practically, numerous marketing decision models are all based on the marketing theories, especially those created by Philip Kotler that provide an overall theoretic support for the marketing engineering, for example, 4Ps theories, 4Cs, etc.

8.2.2 Marketing Decision Models

The marketing decision models are the approaches to explore and solve the marketing issues with stylized tools so as to reach a particular target. Based on the actual marketing problem of the enterprise, they are focused on the core of the issue and derive it by abstraction and construct the correspondent models to aid the decision making of the marketing management. In the decision models, their aims, assumptions, variables, and relationship are all clearly explicated. The aims are usually the reasons to establish the models and define the scope of application; the assumptions provide the models with backgrounds or framework; the variables include those that are controllable, uncontrollable and environmental ones. Marketing decision makers obtain all kinds of models in analyzing the internal and external environmental variables and classifying the data, and then make the correspondent decisions by way of solving, finally carry out them. The commonly used models consist of conceptual, graphic and mathematic ones.

1. Conceptual Model

It is a kind of structure that can reflect the relationships among different parts in words and qualitatively depict the marketing phenomenon. For example, in his marketing process model, Philip Kotler divides various marketing activities into two parts, namely creating value for customers and building relationship with them, acquiring the value from customers as returns (see Figure 8.2).

2. Graphic Model

It is a model that describes and analyzes the marketing phenomenon with figures or tables (see Table 8.1, Figure 8.3). Table 8.1 makes a comparison to the collection method of the basic data and their concrete activities, by which we can distinctly understand the differences among various approaches. Figure 8.3 tells us some market-response models set by Saunders (1997). He explains eight market phenomena with eight figures. In the figures, X represents "inputs", i.e., levels of the marketing efforts or independent variables; Y represents "outputs", i.e., outcomes of the marketing efforts or dependent variables. The definition of the different figures is presented as follows: P1 says that outputs are zero when inputs are zero; P2 says that the linear relationship exists between inputs and outputs; P3 says that the returns decrease with the rise of inputs; P4 tells us that outputs can't surpass a certain level; P5 says that the returns increase progressively with the rise of inputs; P6 says that as inputs increase, the returns increase at first, and then decrease; P7 says that before outputs are produced, inputs must surpass a certain degree; P8 shows us that outputs begin to decrease when inputs have got to a level.

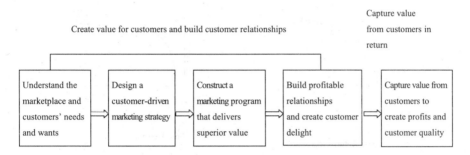

Figure 8.2 A Simple Model of the Marketing Process

Source: Philip Kotler, Gary Armstrong. *Principles of Marketing*. Eleventh Edition. Beijing: Tsinghua University Press, 2008, 5.

Table 8.1 Planning Primary Data Collection

Research Approaches	Contact Methods	Sampling Plan	Research Instruments
Observation	Mail	Sampling unit	Questionnaire
Survey	Telephone	Sample size	Mechanical instruments
Experiment	Personal	Sampling procedure	
	Online		

Source: Philip Kotler, Gary Armstrong. *Principles of Marketing*. Eleventh Edition. Beijing: Tsinghua University Press, 2008, 109.

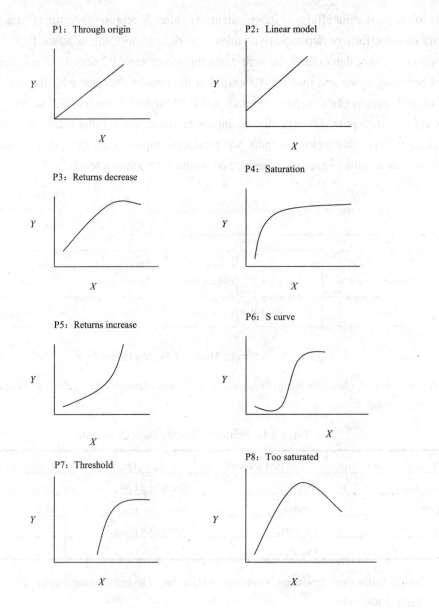

Figure 8.3   Market Response Models

Source: Gary L. Lilien, Arvind Rangaswamy. translated by Wei Liyuan, revised by Chen Dong. *Marketing Engineering*. Beijing: China Renmin University Press, 2005, 41.

3. Mathematic Model

It is an approach in which the quantitative tools are used to analyze the marketing

Chapter 8 Marketing Engineering

phenomenon and solve the marketing problems. In the marketing engineering, mathematic models are applied frequently. For example, the ADBUDG model put forward in 1970 by Little are widely used in the marketing activities as constructing ads and promotion.

ADBUDG model:

$$Y = b + (a-b)\frac{X^c}{d + X^c}$$

For $c>1$, the model shows S shapes; for $0<c<1$, the model shows concave shapes. The floor of the model is b while the top-limit of it is a.

By simulating calculation of the marketing activities, users can obtain correspondent results under different independent variables so as to make it convenient for enterprises to screen and optimize the marketing project. The construction of the marketing decision model with mathematic tools is favorable both to the computerization of the model and to the development of the marketing engineering software. Nevertheless, the models built on the mathematic approaches have their limits, for they are set upon some hypotheses by abstracting the concrete marketing issues. In this way, the decision models for the marketing are not completely the copy of the actual phenomenon, but ideal ones based on certain limited conditions. Therefore, in applying them in the realities, the users must realize these constraints.

8.2.3 Marketing Practice and Engineering Software

Today, more market information may puzzle managers and affect their decision and not have their decision more effective. The application of the marketing engineering, especially the maturity and generalization of the engineering software, will upgrade the decision abilities and efficiency of decision makers by refining the useful information for enterprises. Yet, the users must awake to the fact that the essence of the marketing engineering is still the marketing. The marketing engineering is just a tool to reach the marketing goals. What it gives to the decision makers is an analysis method and platform. The makers should make decisions by synthetically balancing the information about the marketing variables and the simulating results before the final decision project is formed.

The marketing engineering software consists of typical marketing decision models and their analysis. It is the main tool for the decision makers, and not simply the statistic analysis software. The popularization of the marketing engineering software depends on its maturity, which does not need the construction of the decision models by makers themselves, but provides a comparatively perfect platform for them to analyze the key marketing variables and solve the related results in order to give them the reference and advice. At present, the marketing engineering software used widely in the reality is Marketing Engineering Classic v2.4 and Marketing Engineering for Excel developed by Gary L. Lilien and his team. The use of his research results will greatly push the marketing forward.

专栏 8.1　Gary L. Lilien 营销工程软件简介

Gary L. Lilien 营销工程软件主要由三种不同类型的软件模块构成。
(1)　在营销工程软件主菜单下直接运行的 Windows 程序：
- Cluster Analysis (聚类分析程序)
- Multinomial Logit Analysis (多项式分对数分析程序)
- Positioning Analysis (市场定位分析程序)

(2)　在 Excel 下加载运行的电子报表模型：
- ADBUDG (广告预算模型)
- ADVISOR (沟通计划模型)
- ASSESSOR (预测试市场模型)
- Bass Model (巴斯模型)
- Choice-based Segmentation (基于选择的市场细分模型)
- Competitive Advertising (竞争广告模型)
- Competitive Bidding (竞争性投标模型)
- Conglomerate Promotional Analysis (Conglomerate 促销分析模型)
- GE: Portfolio Planning (GE 业务组合规划模型)
- Learning Curve Pricing (学习曲线定价模型)
- PIMS (PIMS 战略模型)
- Promotional Spending Analysis (促销费用分析模型)
- CALLPLAN (销售拜访计划模型)
- Sales Resource Allocation (销售资源分配模型)
- Value-in-use Pricing (使用价值定价模型)
- Visual Response Modeling (可视反应模型)
- Yield Management for Hotels (饭店收益管理模型)

(3)　与主菜单关系松散，激活后就可以执行的独立程序：
- ADCAD (广告方案设计程序)
- Analytic Hierarchy Process (层次分析程序)
- Conjoint Analysis (联合分析程序)
- Decision Tree Analysis (决策树分析程序)
- Geodemographic Site Planning (地理人口网点规划程序)

Chapter 8 Marketing Engineering

- Neural Net Forecasting (神经网络预测程序)

(Source: Gary L. Lilien, Arvind Rangaswamy. translated by Wei Liyuan, revised by Chen Dong. *Marketing Engineering*. Beijing: China Renmin University Press, 2005, 30.)

8.3 Marketing Engineering Methods

Elementary marketing theories, marketing decision models, marketing practice and engineering software conjointly make up a complete system in the marketing engineering. Various components are interrelated, interacted as both cause and effect and embody their inherent laws and relationship among the hypothesis and variables. The methods to link the different components and make them interplay may be qualitative or quantitative. Many methods are used now, but a complete method system is still to be set up. Of numerous approaches, cluster analysis, factor analysis, and decision tree analysis, etc. are often applied in the marketing engineering.

8.3.1 Cluster Analysis

The cluster analysis is usually called "analysis on groups", and is a multivariate statistic technique to study the classification. Its basic idea is presented as follows: in the light of the similarities of the samples or indicators studied, some statistic data that can be used to measure the similarity degree among samples and indicators will be found out and these data are to be regarded as the foundation to classify the groups. The samples with greater similarity are aggregated and those with less similarity clustered until all the samples have been finished classifying.

In the cluster analysis, we can divide the classified objects into two types: one is founded on the variables; the other on the samples. The former will tell us the degree of kinship both among the different variables and among the variable combination; then according to the classified results, allow us to make a regression analysis of the main variables. The latter may classify the samples by way of comprehensively utilizing the information of multiple variables and the classified results can be shown clearly audio-visually. To sum up, the results got by the cluster analysis are more detailed, complete and rational than those by the traditional approaches. In this method, we can formulate a plan of the marketing activities for the target market in differentiating the features of various customers in the target market.

8.3.2　Factor Analysis

The factor analysis aims at describing the linkage among multiple indicators or factors through a few factors, or incorporate several variables closely related into the same type and each type becomes a factor. The type is called a factor because it is unobservable and immeasurable. A few factors will contain most information of the original data. This technique can be beneficial to finding out main elements affecting the customer purchase, consumption and satisfaction and their weights. By this method, one can make a front-end analysis for the market segmentation.

8.3.3　Decision Tree Analysis

The decision tree is produced generally from top to bottom. Each decision or event may trigger two or multiple events and lead to various results. The branch decisions are drawn into an image and the image is much like branches of a tree, so they are called decision trees. The decision tree analysis refers to the following: draw an arrow-line for the structure of the various stages in the decision process and hold a track from roots to leaves. This track is named "rule". The decision tree may have double forks, or multiple forks. The method is mostly used for the choice of multiple projects.

8.3.4　Hierarchy Processing Analysis

The hierarchy processing analysis is used in decomposing the elements relative to decisions into targets, norms, and proposals, on which a quantitative or qualitative analysis is made. This approach is first developed by professor Saaty at the start of 70s of the 20th century. It is a gradation-weight decision analysis method. It has such features as to make decision thought process mathematization based on a little quantitative information so as to have the complicated multi-purpose or multi-norm decision issues simplified by way of deeply analyzing the essence, influencing factors and their inner relationship. It is mainly used in formulating the marketing strategy decision.

8.3.5　Conjoint Analysis

The conjoint analysis method belongs to the multivariate analysis, by which we can decompose multi-factor indicators into several different ones in order to understand sizes and structures affecting the overall indicators by these factors in the sequence calculation, distance analysis, variance analysis, and correlation analysis. In the process of application, the conjoint analysis method may study the element investigated by orthogonal design so as to simplify the operation process.

During the product positioning, to be familiar with the degree affecting consumers' buying process by each factor of the product, generally, we investigate the evaluation value of various features from the consumer directly in the traditional methods and choose the "optimal" value for each factor, and finally, the chosen "optimal" value will be regarded as the essential trait held by new products. Two problems exist at least in the traditional methods: one is that it is difficult for the consumer to give marks to a certain concrete feature; the other is that the "optimal" value of each factor can't co-exist in a new product. In view of the existent problems, we can adopt the conjoint analysis method to solve them, for it doesn't need the consumer to make a direct evaluation of these features, but to do an overall sequencing to the parts tested. For the consumer, the method acts as how to select the products from the same kind in the real life.

8.3.6 Advertisement Budget Methods

Now, numerous methods are used in making the advertisement budget, such as target-task approach, profit percentage method, etc.

1. Target-Task Approach

On the basis of the marketing strategy and aims of the enterprise, the advertisement planning and targets are determined, upon which the advertisement budget is formulated. This method is of much science and also a little delicate. In the course of calculation, a greater deviation will happen to the whole advertisement budget if a certain step goes wrong.

Albert Fery, a marketing expert in the United States, says that the target-task method has the following steps:

(1) Determine the marketing target to be reached in a special period;

(2) Determine the elementary feature in the potential market of the enterprise, such as the awareness degree and attitude of the consumer to the product advertised, purchase situation of the existent consumers;

(3) Analyze the fluctuation of the consumer's attitude and sales volume to the products advertised;

(4) Choose appropriate mass media to make a publication so as to upgrade the popularity

of the product;

(5) Formulate the proper advertisement medium tactics to increase the frequency of the exposure;

(6) Ascertain the lowest advertisement charges, i.e., the total of the advertisement budget.

2. Profit Percentage Method

In the light of the total profit rate in a fixed period, one can make a budget of the publication charges. According to the profit connotation, the method includes net profit percentage and gross profit percentage approaches. Its formula is introduced below.

Advertisement budget costs = profit volume in a fixed period × percentage between advertisement expenditure and profit volume in the same period

The method directly connects the advertisement expenditure and profits and adapts to the advertisement distribution among various products. However, it takes the profits and not the sale promotion into consideration, which may leads to the following deduction: more profits, more advertisement expenditure; less profit, less advertisement expenditure; no profits, no advertisement expenditure. The deduction can't be in line with the reality. When new products are pushed into market, almost no profits are produced at the early stage, but large quantities of advertisement charges are needed to push them on in the market. So, this method is quite passive and should be used carefully.

3. Learning Curve Pricing

The effects of the learning curves are the important causes to lead to the non-linear change of the variable costs. The production of new products has remarkable effects of the learning curves. The unit cost of the product decreases with the increase of the volume of production. Penetration pricing may have the unit cost of the product drop rapidly as to form the market price barriers while the skimming pricing make the product price and cost synchronization.

8.4　Summary

　　伴随着现代经济的发展以及市场营销环境的急剧变化，除了营销理论备受关注，侧重营销实践的营销工程也越来越受到营销界的重视。系列营销工程模型已经建立并用于营销实践。常见的营销工程模型有概念模型、图表模型和数理模型；在模型基础上，还开发出众多营销工程软件，如聚类分析程序、多项式分对数分析程序和市场定位分析程序等。营销工程在研究营销的活动中，常采用聚类分析法、因素分析法、决策树分析法、联合分析法以及广告预算法等，这些工具的使用，使营销工程的研究日趋科学化与精确化。

Key Terms

Marketing Engineering　Conceptual Model　Graphic Model　Mathematical Model　Cluster Analysis　Factor Analysis　Decision Tree Analysis　Conjoint Analysis　Advertisement Budget Methods

【案例】开拓成熟大品牌的新市场蓝海——超人+U系列剃须刀上市策划

2007年9月16日，中国超人集团主办的中国大学生成人仪式在武汉华中科技大学隆重举行，超人集团形象代言人胡军和2007年十名全国新闻热点名人汇聚在华中科技大学大广场，和数千名大学新生一起举行了：由超人+U系列——男人的第一把剃须刀独家赞助的，"腾飞的翅膀，远航的风帆，中国大学生(武汉)成人仪式"。超人集团向与会的大学生赠送了+U剃须刀和成人手册。极富创新意识的大型公益活动吸引了包括来自中央级、湖北本地等60多家媒体莅临现场报道这一精彩消息，下午超人形象代言人胡军又来到武汉最繁华的武汉百货广场举行了"胡军相约武汉"媒体见面会和签名售机活动，隆重推出超人+U系列剃须刀，至此，超人集团以"+U"命名，明确目标对象、精准细分市场的副品牌系列剃须刀在武汉闪亮首发。大学生成人仪式上派发避孕套的新闻迅速在全国形成社会焦点话题，超人+U剃须刀随着公众的关注而声名鹊起，拉开了超人品牌的新市场蓝海的序曲。

一、产品同质化，市场创新天

随着中国市场化程度不断深入，市场竞争日趋加剧，中国小家电市场更是被看成香饽饽，大家纷纷投入其中。特别是大家电企业，它们借助自身的渠道优势，把小家电市场搞成六国大战，它们不能撼动外资大品牌，只能从国内品牌市场中分食一杯羹。中怡康的报告可以充分说明，几年来飞利浦的市场份额几乎没有变化，变化的是小品牌的占有率。小家电市场竞争到现在，两个方面的事实已经摆在营销人面前。一方面，小家电产品的同质化已经非常严重，国内企业没有核心技术竞争力；另一方面，老产品竞争力丧失，一步一步萎缩直到完全退出市场。国内品牌靠不断开发新产品(仅仅是简单的外形变化)来保持销售量，国内两大剃须刀品牌每年推出的新产品都在数十款，是外资品牌新品量的几倍，甚至几十倍，但是由于缺乏上市的全面规划和核心竞争力，其成功率非常低。据相关统计表明，近年来小家电新产品上市已经由3年前的30%成功率下降到20%左右。这是个足以让生产企业的研发人员和营销人员震惊的数字，因为你在为新产品上市所做的艰苦工作中，已经命中注定80%做的是无用功。面对这个市场现状，超人集团十分重视市场部的工作，让其不断地在市场营销的各个环节上精耕细作，从消费者需求分析、新产品开发信息输入、上市规划开始，做到新产品的定位研发、定时上市，保证新产品成功的第一步；面临国际品牌知名度、美誉度高于本土品牌的竞争优势，超人品牌在生存压力中寻找全新的细分市场，争取实现错位竞争，根据超人品牌的市场定位，研发适合青年学生使用的时尚、实用、高性价比产品,同时开发年轻一代聚集的高校零售市场,从容应对飞利浦、松下等国际品牌低中高端价格带市场通吃的策略。有了产品,明确了细分市场之后,如何让新产品在这个新市场里成功成了超人市场人员的困惑。超人市场人员在与关键点公关策划公司共同策划形象代言人活动的过程中,敏锐地发现了其组织"成人仪式"创意的闪光点,果断和策划公司签订了合作协议,全面完成了上市策划项目,成就了超人+U"男人第一把剃须刀"。

二、精准品牌定位,创造价值蓝海

有了闪光的创意,还需要通过缜密的认证和全面的策划,完成系列化、完整的市场方案。他们首先进行了系列市场调研,发现一个足以让所有人兴奋的事实。通过消费行为调查表明,男性消费群体对于第一次剃须经历特别重视,人生中初次使用的品牌往往会影响其一生的购买行为。按照男性生理特性分析,第一次剃须体验往往发生在大学时期,因此,大学市场会成为电动剃须刀一个全新的市场,这个细分市场做大后,对超人的市场份额贡献不容低估。这个调查结果证明了创意的方向是正确的,鼓舞着超人市场人员继续不断地创新。切分大学生市场作为超人的蓝海市场,得到超人集团从上至下的一致认同。但是,经过历史营销的分析研究发现,对于剃须刀这类产品而言,大学校园往往看上去很美,进入后很惨,由于大学生消费的冲动性、消费水平等种种不确定因素,包括飞利浦等众多品牌均在这个细分市场中做过营销努力,但到最后均无功而返。但是以怎样的方式,如何利用"成人仪式"成功开拓包括大学生在内的青年人市场,创造超人品牌价值的新蓝海市场成为项目组的研究课题。发现了大学生这个具有战略意义的目标消费群体,紧接着就是找到一个让消费者充分信赖的购买理由,项目组通过十多次的头脑创意风暴会,"男人的第一把剃须刀"这一品牌定位完美呈现出来。"男人的第一把剃须刀"从五个方面抢占了竞争力:第一,"第一把"、"第一次"是"成人仪式"最贴切、最佳的形容词,成人仪式是我们从孩子到成人的一个里程碑,是成人后的第一次活动,之后的每一件事均是他们的第一次,包括第一次剃须、第一次恋爱,等等;第二,"第一把"不仅有效地区别于竞争对手,而且成功地用"第一把"的定位抢占了消费者的心智空间;第三、"男人的第一把剃须刀",其目标群体针对大学生,大学生的购买能力相对较弱,超人的中低价格符合广大青年群体的购买能力,这种定位成功地促使超人品牌跳出了"低质低价"、"低端"、"低档"的品牌形象;第四,超人通过"男人的第一把剃须刀"的品牌诉求,为超人品牌培养了顾客终身品牌忠诚度;第五,"第一把"与关注的这个年龄层目标消费群众多特征不谋而合,让超人剃须刀成为大学生众多"第一次"的一员,从而形成人生中无法忘却的记忆。

三、好名字唱响品牌,副品牌成就新品

明确了向目标消费群体推荐的理由后,超人结合年青群体胡须柔软、面部娇嫩的特征,为大学生量身开发了一系列适合大学生使用的剃须刀。根据大学生的消费能力,产品定价为100元左右。有了一个极具需求的群体,有了一个好的品牌定位后,一个好的产品命名会起到事半功倍的效果。项目组结合超人品牌的历史和现状，决定采用主副品牌命名的策略。为了能够产生一个真正迎合目标对象喜好，又能够符合超人品牌"我就要超人"的品牌理念的名称，通过十几次的创意评选，并进行针对性的目标对象征询评议，最终"超人+U"从100多个备选名称中脱颖而出，实现了名字创意的所有要求。首先，"+U"的命名方式完全与年青群体追求的时尚流行文化吻合，这种用词在成年人的世界里却属于胡乱造词的范畴。"+U"的命名方式抓住了新新人类喜欢专属与特立独行的个性特征，能轻而易举地获得目标对象的认可和接受。其次，"+U"的谐音是"加油"，寓意是希望年轻人加油，学习加油、生活加油、工作加油，倡导一种积极向上的精神风貌，主副品牌连读是"超人+U"——超人加油，鼓励年轻人成人、成超人，这就是超人品牌内涵的深化和发展的最佳表现。品牌定位找准了，目标消费对象找到了，目标市场明确了，产品创意完成了，产品名称有了，万事俱备，只欠东风，接下来要解决的就是如何使超人+U新产品系列的上市和成人仪式的配合，能够做到天衣无缝，相得益彰，实现"超人+U"剃须刀一举成名天下知，树立"男人的第一把剃须刀就是超人+U系列"的形象。

四、武汉成人礼，超人+U忙

在思考上市推广的时候，项目组把思路引回超人+U品牌定位上，"男人的第一把剃须刀"强调的是庄重时刻的特殊产品，从这个方向上，项目组把关切到大学新生重要的人生时刻一一罗列出来。在众多的重要时刻中，终于找到了一个重要机会。从高中到大学阶段，要完成从少年到成人的转变，而这个转变正是人生中无数"第一次"中最重要的一次，如果在"最重要的一次"中把"男人的第一把剃须刀"植入其中，那么超人+U上市推广的问题必将迎刃而解。于是超人决定举办一场大一新生成人仪式，决定对成人仪式进行革命性的突破与颠覆，一旦成功必将成为一个市场引爆点。

(1) 超人+U系列推广活动第一波。2007年9月16日清晨，超人"中国大学生(武汉)成人仪式"准时举行，超人形象代言人、影视明星胡军早早来到仪式现场，成就了他第一次早起，创造了明星清晨参加活动的第一早，因为这次活动的意义吸引了他，"展开腾飞的翅膀，扬起远航的风帆，做新一代的超人，成为社会的超人"，仪式深远的意义和巨大的社会责任感感动了他。同样也感动了应邀参加仪式的来自全国的2007年10名热点"超人"，更是让广场上2000名18岁的大学新生群情激昂，感动无限。当他们接过明星们送上的蕴含了加油鼓劲深刻含义的成人礼物——超人+U系列剃须刀和成人手册时，成人，成超人必将成为每个青少年心中的梦想，也是每位父母对子女的深切期望，他们一定会记住这动人时刻，记住超人的陪伴。

(2) 超人+U系列推广活动第二波。紧接着2007年中国新闻热点人物代表进行生动的超人群英报告会，80后IT亿万富翁茅侃侃先生，"感动中国"2005年度人物、中国十大杰出青年洪战辉先生，中国102万乡村医生的杰出代表李春燕女士，疯狂做好事誓为河南人正名的李高峰先生，挽救22条生命的"活雷锋"张猛先生，192个艾滋病孤儿的爱心妈妈张颖女士，深入传销组织、解救大学生的卧底三人组成员王勇先生，防艾大使、全国大学生年度人物提名陶颖女士，欲与于丹比肩的超级保安谭景伟先生等，分别做了生动的报告，还与大学生进行了互动交流，加深了超人+U系列与大学生和新闻媒体的接触。会上，来自全国的40余家媒体进行了采访和报道。

（3）超人+U系列推广活动第三波。16日下午，完成了在成人礼上与目标消费者的交流后，超人来到了广大消费者面前，开始了真正的产品销售推广：超人集团2007年胡军武汉广场签售会隆重举行。当著名影星胡军出现在舞台上时，全场气氛达到了高潮，影迷纷纷购买超人+U剃须刀，整个武汉广场始终被超人的气氛包围着。随着三波活动的隆重举办，超人+U剃须刀与武汉消费者见面，同时通过60余家新闻媒体的新闻报道，透过电视、广播、报刊和网络与全国消费者也见面了，加之创新的成人礼引发了媒体的大讨论、大宣传，使新产品完成了第一轮导入。

（4）超人+U系列推广活动第四波。为了进一步延续武汉成人仪式的影响，同时把活动引向深入，超过50万的网友踊跃参加的"大学生心中的超人——2007年度十大新闻人物评选"揭晓十位火爆人气超人。经过第三方数据公证，包白龙、阮鹏、高燃、茅侃侃、陶颖、谭景伟、李高峰、吴莹莹、张颖、李春燕最终"登顶"，荣膺"大学生心中的超人——2007年度十大新闻人物"。评选过程高潮迭起、惊喜连连、精彩不断，出席了武汉活动且呼声较高的"美女副总裁"吴盈盈和IT精英茅侃侃等，并没有像预期那样脱颖而出，而是由半路杀出的"四匹黑马"抢先占据榜单的前四位，这是因为他们最大限度激发了自己"超人"的潜质，反映出80后坚韧不屈、百折不挠的精神，更符合80后心目中的超人形象。他们面对困难，勇敢地挑战自我、战胜自我，这种乐观、自强不息的精神深深感染了全体参加活动的大学生。媒体评价超人集团举办的"超人"评选活动为当代年轻人树立了"榜样"的力量。"超人"背后共同折射的积极乐观的生活态度，不懈努力进取的精神，勇于承担社会责任的品质，推动社会文明进步的中坚精神，正是当代年轻人身上逐渐流失的"超人"人格精华，正是当代年轻人思想成长所急需的精神"面包"。今天互联网时代是一个造就超人的时代，人们追求的是更具个性化的超人。在共建和谐社会的主旋律下，具有积极乐观的生活态度和勇于承担社会责任的优良品质、积极创造社会价值的人，都应该是值得我们敬佩的超人。超人加油！超人+U系列产品以一个文明进步使者的形象站在了广大消费者的面前，特别是年轻人的面前，它必将真正成为男人的第一把剃须刀，引导陪伴年轻一代实现成人、成超人的理想。

回顾2007年利用新闻热点人物的活动，其成功原因主要有以下几点。一是活动策划的精准：超人品牌的内涵和个性与新闻热点人物具有天生的结合性，用茅侃侃等新闻热点人物集中"代言"超人品牌是一个突破式的品牌与营销解决方案，引发上百家平媒、上万家网站竞相报道，形成主动传播热潮。二是活动和产品的有机结合：在新闻传播此起彼伏的热浪中，超人+U迅速锁定目标群体实现精准传播，创下校园营销里程碑式的影响。三是积极有效的危机预防，保证了品牌传播效果。四是连续作战，巩固成效，持续性为品牌文化建立推广平台。事件营销犹如一股旋风，总有归于平静的一天，成人仪式结束后，超人集团迅速启动了"大学生心目中的超人——2007十大新闻人物评选"，把整个活动效果贯穿到2007年下半年，让品牌持续传播。

(资料来源：计哲. 开拓成熟大品牌的新市场蓝海 超人+U系列剃须刀上市策划.
[2008-06-09]. http://www.ppzw.com/ppzwzs/.)

【案例分析】

中国超人集团主办的中国大学生成人仪式在武汉华中科技大学隆重举行并获得了成功。分析其成功的原因，主要有以下几点，一是极富创新意识的大型活动的公益性，关注目标市场群体的成长，如超人集团形象代言人胡军和2007年十位全国新闻热点名人汇聚在华中科技大学大广场，和数千名大学新生一起举行了由"超人+U系列——男人的第一把剃须刀"独家赞助的，"腾飞的翅膀，远航的风帆，中国大学生(武汉)成人仪式"，超人集团向与会的大学生赠送了+U剃须刀和成人手册。二是活动策划的精准性。三是活动和产品的有机结合。四是积极有效的危机预防，保证了品牌传播效果。五是连续作战，巩固成效，持续性为品牌文化建立推广平台。在这些原因中，"精准性"、"有机结合"以及"有效的危机预防"是关键，要达到这些目的，营销人员必须进行广泛而深入的市场调研与分析，借助于相应的营销手段，才能达到活动开展时的有的放矢，才能提出具有前瞻性的预防措施。

【思考题】

1. 分析案例中传播、推广新产品的主要途径。
2. 案例成功向市场推广新产品的关键点有哪些？
3. 从营销工程角度分析，可以从哪些方面为该案例构造出相应的营销活动模型？

Chapter 9

Marketing Investigation and Market Forecast

Focus on:

1. Types and functions of the marketing information.
2. Make-up of the marketing information system.
3. Contents and basic methods of the market investigation.
4. Contents and elementary approaches of the market forecast.

9.1 Marketing Information Systems

Information is the foundation to launch the marketing activities for enterprises and large quantity of it now has been the rich sources available for them.

9.1.1 Functions of Marketing Information

1. Definition of Marketing Information

Marketing information is defined as comprehensive reflection to the existence, movement and reception response of various matters and things related to the firm's marketing activities in the given time and conditions such as the trend of the marketing environment, changes in corporate sales, corporate advertising effectiveness, etc. Marketing information is generally manifested as language, text, data, and symbols.

2. Functions of Marketing Information

(1) Marketing information is the prerequisite and basis for decision-making.

In the course of marketing, the firm must base its decisions whether they are strategic as marketing aims and orientation or they are tactics as products, pricing, place and promotion and so on upon the precise marketing information obtained.

(2) Marketing information is the basis for formulating corporate marketing plans.

The detailed marketing plan that is used to determine the concrete measures and paths to

Chapter 9 Marketing Investigation and Market Forecast

realize the marketing targets has to be changed according to the market demands on the base of the marketing decision.

(3) Marketing information is a necessary condition to carry out marketing control.

The fluctuation of the market environment decides that the firm must adjust its marketing plans in line with the feedback information so as to effectively control the marketing activities and make them advance towards the fixed target.

(4) Marketing information is the basis for internal and external coordination.

The marketing information ought to be kept on being collected in order to coordinate the relationships among the inner conditions, outer environment and marketing targets in the light of market changes and to optimize the firm's marketing activities.

9.1.2 Types of Marketing Information

On the basis of various classification standards, the marketing information can be divided into different types.

1. Internal and External Information

According to its source of information, the marketing information can be divided into the external and the internal information.

The external information primarily refers to that from politics, economy, technology, demography, society, statute, culture, psychology, ecology, competition, etc.

The internal information is that in the marketing from the various statements and reports, plans, records, and files of the business.

2. Strategic, Management and Operational Information

In the light of the levels of decision-making, marketing information can be divided into strategic information, management information and operational information.

The strategic information is used to make decisions by the firm's senior leadership. It includes the development of new products, development of new markets, investment in equipments and change of services.

The management information means that needed by the managers in decision-making. It includes the information of the micro-management in formulating, and implementing plans about the resource distribution, use and control, etc. and that of the macro-management such as economic policy, economic leverage, economic laws and regulations and so on which the governments adopt to manage and regulate the enterprise.

The operational information is that about daily business activities of enterprise, including the information on production and supply of goods, commodity demands and sales, and competitors.

Besides, according to the expression form, the information is divided into text messages and data ones; to the processing degree, it can be divided into initial ones and processed ones; to its stability, it is divided into fixed and mobile ones.

9.1.3 Marketing Information Systems

The marketing information system consists of such interactive elements as human beings, machines and programs, by which the enterprise uses to collect, select, analyze, and assess the information so as to formulate, improve, implement and control the marketing plan. It includes traditional manual information systems and modern information ones.

The traditional manual information systems collect process and transmit information through artificial calculators, typewriters, copiers, telephones and other tools, etc. It transmits information and forms the marketing information systems among the staffs of the firm with the help of statements, reports, accounts and other material carriers.

The modern information systems are centered on computers, analyze and process the information input and then output the useful information. It transmits the messages by the computer linkage and forms the marketing information system.

1. Information System Establishment Principles

(1) Integrity principle

The marketing information system in a firm must take all the marketing activities as a whole, straighten out the relationships inside the firm and care about the development both in the realities and in the future. In the meanwhile, the information content should be harmonious from inside to outside, between the current demands and the long-term ones, and between the communication form and transmission language.

(2) Simple and appropriateness

The transmitted information ought to be simple and clear and the appropriateness is the main standard to screen the messages in order to accelerate the circulation of the information, and to raise its effectiveness.

(3) Effectiveness

The firm's marketing information system must be able to satisfy the needs of the marketing activities and cater for the marketing decision and management. Therefore, the system should eliminate the ineffective messages and select appropriate ones.

2. Structure of Marketing Information System

The marketing information system in a firm consists of the internal reporting system, the external latest information systems, marketing research system and marketing analysis system, by which the information communication is completed (see Figure 9.1).

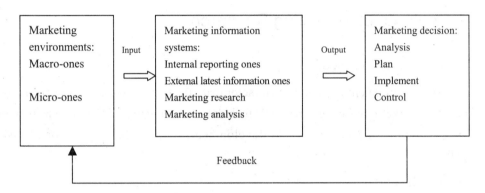

Figure 9.1 Structure of the Firm's Marketing Information System

(1) Internal reporting system

The internal reporting system provides sales information, inventory information, customer information, and customer management. Currently, many enterprises have set up computer management system, and decision makers can access the computer information about business marketing at any time.

(2) External latest information system

The external information system obtains the latest information through the Internet and various publications, advertising, information, etc. and also from consumers, suppliers, distributors, competitors, and internal employees.

It functions primarily in the collection and accumulation, processing and transmission of the external information.

(3) Marketing research system

The marketing research system can scientifically collect, analyze and present data, raise the level of the enterprise marketing survey. The system's main task is to evaluate and transfer all the necessary information needed by decision-makers.

(4) Marketing analysis system

The marketing analysis system, also known as marketing decision support system, aims at providing the quantitative conclusions for policy-makers and thus raising policy recommendations for the decision makers by analyzing the information and documents given by the above-said sub-systems. It often runs by means of series of statistic models or marketing decision ones and is the advanced marketing information processing system.

9.2 Marketing Research

9.2.1 Contents of Marketing Research

1. Environmental Investigation

The market environment is an important factor that affects the market demand and corporate marketing. The market environment research includes the following: (1) policy changes in the statute, (2) economic and technological development, (3) population, (4) social fashion, (5) competition.

2. Market Research

(1) Total market investigation

The main contents to be investigated in the total market consist of the total disposable currency in the market, the monetary able to be used for commodity, supply and demand status and fluctuation, etc.

(2) Market segment survey

The actual demands and sales in all segments and target markets are to be understood and the maximum hidden demands and capacities, saturation points and the relationship between demands and industry in all the segments are to be studied.

(3) Investigation of the market share and its changes

Marketers ought to be familiar with the market position, market share and its fluctuation of the firm itself and its rivals, and also master the demand features and change regularities of certain products.

3. Product Analysis

Product survey includes the following aspects in the angle of marketing: (1) property and quality of products, (2) profile and package of products, (3) services of products.

Property and quality of products includes the following: analysis of product life cycle in the market; investigation of the characteristic requirements of consumer products; understanding of the particular consumer product requirements and changes such as food sweetness, color, and taste, etc.

Chapter 9 Marketing Investigation and Market Forecast

The product profile and package in the various markets includes the colors, patterns or the preferences of customers for the outer package of the product, the symbolic meaning and emotion in a variety of colors and patterns; the market requirements of product specifications such as size, weight, etc. As for the transportation packing, it concerns loading and unloading, storage, anti-stealing, and so on. For the industrial products, the requirements for the identification, package opening, partial packing and recycling, etc. should be cared for while for the consumer products, more attentions ought to be paid to the colors, designs, etc.

The services of products mean an understanding of the market requirements and the effect of a range of services in the business activities so as to improve service levels.

4. Price Research

Price studies care much for the product cost, price comparison, the relationship among price, supply and demand, pricing effects.

(1) Product cost and price comparison refer to understanding the various costs in the production and operation in order to provide the basis for reasonable pricing; understanding the relationship of the prices to different related products in the same market; understanding differential prices of the similar products acceptable by consumers.

(2) Relationship among price, supply and demand means an investigation into the supply and demand curves and elasticity for various products to provide a reasonable basis for pricing strategy.

(3) The pricing effects include understanding of price differences and their influence on demands from the firm's products or from the similar ones of its competitors; understanding the rationality and effectiveness of its pricing strategies; investigation into feasibility and expected results of the adjusted prices and pricing strategy.

5. Sales Channel Research

The study consists of analysis of the existing sale channels, distribution investigations, adjustment of the sales channels.

(1) Analysis of the existing sale channels

The analysis concerns the components of the existing sale channels, their functions and inventories, the situation that the components are used by competitors, the price reduction and promotion in the channels.

(2) Distribution investigations

The image, scales, volumes, promotions, customers and services provided in the distributors should be all cared for.

(3) Adjustment of the sales channels

The costs, expenses and expected benefits in the new channels ought to be surveyed in order to provide the foundation for readjusting the sale channels.

6. Advertising and Promotion Status

Advertising and personal selling, sales promotion, public relations and the rational use of the other promotional measures are playing an important role in the sales of enterprise products. The study of advertising and sales promotion focuses on their objects, their subjects, media, audience, and their effects.

7. Corporate Image Research

Corporate image refers to the status in the public perception of the company and its products. Corporate image studies pay much attention to the company's operational idea, the behavior, the visual transmission of the image.

9.2.2 Marketing Research Process

Marketing research composes of series of planned, organized activities and must obey certain process before achieving expected results. Its steps are presented as follows:

1. Determination of Research Themes and Objectives

In the organization of marketing research activities, each candidate should first identify the most critical and most pressing problems, select the theme of the investigation, and define clearly what tasks to be accomplished, what goals to be achieved.

According to the survey topic and purpose, investigators can be divided into three types: exploratory research, descriptive survey and causal investigation.

(1) Exploratory research

Exploratory research can understand the situation, identify problems and find the factors in the new marketing that are helpful to the decision making.

(2) Descriptive survey

Descriptive survey stresses the data collection and recording of information, and focuses on the objective facts of the static description.

(3) Causal investigation

Enterprises often face various relationships among different factors in the business activities and causality survey can also be used to understand the market response to changes in the marketing decision making. Causal investigation as an experimental method is often used to

Chapter 9 Marketing Investigation and Market Forecast

collect data and has active and dynamic characteristics.

2. Formulation of Survey Plan

Survey plan includes the sources of information, survey objects, survey methodology, cost estimation and other items.

(1) Sources of information

The survey plan must take into account the choice of information sources. According to their sources, the survey data can be divided into first-hand information and secondary sources.

The first-hand information refers to the original documents collected for the purpose of the survey. Most marketing research projects need to collect the first-hand information. The cost of collecting first-hand information is generally higher, but the information obtained is usually related to the problem to be solved more closely. The first-hand information is often collected by field investigations.

The secondary data collection refers to the ready-made survey data for the purpose of study. Compared with the first-hand information gathered, the cost of collecting the secondary data is usually much lower, and less time spent. However, the market research is hard to find the ready-made second-hand information.

(2) Survey objects

According to the survey object, the marketing research can be divided into two categories, namely, universal surveys and sample ones. In the marketing research, the former is rarely used while the latter is commonly used, which means a survey into numerous individuals of the population to be investigated.

Main types of sample surveys include non-random sampling and random sampling. The samples of non-random sampling are usually selected by experience of the investigators. Therefore, they are affected by the investigator's subjective judgment, which often causes a great error. However, if the investigator is well experienced, it is sometimes a simple tool for the survey. It mainly consists of sampling by convenience, by judgment and by quota.

The random sampling is defined as follows: the determination of its samples is not controlled by the investigator's subjective idea and they are sampled in some statistic methods. So, each individual in the population to be surveyed has equal chance to be chosen. It includes such approaches as pure random sampling, systematic sampling, rank random sampling and group random sampling.

(3) Survey methods

Three commonly used methods are adopted in the market survey data collection: inquiry, observation and experiment.

Inquiry method is a two-way communication survey, which includes verbal and communicative survey.

Observation method is a one-way investigation mainly through the direct observation of people's behavior, and field recording by the market research staff so as to obtain the required information.

Experimental method is a more formal approach. Experiment is done by the investigators as hereinafter: first, group the objects to be surveyed and each team is an experiment group under the conditions unchanged; then, compare changes in different groups by experiment; next, observe the impacts on the objects for the changing conditions.

(4) Cost estimation

Market research staff must carefully estimate the cost for market research in formulating the survey plan, and also cost estimation will be incorporated into the survey program, which should be reported to the competent department or supervisor for approval.

3. Implementation of the Survey Plan

The implementation of the survey plan includes three steps: data collection, processing and analysis.

Data collection is most expensive and most inclined to errors. So the responsible marketing research must closely supervise the survey field activities so as to avoid the deviation happening in the survey.

Data processing includes the classification, arrangement and integration of the survey data in order to ensure the accuracy and completeness of them.

After the survey data are processed, you can analyze them to obtain the findings. The analysis approaches include quantitative and qualitative ones, experienced and mathematic ones, etc. Currently, more and more enterprises adopt the mathematic analysis method to handle the documents surveyed.

4. Investigation Report

The findings of the investigation should be expressed in the form of summary reports. There are two common forms of the marketing research report: technical report and conclusion report. The former focuses on the process of the market investigation and its contents include the aims, methods, data processing techniques, extracts from the survey documents, and conclusion, and so on. It aims at providing references for the market surveyor. The latter emphasizes the outcomes of the market survey where the investigators should present the suggestion and conclusion for reference to the decision-makers.

9.3 Marketing Forecasting

9.3.1 Types of Marketing Forecasting

Marketing forecasting aims at analyzing the marketing information, finding the changing laws of market, and inferring the future by them. The marketing forecasting can be divided into different types according to different criteria.

1. Macro and Micro Forecasting

Macro forecasting means a prediction to the overall market conditions affecting marketing. It mainly includes the level of the purchasing power, total demand and composition of the commodity, and the impact of economic policies on the supply and demand. Micro forecasting refers to predicting the future of supply and demand in the angle of a firm, a partial market or a product. It consists of commodity resources, sales, inventory and business market share and operating effectiveness, etc.

2. Long-Term, Medium-Term and Short-Term Forecasting

Generally, long-term forecasting refers to a prediction more than 5 years; medium-term forecasting is one from 1 to 5 years; short-term forecasting is less than 1 year.

3. Qualitative and Quantitative Forecasting

Qualitative prediction aims at estimating the marketing changes in the period of time by analysis and inference based on survey data and subjective experience. It is a commonly used approach in the marketing forecasting, of which the market survey forecast and judgment by experience are two cases.

Quantitative prediction is based on changes in marketing data, adopts mathematical and statistical methods, tries to find out the general rules of the marketing changes, and then makes a quantitative estimation to the prospect of marketing changes.

In the forecast, the qualitative and quantitative approaches are often combined to make a comprehensive forecast.

9.3.2 Marketing Forecast Steps

There are four steps: identify prediction target, collect data, select prediction method, analyze forecasting error.

1. Identifying of the Prediction Target

The target can be identified by the tasks in various periods, assignments from the leader, requirements to formulate a plan and the problems urgent to be solved in the firm.

2. Collecting the Data

Based on the forecasting target, marketing investigation is made so as to obtain and arrange the needed documents and to be well prepared for the forecasting.

3. Choosing the Forecasting Approaches

The commonly used forecasting methods consist of market survey approach, regression analysis, time series analysis, etc. One must make a choice among them in the light of the forecasting requirements.

4. Final Forecasting by Adjusting the Error

The outcomes from the various quantitative forecasting ought to accept a feasible study by correlation test, hypothesis test, and so on. Then the final forecasting can be presented after an error adjustment combined with the political and economic situation.

Examples of the Forecasting Methods

专栏9.1　　　　　　　　销售人员综合意见法

例如，某百货公司有正副经理2人，负责某商品销售的营业员3人，他们对下期的销售情况作了如下估计，如表9.1所示。

表9.1　各类人员对下期销售情况的预测

		营业员			经理	
		甲	乙	丙	正	副
最低	销售量	240	200	250	280	300
	概率	20%	10%	10%	15%	10%
最可能	销售量	300	280	320	340	350
	概率	60%	70%	80%	75%	75%
最高	销售量	350	320	400	400	400
	概率	20%	20%	10%	10%	15%

首先计算每个人的期望预测值。营业员甲的预测值为：
240×20% + 300×60% + 350×20%=298

Chapter 9　Marketing Investigation and Market Forecast

同理可计算其余每个人的期望预测值分别为：

营业员乙：280

营业员丙：321

正经理：337

副经理：352.5

然后，计算各类人员的平均预测值。假定三个营业员的预测水平相当，此时，

营业员的平均预测值=(298+280+321)÷3≈300

假定两经理的预测水平也基本相同，那么，

经理的平均预测值=(337+352.5)÷2≈345

最后，计算综合预测值。假定在该企业中，经理们由于掌握情况比较全面，预测能力也比营业员要强一些，因此，分别给予经理和营业员权数2和1，进行加权平均。得：

综合预测值=(345×2+300×1)/3=330

由此，可以预测该商品下期销售量可能是330单位。

(资料来源：梁东，刘建堤，孙安彬，谭学英. 市场营销学. 北京：清华大学出版社，2007.)

5. Quantitative Analysis

For the use of quantitative prediction method, there must be a lot of statistical data and statistical methods and relevant statistical and mathematical knowledge as a basis. Commonly used methods include time series analysis forecasting and causal analysis forecasting.

Application Examples

专栏9.2　　　　　　　　　　市场研究预测法

对于某地区某家用电器的需求量的预测用市场研究预测法进行预测的过程如下。

由于消费者对耐用消费品购买的计划性，使得市场研究预测法在耐用消费品的需求预测中得以成功运用。预测步骤如下：

(1) 取得样本资料。以固定样本(如家计调查点)或根据预测需要以典型抽样或随机抽样所抽取的样本作为调查对象，通过对调查对象的直接访问或问卷调查，了解该商品的社会拥有量以及计划期间需要购买的数量、品种、规格、购买能力、购买要求等。

(2) 统计计算。根据调查取得的样本资料，计算每百人(户)的拥有量(即：样本拥有量÷样本数×100)、计划期间每百人(户)的需求量(即：样本需求量÷样本数×100)以及各收入层需求情况，对各不同规格商品的需求情况等。

(3) 推算计划期间该商品的需求量。根据计划期间每百人(户)的需求量及该地总人(户)数进行推算。计算公式为：计划期需求量=每百人(户)需求量×总人(户)数÷100。

如某地通过对400户家计调查点的问卷调查得知，在计划期间准备购买该产品的有20

户。由此可知，计划期间每百户对该产品的需求量为 20÷400×100=5(台)，进而推算出该地16万户居民计划期间对该产品的需求量 5×160000÷100=8000(台)。

(资料来源：梁东，刘建堤，孙安彬，谭学英. 市场营销学. 北京：清华大学出版社，2007.)

专栏9.3　　　　　　　　　　　时间序列法

季节性商品的销售往往随着时间的推移呈现出比较规则的周期性波动。对于季节性商品的销售量 Y 的预测，一般是依据五年以上的时间序列资料，通过对时间序列的长期趋势 T 的分析，以及不同时期受季节因素影响的季节指数 S_i 的分析，由时间序列与各分量之间的关系来实现。时间序列可分解为长期趋势 T、季节因素 S、循环因素 C 和随机因素 E 等分量。当循环性和随机性等不可控因素的影响作为误差处理时，时间序列与 T、S_i 间的关系可近似地表示如下：

$$Y=TS_i$$

上式即为季节性商品的预测模式。

式中的长期趋势值 T，在时间序列资料较少，或者是上升、下降趋势不明显时，可以近似地用近期各月(季)的平均值来代替。当上升或下降趋势明显时，可以由各年的销售实绩资料，用直线趋势外推法求出预测期年销售预测值，从而求得月(季)平均值作为趋势值 T；或由各月(季)销售实绩资料，用直线趋势外推法求得各月(季)趋势预测值；还可以用移动平均法求得长期趋势值。

季节指数 S，又称为季节比率或季节变动系数，它表示在季节因素影响下，各时期的时间序列值与趋势值之间的比率。季节指数 S 的计算方法如下：

首先，计算同季的平均数 $\bar{X}_i$。

$$\bar{X}_i = 各年度同季实际值之和 \div 年度数$$

其次，计算总平均数 $\bar{X}$。

$$\bar{X} = 各年度实际值之和 \div (年度数 \times 季度数)$$

再次，计算季节指数 S_i。

$$S_i = \frac{\bar{X}_i}{\bar{X}}$$

最后，计算调整季节指数 S_i^*。

$$S_i^* = S_i \times 季度数 \div \sum S_i$$

例如，表9.2所列出的是某商品5年的分月销售实绩(单位：件)，以此为依据即可计算各月的平均数、总平均数，进而计算季节指数 S_i 及调整季节指数 S_i^*。

Chapter 9 Marketing Investigation and Market Forecast

表 9.2 平均数法季节指数计算表

月\年	1	2	3	4	5	月平均数	季节指数 S_i	调整季节指数 S_i^*
1	50	70	85	100	120	85.0	0.791	0.772
2	48	70	90	110	140	91.6	0.852	0.831
3	60	75	90	115	110	90.0	0.837	0.817
4	70	86	95	120	124	99.0	0.921	0.899
5	64	84	100	110	130	97.6	0.908	0.886
6	52	86	96	105	135	94.8	0.882	0.861
7	88	100	110	140	180	123.6	1.450	1.415
8	80	90	105	130	160	113.0	1.051	1.025
9	73	80	100	125	150	105.6	0.982	0.958
10	90	92	90	115	145	106.0	0.990	0.966
11	81	90	105	130	150	111.2	1.035	1.010
12	110	150	160	200	240	172.0	1.600	1.560
Σ	866	1073	1226	1500	1784	107.45	12.299	12.000

由 5 年的年销售实绩看出,销售量呈明显上升趋势,在预测时可以年销售实绩资料为依据,用直线趋势外推法求出下年销售量趋势值,如表 9.3 所示。

表 9.3 直线趋势外推法计算表

时间编号	年销售量 Y	t^2	tY
−2	866	4	−1732
−1	1073	1	−1073
0	1226	0	0
1	1500	1	1500
2	1784	4	3568
Σ	6449	10	2263

模式: $T = a + bt$
其中: $a = \Sigma Y \div n$, $b = \Sigma tY \div \Sigma t^2$
由最小二乘法得:
$a = 6449 \div 5 = 1289.8$, $b = 2263 \div 10 = 226.3$
由此,预测得出下年销售趋势值(即 $t=3$ 时)
$T = 1289.8 + 226.3 \times 3 = 1968.7$(件)

进而预测各月的销售量，其公式为：

$Y = T \div 12 \times S_i^*$

例如，要预测下年三月份的销售量，则：

$Y = 1968.7 \div 12 \times 0.817 = 134(件)$

若年销售量反映出没有显著上升、下降趋势时，不必用直线趋势外推法来计算年销售趋势值，只需用上年的月平均值来代替，即

$T = 1784 \div 12 = 148.67(件)$

由此预测得下年三月份销售量为：

$Y = 148.67 \times 0.817 = 121(件)$

(资料来源：梁东，刘建堤，孙安彬，谭学英. 市场营销学. 北京：清华大学出版社，2007，137-140.)

9.4 Summary

市场营销信息系统由四个子系统构成：内部报告系统、外部最新信息系统、市场营销调研系统和市场营销分析系统。市场营销信息系统由人、设备和程序组成，为营销决策收集、筛选、分析、评估和分配及时、准确的信息。市场营销调研是运用科学的方法，有目的、有计划地收集、整理和分析有关营销的信息，提出建议，作为市场预测和营销决策的依据。市场预测是在营销调研的基础上，对未来的市场需求量及影响需求的因素进行分析研究和预测。在此过程中包括定性分析研究和定量分析研究。

Key Terms

Marketing Information Systems External Information Internal Information Internal Reporting System External Latest Information System Marketing Research System Marketing Analysis System Environmental Investigation Exploratory Investigation Descriptive Survey Causal Investigation Macro Prediction Micro Forecasting Qualitative Forecast Quantitative Forecast

【案例】扩展市场，别舍不得做市场调查

一、问题描述

一个德国信号发生器制造商打算实行一个全新而大胆的策略：气势磅礴地开展国际市场的销售。这家公司已自行察觉到一个既存的问题，即该公司产品在国外14个国家中销售虽已有15年历史，但国内销售额仍占总销售额的45%，这显示过去的全球营销策略有盲点。北京一家技术公司应制造商的要求，向其提出改进建议。正如同大多数工程背景的公司一样，这家制造商过去曾做过的唯一的市场调查就是阅读相关的贸易期刊和杂志。而并不令

人感到意外的是，这家年营业额高达五千万美元的公司，仅愿意花一千美元的调研费，来支持一个超过一千万美元的全球扩展计划。

二、调查设计

由于经费太少，在北京康斯技术发展公司所能有效追踪评估的市场指标中，唯一的选择就是价格。他们决定调查该公司全球营销策略起作用最大的前五个国家的定价情况，包括美国、英国、荷兰、日本与法国。他们同时列举出五种同级产品的25家经销商的销售价来比较价格差异。资讯搜集方式采用竞争者访谈，询问各公司在不同国家的定价策略与价格。

三、调查结果

调查结果令所有人感到吃惊(参见表9.4与图9.2到图9.3)，甚至这家公司的总裁，在看到这项为期两周的调查的结果后也深感惊讶，他最后承认，这项调查或许是他曾经做过的最佳投资。

表9.4　竞争品牌在各国的定价情况

单位：美元

国家＼品牌＼定价	German X1140	American H3591	British WG110	Japanese S2000	American W45941
德国	12 560	20 492	17 350	14 351	17 985
法国	19 100	19 025	17 250	15 443	18 095
英国	20 856	18 980	14 110	13 942	18 750
荷兰	19 205	19 642	16 950	15 650	18 942
美国	22 500	16 500	15 300	16 000	9 500

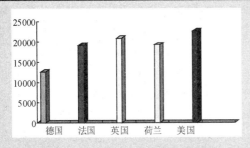

图9.2　X1140在各国的定价情况

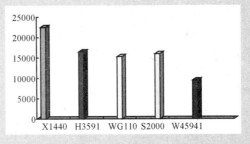

图9.3　竞争品牌在美国的定价情况

以下为本案例调查的一些发现：

(1) 公司产品在国内的销售价过低，为了占有市场几乎是以出厂价销售，对公司的赢利毫无贡献。

(2) 很多欧洲的客户不在本国购买该公司产品，而是避开经销商直接到德国购买，这样可以节省40%的开支。

(3) 发现新的竞争对手，日本厂商正企图以低价策略侵入市场，S2000型为其探路石，

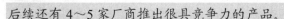

后续还有 4~5 家厂商推出很具竞争力的产品。

(4) 该公司产品在美国的定价过高,特别是考虑到美国是该公司全球开发最重要的目标市场。

(5) 给经销商的价格过高,使其获利过低,造成经销商自行抬高价格,以获取足够的利润。

四、行动策略

很明显,日本厂商加入后将使价格竞争更加激烈。为面对日本厂商的低价竞争,公司生产部门推行自动化与即时技术来降低成本。

公司降低给经销商的价格,并要求经销商以统一价格销售该公司产品。

该产品的德国市场价格提高 40%。

整合并统一公司的全球定价政策,在各国市场的同类产品中采取最高策略,并以完善的客户支持、售后服务与培训来赢得客户。

进行更多的竞争分析与市场策略调查。

五、市场影响

虽然德国境内售价提高 40%,但销售额仍保持稳定。

两年后,国际市场的销售比重由 55%增至 75%。

由于产品售价的提高,同时降低了 19%的销售成本,该公司的利润提高了 3 倍。

即使日本厂商加入并在 3 年内占领了 15%的市场,该公司的市场占有率仍然提高了 4%。

【案例分析】

在开始一个投资高达一千万美元的全球扩展计划之前,最好先投资得到一张精确的市场分析图。那么,企业就应舍得花钱做市场调查。在采取行动之前,要获得有关的市场信息和情报资料,以免做出错误的决策,减少风险,提高效益。如今,市场情况变化万千,顾客需求愈来愈多样化,顾客的爱好、动机、欲望对市场营销的影响很大。因此,企业要了解哪种产品是顾客所需要的,如何定出适宜的价格,怎样合理地选择分销渠道,选择适当的销售方式,适时适地地满足顾客需求,了解潜在市场情况……实现这些目标,都需要做好市场调查工作,从多方面获取市场情报资料,敏感地捕捉这些信息,分析和研究市场需求变化的规律,用以指导企业的经营决策,有预见地安排市场营销活动,提高企业的经营管理水平,促进企业更好地生存和发展。

过去,我们很多企业根本没有这种观念。在节约成本的指导思想下,就把做市场调查的这部分给节约掉了,或者只愿意花很少的代价,如本案例中那个德国制造商一千万美元的扩展计划只愿意花一千美元做市场调查,尽管如此,也取得了相应的收获。如果他用更多资金做包括价格在内的全面调查分析,就会获得更大的收益。

(资料来源:曹刚,李桂陵,王德发等. 国内外市场营销案例. 武汉:武汉大学出版社,2003. 案例根据北京康斯技术发展公司报告改编)

Chapter 9　Marketing Investigation and Market Forecast

【思考题】
1. 价格是否是市场测量的唯一项目？为什么？
2. 市场调查的必要性表现在哪？
3. 影响调查结果的因素有哪些？
4. 市场调查有何作用？
5. 新的市场营销观念的核心是什么？

Part IV Marketing Mix

Chapter 10

Product Strategies

Focus on:

1. Connotation and types of the product.
2. Elements of the product strategy.
3. Analyze the product strategy by using "Dog-Cow Figure".
4. Roles of the brand in the product marketing.

10.1 Generalities

The main part of the product/service program of an enterprise is the product or the service (product policy). In addition, a company may offer products/services by creating a certain range (range policy), by packaging the ware (packaging policy), by using brands for labeling (brand policy), by granting warranties for damage (warranty policy) and by offering customer services (service and customer service policy).

10.1.1 Term "Product"

The term "product" does not only denote an object. A product is an "object" that satisfies desires or needs on the market. These may be

(1) objects such as a car or a book,

(2) organizations representing ideas or political parties,

(3) places and locations such as a hotel, a tourist town, a health spa, and

(4) persons leading and representing an enterprise, or politicians who want to be elected.

A product has 3 dimensions:
- The core product: i.e. the basic benefit. This is the solution to the problem or the benefit sought by the customer.
- The real product: Here the core product takes on a real shape. The real product is defined by 5 characteristics:
  - Packaging
  - Functionality
  - Appearance/design
  - Brand
  - Quality
- The extended product: additional benefits. The goods themselves are often not enough. They have to be supplemented by additional benefits such as warranty or guarantee, delivery and payment conditions, installation, explanation and training, support in case of malfunction (maintenance, repair), or a telephone hotline.

10.1.2 Types of Products

With a view to better marketing, experts have classified products into types characterized by specific properties.

1. Consumer Goods

These are goods the customer purchases for his own personal use. Among them are "everyday commodities" such as food, "shopping goods" such as clothes, household goods and furniture, "specialties" such as musical instruments and luxury goods, and "unknown goods" which the customer does not know yet and to which advertising has to draw his attention.

2. Industrial Goods

They are meant for professional and economic use. Among them are services (window-cleaning, legal consultation, etc.), operational supply items (nails, paper, etc.), producer goods (factory premises, office buildings) and raw materials.

Consumer goods such as a lawn mower, can be classified as industrial goods if used for professional purposes.

All marketing measures within the marketing mix aim to further the sales of a specific product (or service) or of a product range. Decisions about the product range are therefore essential marketing-policy decisions. These measures include Product Range Policy ("Product

Policy"), Remunerative Policy ("Price Policy"), Distributive Policy ("Distribution"), and Communicative Policy ("Promotion").

10.2 Product Policies

The instruments of product policy are
(1) Product innovation,
(2) Product variation,
(3) Product elimination.

10.2.1 Product Innovation

Products can only be sold on the market if they correspond to the requirements and expectations of the customers. The expectations of the customer are primarily geared towards the solution of a specific problem. In this case, we speak of the benefit a product offers to the customer.

1. Product Use = Basic Use + Additional Use

Basic use: satisfies the actual or original requirement of the customer.
Example: the original need of a driver consists in getting from A to B.
Additional use: satisfies a requirement that is related to the basic one but can go far beyond it.
Example: In addition to our driver's basic requirement, he could desire the following factors: prestige, comfort, lots of HP, security, low fuel consumption, etc.

2. Product Innovation = Development of New Products

The development of new products is of great importance for all enterprises. For new products there is no saturated market and thus no struggle to drive competition out of the market.

A continual renewal of products does, however, not only contribute to the safeguarding of the enterprise potential, it also conceals the danger of expensive false developments. Proceeding in a methodical and systematic way in the domain of product innovation can protect against such "failures" or "flops".

3. Innovation Process

The sequence of innovation is as follows:
- Search for ideas;
- Pre-selection of product ideas;

Chapter 10 Product Strategies

- Rentability analysis;
- Product development and product testing;
- Market testing;
- Introduction of the new product.

(1) Search for ideas

Methods for the attainment of new ideas (creativity techniques) include the following:

- Brainstorming
- Brain writing (6-4-5 method)
- Brain-writing pool
- Morphological box
- Science fiction method
- Lexicon method
- Synectics

In the case of all these methods, it is indispensable to establish a common and exact definition of the subject and/or problem and the goals. Furthermore, all the participants have to be familiar with the rules valid for the respective method and must stick to them.

(2) Pre-selection of product ideas

Pre-selection (also called screening) has the task of selecting from the collected ideas and suggestions of the first phase those which promise the greatest success for the enterprise. The selection can proceed via various methods. The most current are checklists and point system models ("Scoring").

(3) Rentability analysis

Now, the product ideas remaining after the pre-selection have to be examined with respect to the expected costs of development, production, sales and revenue. Methods for this are e.g. the break-even analysis (profit-threshold analysis) and also the individual investment calculation methods.

(4) Product development and product testing

In the context of this phase, a first product ready for testing (prototype) is developed by structuring the basic elements of the product. The product development is concerned in this respect with the actual product function (basic use) of the product, its physical, functional, aesthetic and symbolic characteristics, and with the additional product functions related to the product.

(5) Market testing

This refers to the sale of new products on a trial basis under controlled conditions in a limited market and with the application of selected marketing tools or of all marketing tools. With Me-Too-Products (=easily imitable products), market tests are not meaningful since the competition can enter the market simultaneously or with only a short delay.

(6) Introduction of the new product

Despite detailed checks and tests, it can happen that newly introduced products cannot survive in the market. The most frequent reasons for this are as follows:

- Wrong choice of the moment of introduction;
- Insufficient distribution policy;
- Too early or too late introductory advertising;
- The "wrong" price, i.e. one not corresponding to real market conditions.

10.2.2 Product Variation

In product variation, already existing products are altered. The variation can consist of a modification, differentiation or a diversification of the product (see Figure 10.1).

Products	Products	Products	Products	
A1 + B1	A1 + B1	A1 + B1	A1 + B1	+ C1 new
A2 + B2	A2 + B2	A2 + B2	A2 + B2	+ C2 new
A3 + B3	A3 + B3	A3 + B3	A3 + B3	
A4	A4 new	A4	A4	
		A5 new		
		A6 new		
Original range	Modification	Differentiation	Diversification	

Figure 10.1 Product Variation

1. Modification

A modification is when one or more elements of an initial product are altered and the newly formed product replaces the initial one. The range of products remains unaffected by this.

2. Differentiation

A differentiation occurs when one or more elements of an initial product are altered. The new product arising from this is, however, now in the range alongside the initial product (=alteration of the depth of the range).

Chapter 10 Product Strategies

3. Diversification

Diversification occurs when an enterprise includes additional products in the range (=alteration of the breadth of the range).

10.2.3 Product Elimination

This means the exclusion of products from the range.

1. Product Life Cycle

The product life cycle model attempts to represent the career of a product measured in terms of turnover, profits or losses between its introduction onto the market and its exit from it. The fundamental evidence of the model is that every product, independent of the course of its specific turnover, at first achieves rising and then falling sales, and that every product goes through quite determined phases independent of its absolute life span.

One differentiates between the following phases:

(1) Research and development

The efforts of enterprises in the R&D area (Research and Development) are in part very great. On the one hand, this is an attempt to dodge the struggle to drive competition out of the market and on the other hand to improve one's own market position. Although the risk is high, it is, above all, in both cases possible to achieve higher profits.

(2) Introduction

In the case of a completely new product, the pioneer enterprise has a quasi-monopoly position. The new product is adopted hesitantly by the so called "innovators". This phase is characterized by slowly rising sales and with the help of extensive advertising and sales promotion. The proceeds which are still small cannot cover the high costs of research, development and advertising etc., so that, in this phase, losses are made.

(3) Growth

In this phase, the market breakthrough has to be made, and a sales boom begins, if the product doesn't prove to be a flop. In the growth phase, the new product is imitated by competitors for the first time. The "early majority" of users are added to the customer group. By means of intensive market extension, the suppliers achieve a high growth in turnover with high profits.

(4) Maturity

The suppliers are joined by those conservative enterprises which only produce problem solutions that have already succeeded on the market. The market becomes polypolistic. The "late majority" of users now make their entry as customers. The competition leads to price wars (price reductions) and to falling profits (above all because of the ever increasing number of variations which raise costs again).

(5) Saturation

On the consumer side, the "late customers" arrive, the market volume is already highly saturated, and sales stagnate. The variations (differentiations) often lead to excesses. Profits fall further.

(6) Degeneration

In this phase, most of the suppliers drop out because of too low profits. The reason for the decline of the product is that the need which the product satisfied, is now better, more cheaply and more conveniently satisfied by different, new products.

Figure 10.2 shows the ideal type of the course of a product life cycle.

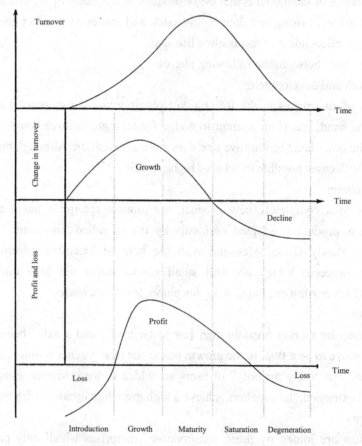

Figure 10.2　Course of a Product Life Cycle

2. Re-Launch

Re-launch is when, during the maturity phase, the product is newly adapted to the market. With this adaptation (technology, packaging, design, advertising, etc.), elimination is avoided and an increase in turnover achieved.

10.3 Product Positioning

Product positioning describes the position of the various products on the market. Central questions which can be answered in connection with such positioning models are as follows:

(1) How are the products of the competition placed in my product area?
(2) To what product qualities do customers react and how do they react?
(3) Can market niches be recognized?
(4) What placing in the product area is suitable for an existing product?

Portfolio Analysis

Portfolio analysis is concerned with determining a balanced product program with respect to the future revenue development. Since enterprises are generally multi-product businesses, it is recommended that the individual products be placed in so called strategic business fields (SBF) or strategic business units (SBU).

The base model (see Figure 10.3) of portfolio analysis is the so called "4-field matrix" of the BCG (Boston Consulting Group). A "9-field matrix" can also be drawn up (see Figure 10.4).

Two parameters must be established for the positioning of the Strategic Business Units: The attractiveness of the market (future market growth) and the relative competition advantage (relative market share).

1. Market Attractiveness

The market attractiveness is looked at independently of your own enterprise, whereby the following principles are to be considered:

(1) How favorably is the attractiveness of the market judged from the point of view of the market outsider who is considering entering the market?
(2) How does the market insider see the attractiveness of the market?

From these results, the general evaluation rules are as follows:

(1) The more difficult the demands on the supplier are, the greater is the attractiveness for the market by reason of the difficult market entry.

(2) The more demand promises success, the greater the attractiveness of the market.

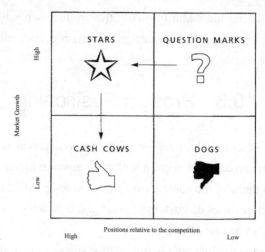

Figure 10.3　Business Portfolio

The evaluation can be determined as
(1) High;
(2) Medium;
(3) And low.

2. Relative Competition Advantage

In the evaluation of the relative market share, it is a matter of looking at ones own Strategic Business Units in proportion to the strongest or most important competitors.

Here, too, the evaluation can be determined as
(1) High;
(2) Medium;
(3) And low.

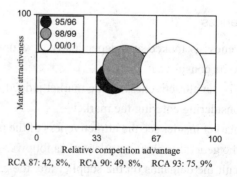

RCA 87: 42, 8%,　　RCA 90: 49, 8%,　　RCA 93: 75, 9%

Figure 10.4　Examples from Real Situations

Chapter 10 Product Strategies

10.4 Product Strategies

10.4.1 Strategy: Bringing Under Control

Initial position: Through obsolescence of the products increasing losses in turnover and danger of the loss of market leadership.

Strategy: Defense of market leadership, compensation for turnover losses through new development and program streamlining (see Figure 10.5).

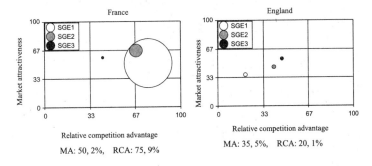

Figure 10.5 Actual Portfolio

10.4.2 Strategy: Defense

Initial position: The position of the business units is at the interface between growth and maturity phase.

Strategy: Defense of domestic market leadership; safeguarding of further growth by fostering of products; market extension (see Figure 10.6).

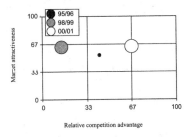

RCA 87: 42, 9%,   RCA 90: 14, 6%,   RCA 93: 67, 1%

Figure 10.6 Portfolio Analysis

10.4.3　Strategy: Expansion

Initial position: Product range in growth phase.
Strategy: Expansion, market extension (see Figure 10.7).

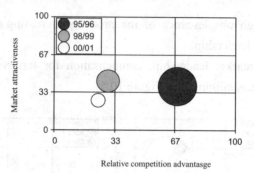

RCA 87: 67, 8%,　　RCA 90: 29, 4%,　　RCA 93: 24, 7%

Figure 10.7　Portfolio Analysis

10.4.4　Strategy: Holding

Initial position: Positive development through economic growth but weaknesses in partial areas.
Strategy: Maintenance of market leadership; gradual product streamlining (see Figure 10.8).

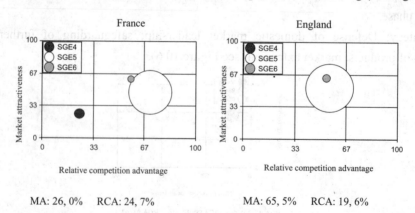

MA: 26, 0%　　RCA: 24, 7%　　　　　MA: 65, 5%　　RCA: 19, 6%

Figure 10.8　Actual Portfolio

10.4.5 Strategy: Exit

Strategy: Gradual Exit from this business area; positioning of replacement products at the interface U/M; skimming of still positive DB.

The portfolio analysis makes it possible to enter the product life cycle of an individual product (see Figure 10.9).

Portfolio	Life Cycle Phase	Standard Strategy
Question Marks	Introduction Phase, Start of Growth Phase	Increase market share or abandon (flop)
Stars	Growth Phase	Increase market share
Cash Cows	Maturity Phase	Maintain market share
Dogs	Saturation Phase, Degeneration	Elimination of product

Figure 10.9 Portfolio Analysis

A portfolio analysis also provides the possibility of registering not only actual states but also nominal values at the same time.

10.5 Brands

Strong brands are a valuable asset for the seller. A brand can help build up customer loyalty. However, there is less consideration of brands among the younger generation, who are less loyal to brands than older customers.

A brand is more than just a name or a logo; it enhances perception among the consumers and also generates emotions. A key decision concerns the choice of "brand name". The brand name must be memorable, delineate the benefit of the product, be easy to pronounce and be recognizable in all languages.

An enterprise can combine several brands under its roof. The brands can serve different products, and even one and the same product marketed to different target groups.

10.6 Summary

产品或服务是企业生产和经营活动的主要目的,包括有形和无形的产品与服务。产品由 3 个维度组成，即核心产品、形式产品和延伸产品。根据产品适用的对象，产品可以分为消费品和工业品。不论是消费品还是工业品，都是为了最大限度满足市场需求，从而实现企业利润。

企业为了在激烈的市场竞争中求得生存，必须根据市场变化调整自己的产品策略，常见的产品策略有产品创新策略、产品多样化策略以及产品淘汰策略。产品策略的选择依赖于产品业务组合的分析和基于业务分析的产品战略定位，因此，我们可以采用"狗牛图"矩阵分析企业业务，确定企业产品定位战略。主要产品战略包括：市场领先地位控制战略、国内市场保持与延伸战略、拓展战略、维持战略与撤退战略。同时，品牌也是产品生产与经营以及吸引和保留客户必须关注的问题。

Key Terms

Products   Product Innovation   Product Variation   Product Elimination   Portfolio Analysis   Product Strategy   Brand

【案例】 宝洁公司多品牌策略

品牌延伸曾一度被认为是充满风险的事情，有的学者甚至不惜用"陷阱"二字去形容其风险之大。然而，纵观世界一流企业的经营业绩，我们就不难发现，这其中既有像索尼公司那样一贯奉行"多品一牌"这种"独生子女"策略的辉煌，更有像宝洁公司这样大胆贯彻"一品多牌"策略，在国际市场竞争中纵横驰骋尽显"多子多福"的风流。

宝洁公司是一家美国企业。它的经营特点一是种类多，从香皂、牙膏、漱口水、洗发精、护发素、柔软剂、洗涤剂，到咖啡、橙汁、烘焙油、蛋糕粉、土豆片，到卫生纸、化妆纸、卫生棉，到感冒药、胃药，横跨了清洁用品、食品、纸制品、药品等多种行业。二是许多产品大都是一种产品多个牌子。以洗衣粉为例，他们推出的牌子就有汰渍、洗好、欧喜朵、波特、世纪等近10种品牌。在中国市场上，香皂用的是舒肤佳，牙膏用的是佳洁士，卫生巾用的是护舒宝，仅洗发精就有"飘柔"、"潘婷"、"海飞丝"三种品牌。要问世界上哪个公司的牌子最多，恐怕非宝洁莫属。

宝洁公司是如何实施多品牌策略的？

一、寻找差异

如果把多品牌策略理解为企业多到工商局注册几个商标，那就大错特错了。宝洁公司经营的多种品牌策略不是把一种产品简单地贴上几种商标，而是追求同类产品不同品牌之间的差异，包括功能、包装、宣传等诸方面，从而形成每个品牌的鲜明个性，这样，每个品牌都有自己的发展空间，市场就不会重叠。以洗衣粉为例，宝洁公司设计了9种品牌的洗衣粉，汰渍(Tide)、洗好(Cheer)、格尼(Gain)、达诗(Dash)、波特(Bold)、卓夫特(Dreft)、象牙雪(IvorySnow)、奥克多(Oxydol)和时代(Era)。他们认为，不同的顾客希望从产品中获得不同的利益组合。有些人认为洗涤和漂洗能力最重要；有些人认为使织物柔软最重要；

还有人希望洗衣粉具有气味芬芳、碱性温和的特征。于是就利用洗衣粉的9个细分市场，设计了9种不同的品牌。

宝洁公司就像一个技艺高超的厨师，把洗衣粉这一看似简单的产品，加以不同的佐料，烹调出多种可口的大菜。不但从功能、价格上加以区别，还从心理上加以划分，赋予不同的品牌个性。通过这种多品牌策略，宝洁已占领了美国更多的洗涤剂市场，目前市场份额已达到55%，这是单个品牌所无法达到的。

二、制造"卖点"

宝洁公司的多品牌策略如果从市场细分上讲是寻找差异的话，那么从营销组合的另一个角度看是找准了"卖点"。卖点也称"独特的销售主张"，英文缩写为USP。这是美国广告大师罗瑟·瑞夫斯提出的一个具有广泛影响的营销理论，其核心内容是：广告要根据产品的特点向消费者提出独一无二的说辞，并让消费者相信这一特点是别人没有的，或是别人没有说过的，且这些特点能为消费者带来实实在在的利益。在这一点上宝洁公司更是发挥得淋漓尽致。以宝洁在中国推出的洗发精为例，"海飞丝"的个性在于去头屑，"潘婷"的个性在于对头发的营养保健，而"飘柔"的个性则是使头发光滑柔顺。在中国市场上推出的产品广告更是出手不凡："海飞丝"洗发精，海蓝色的包装，首先让人联想到蔚蓝色的大海，带来清新凉爽的视觉效果，"头屑去无踪，秀发更出众"的广告语，更进一步在消费者心目中树立起"海飞丝"去头屑的信念；"飘柔"，从牌名上就让人明白了该产品使头发柔顺的特性，草绿色的包装给人以青春美的感受，"含丝质润发素，洗发护发一次完成，令头发飘逸柔顺"的广告语，再配以少女甩动如丝般头发的画面，更深化了消费者对"飘柔"飘逸柔顺效果的印象；"潘婷"，用了杏黄色的包装，首先给人以营养丰富的视觉印象，"瑞士维他命研究院认可，含丰富的维他命原B5，能由发根渗透至发梢，补充养分，使头发健康、亮泽"的广告语，从各个角度突出了"潘婷"的营养型个性。

从这里可以看出，宝洁公司多品牌策略的成功之处，不仅在于善于在一般人认为没有缝隙的产品市场上寻找到差异，生产出个性鲜明的商品，更值得称道的是能成功地运用营销组合的理论，成功地将这种差异推销给消费者，并取得他们的认同，进而心甘情愿地为之掏腰包。

三、能攻易守

传统的营销理论认为，单一品牌延伸策略便于企业形象的统一，减少营销成本，易于被顾客接受。但从另一个角度来看，单一品牌并非万全之策。因为一种品牌树立之后，容易在消费者当中形成固定的印象，从而产生顾客的心理定势，不利于产品的延伸，尤其是像宝洁这样的横跨多种行业、拥有多种产品的企业更是这样。宝洁公司最早是以生产"象牙牌"香皂起家的，假如它一直沿用"象牙牌"这一单一品牌，恐怕很难成长为在日用品领域称霸的跨国公司。以美国Scott公司为例，该公司生产的"舒洁牌"卫生纸原本是美国卫生纸市场的佼佼者，但随着"舒洁牌"餐巾、"舒洁牌"面巾、"舒洁牌"纸尿裤的问世，使Scott公司在顾客心目中的心理定势发生了混乱——"舒洁该用在那儿?"一位营销专家曾幽默地问：舒洁餐巾与舒洁卫生纸，究竟哪个品牌是为鼻子设计的?结果，舒洁卫生纸的头把交椅很快被宝洁公司的Charmin卫生纸所取代。

可见，宝洁公司正是从竞争对手的失败中吸取了教训，用一品多牌的策略顺利克服了顾客的"心理定势"这一障碍，从而在人们心目中树立起宝洁公司不仅是一个生产象牙香皂的公司，还是生产妇女用品、儿童用品，乃至药品、食品的厂家。

许多人认为，多品牌竞争会引起经营各个品牌的企业内部各兄弟单位之间自相残杀的局面，宝洁则认为，最好的策略就是自己不断攻击自己。这是因为市场经济是竞争经济，与其让对手开发出新产品去瓜分自己的市场，不如自己向自己挑战，让本企业各种品牌的产品分别占领市场，以巩固自己在市场中的领导地位。这或许就是中国"肥水不流外人田"的古训在西方的翻版。

从防御的角度看，宝洁公司这种多品牌策略是打击对手、保护自己的最锐利的武器。

一是从顾客方面讲，宝洁公司利用多品牌策略频频出击，使公司在顾客心目中树立起实力雄厚的形象；利用一品多牌从功能、价格、包装等各方面划分出多个市场，能满足不同层次、不同需要的各类顾客的需求，从而培养消费者对本企业的品牌偏好，提高其忠诚度。

二是对竞争对手来讲，宝洁公司的多品牌策略，尤其是在像洗衣粉、洗发水这种"一品多牌"的市场中，宝洁公司的产品摆满了货架，就等于从销售渠道减少了对手进攻的可能。从功能、价格诸方面对市场的细分，更是令竞争者难以插足。这种高进入障碍无疑大大提高了对方的进攻成本，对自己来说就是一块抵御对手的盾牌。

（资料来源：曹刚，李桂陵，王德发等. 国内外市场营销案例. 武汉：武汉大学出版社，2003. 案例根据北京康斯技术发展公司报告改编）

【案例分析】

综上所述，我们从宝洁公司的成功中看到了多品牌策略的多种好处，但这并非是坦途一条。俗话说"樱桃好吃树难栽"，要吃到多品牌策略这个馅饼，还需要在经营实践中趋利除弊。

一是经营多种品牌的企业要有相应的实力，品牌的延伸绝非朝夕之功。从市场调查，到产品推出，再到广告宣传，每一项工作都要耗费企业的大量人力物力。这对一些在市场上立足未稳的企业来讲无疑是一个很大的考验，运用多品牌策略一定要慎之又慎。

二是在具体操作中，一定要通过缜密的调查，寻找到产品的差异。有差异的产品品牌才能达到广泛覆盖产品的各个子市场、争取最大市场份额的目的。没有差异的多种品牌反而给企业加大生产、营销成本，给顾客的心理造成混乱。

三是要根据企业所处行业的具体情况来衡量。如宝洁公司所处的日用消费品行业，运用多品牌策略就易于成功，而一些生产资料的生产厂家则就没有必要选择这种策略。

【思考题】
1. 宝洁公司多品牌策略有何特点?
2. 哪类企业和产品适于实施多品牌策略?
3. 实施多品牌策略有哪些利弊?
4. 宝洁如果采用统一品牌,结果会不会更好?
5. 在什么情况下应采用统一品牌战略,什么情况下采用多品牌战略?

Chapter 11

Price Strategies

Focus on:

1. Various factors affecting the pricing.
2. How to price the product or service.
3. Pricing strategies and their merits and drawbacks.

This chapter examines the price element of marketing mix, which needs to be considered from several perspectives. Customers respond to price just as they do to product, place and promotion. A price that is either too low or too high may not only discourage customers from buying, but may also affect their attitudes towards and perception of the product. Price is especially important because it affects the number of sales an organization makes and how much money it earns.

11.1 Factors Affecting Pricing

With the increasing complicated marketing environment, developing, choosing and implementing pricing strategies become more difficult. Marketing managers should consider not only cost compensation, but also attitude of customers towards pricing and competitive environment when develop pricing strategies. There are diverse factors affecting pricing which include pricing objectives, costs, market demands, competition, other marketing mixes and legal regulations.

11.1.1 Pricing Objectives

Pricing objectives seek to achieve expected objectives by developing prices of products or services. There are three pricing objectives which are profit-oriented price objectives, sales-oriented price objectives and status quo price objectives.

Chapter 11 Price Strategies

1. Profit-Oriented Price Objectives

Profit-oriented price objectives which are the important components of corporate pricing objectives seek to achieve profit. They are adopted by most companies since gaining profit is necessary for their survival and development. There are three types in practice, namely, profit maximization, expected rate of return on investment, and satisfactory profit objective.

2. Sales-Oriented Price Objectives

A sales-oriented price objective seeks some level of unit sales, dollar sales or share of the market, without reference to profit. Its main indicators include sales growth and market share. Sales growth objective is sought by marketers wanting to set prices so that sales volumes increase. A market-share price objective seeks to gain some specific share of a market.

3. Status Quo Price Objectives

Status quo price objectives aim to stabilize prices, meet competition or even avoid competition. Price stability seeks to manage the market price by pricing its own products to avoid unnecessary price fluctuation. In order to avoid and meet competition, companies may set prices lower or higher than their competitors or just set the same price as their competitors.

11.1.2 Product Costs

Generally speaking, two basic factors determine the boundaries within which market prices should be set. The first is the product cost, which establishes a price floor, or minimum price. Second, prices for comparable substitute products create a price ceiling, or upper boundary. Product costs refer to the sum of various costs of producing a product or delivering a service. Any pricing method that involves the cost must consider the various types of costs and how they change in different ways as output changes. To have better understanding of product costs, six types of costs must be defined.

1. Fixed Costs

Fixed costs are those that are fixed in total, no matter what quantity is produced. Among these fixed costs are rent, depreciation, managers' salaries, and property insurance.

2. Variable Costs

Variable costs are those variable expenses that are closely related to output, including expenses for parts, wages, packaging materials and sales commissions.

3. Total Costs

Total costs are the sum of total fixed and variable ones. Changes in the total cost depend on variations in total variable costs, since the total fixed cost remains unchanged.

4. Average Fixed Cost

The average fixed cost is obtained by dividing total fixed costs by the related quantity.

5. Average Variable Cost

The average variable cost is obtained by dividing the total variable cost by the related quantity.

6. Average Cost

The average cost is obtained by dividing the total cost by the related quantity.

11.1.3 Market Demands

Between the lower and upper boundary for every product there is an optimum price, which is a function of the demand for the product as determined by the willingness and ability of customers to buy. If market supply cannot satisfy demands, price increases. On the contrary, when supply is bigger than market demands, price drops consequently. Meanwhile, price affects market demands and sales volumes as well. Therefore, organizations should understand the degree that market demands are affected by pricing changes.

Price elasticity is the index to show how responsive demand will be to a change in price. The price elasticity of demand is given by the following formula:

Price Elasticity of Demand = % change in quantity demanded ÷ % change in price

11.1.4 Competition

Pricing policies are depending on not only reactions of customers, but also competitors. Competition behavior changes when competitive environment and competitive advantages change in different market structures. There are four basic kinds of market situations: pure competition, oligopoly, monopolistic competition and monopoly. Companies apply different pricing methods in different market structures. In pure competition situation, prices are set completely by the market. Companies accept market prices and have no right of price setting. In monopolistic competition, companies produce differentiated products and set prices according to product differentiation degree and prices set by competitors. In oligopoly situation, companies are dependent on and influenced by each others, therefore, price setting should consider reactions of competitors. Any price fluctuation will lead to responding reactions. In the perfect monopoly situation, there is no competition and the only seller has total control on market price.

11.1.5 Legal Aspects of Pricing Policies

In order to help the economy to operate more effectively in the interests of customers, governments use legislations and policies to manage organizations' pricing decisions. Pricing legislations normally focus on price composition, changes of pricing, price level and price management. Organizations therefore need to understand and follow pricing legislations to make the right pricing decisions and protect their own interests. Furthermore, in the daily operation organizations should pay close attention to policies and legislations concerning currency, finance, commerce and distribution.

11.2 Elementary Pricing Methods

Pricing methods which are guided by specific pricing objectives of corporate apply price decision theories to set prices with the consideration of cost, demand and competition. Prices may be developed in various ways. These methods may be divided into three basic categories: cost-oriented pricing, demand-oriented pricing and competition-oriented pricing.

11.2.1 Cost-Oriented Pricing

Cost-oriented approaches which are the most commonly used pricing methods set prices according to costs. Prices must be equal to or higher than the cost of products. Normally, organizations which apply cost-oriented pricing set prices by adding a given amount of profits to the cost of a product. There are some categories of cost-oriented pricing which include cost plus pricing(mark-up), average-cost pricing, target return pricing and break-even analysis pricing.

1. Cost Plus Pricing

Some organizations set prices by using a cost plus method – that is, a given amount added to the cost of a product, to obtain the selling price. Suppose a supermarket buys a brand of sunscreen for $8. In order to make a profit, the store must sell the sunscreen for more than $8. If $4 is added to cover operating expenses and provide a profit, the store is marking up the item by

$4.

The cost plus is usually stated as percentage, rather than dollar amounts. A mark-up of $4 on a cost of $8 is a mark-up of 50 per cent. If the mark-up is calculated as a percentage of the selling price of $12, it is 33.3 per cent. It is normal to use the term mark-up percentage in relation to the cost, rather than the selling price.

The price calculation formula is as follows:

Selling price = Total cost per unit × (1 + Mark-up)

Case 11.1

A company produces 2,000 sets of TV, total fixed cost is ¥6 million, variable cost per unit is ¥1,000, if mark-up is 25%, the selling price is calculated as follows:

Fixed cost per unit = 6,000,000 ÷ 2,000 = ¥3,000

Total cost per unit = 3,000 + 1,000 = ¥4,000

Selling price = 4,000× (1 + 25%) = ¥5,000

This approach has some advantages. Firstly, it is simple and makes good sense. Secondly, if different companies in the same industry use the cost plus to set prices, they often use similar mark-up percentages because their operating expenses are similar. Consequently, products are sold at about the same price and the price war can be avoided. Lastly, this method is acceptable to both sellers and buyers. To the seller, it covers total expenses and provides a given amount of profits. Buyers are happy as well since prices are affordable.

2. Average-Cost Pricing

Average-cost pricing involves adding a reasonable mark-up to the average cost of a product. Average cost per unit is identified from past records. Dividing the total cost for the past year by the number of units produced or sold in that period provides an estimate of the average cost per unit for the next year. The producer sets the price by applying a mark-up to the estimated average cost per unit.

Average cost per unit = Total cost (past year) ÷ Number of units produced or sold (past year)

Selling price = Average cost per unit × (1 + Mark-up)

The success of the average-cost pricing depends on some estimate of demand in the coming period to allow the calculation of a realistic average cost. In stable situations, prices set by this method may yield profits. When demand is variable, the average-cost pricing is even more risky.

The average-cost pricing is simple, and it may work well if the company sells at least the quantity used to estimate the average cost per unit. Losses may occur if actual sales are significantly below the anticipated level or if costs increase.

The major limitation to this approach is that no consideration is given to cost variations at different levels of output. Typically, the average cost per unit is relatively high with low volumes of production, while larger volumes produce economies of scale and the average cost per unit declines. Another danger of average-cost pricing is that it ignores competitors' costs and prices. It is not just the organization's own product price that influences demands; the price of available substitutes may also have a real impact.

3. Target Return Pricing

Target return pricing adding a target return to the cost of a product has become a popular strategy. The price setter seeks to earn a percentage return on investment, or a specific total dollar return. While the expected quantity is not sold, the return is much lower than the expectation.

> **Case 11.2**
>
> The total investment of the TV manufacturer is 8 million, the investment payoff period is 5 years, and the selling price per unit is calculated as follows:
>
> Target return rate = 1 / investment payoff period × 100% = 1/5 × 100% = 20%
>
> Target profit per unit = Total investment × Target return rate ÷ Predicated sales
> $$= 8,000,000 \times 20\% \div 2,000 = ¥800$$
>
> Selling price per unit = Total fixed cost ÷ Predicated sales + Variable cost per unit + Target profit per unit = 6,000,000 ÷ 2000 + 1,000 + 800 = ¥4,800

4. Break-Even Analysis Pricing

Break-even analysis evaluates whether the organization will be able to break even, that is, cover all of its costs with a particular price. This method focuses on the break-even volume, that is, the quantity at which the organization's total cost will just equal its total revenue.

The break-even volume can be calculated using the following formula:

Break-even volume = Fixed cost ÷ (Price – Variable cost)

Break-even price = Total fixed cost ÷ Break-even volume + Variable cost per unit

> **Case 11.3**
>
> The fixed cost of a company is ¥100,000, variable cost is ¥30 per unit, if the break-even volume is 2,000, the break-even price is calculated as follows:
>
> Break-even price = 100,000 ÷ 2,000 + 30 = ¥80

Break-even analysis is a useful tool for analyzing costs and evaluating profits in different market environments. However, it does not consider the effect of price on the quantity that customers will be willing to purchase. To achieve the most profitable price, marketers should attempt to estimate demands. While break-even analysis is a simple and helpful tool for evaluating options, it is often misunderstood. Beyond the break-even volume, profits seem to be growing continually. However, this is rarely true. Most managers face downward-sloping demand curves and total revenue curves do not continue to climb.

11.2.2 Demand-Oriented Pricing

Demand-oriented pricing can be called as "customer-oriented pricing" or "market-oriented pricing". It focuses on customer needs and sets prices according to market demands and customers' price sensitivity. Demand-oriented pricing does not have direct relation with costs and is flexible to change while market demands are changing.

1. Perceived-Value Pricing

Organizational buyers evaluate how a purchase will affect their total costs and many marketers take this into account when estimating demand and setting prices. They utilize perceived-value pricing, which involves setting prices that will capture some of what customers will save by substituting the company's product for the one currently being used.

For instance, a producer of computer-controlled machines used in car assembly may recognize that the new machine does not just replace a standard machine, it also reduces labor costs, quality control costs and after the car is sold, costs of warranty repairs. The potential savings might be different for different customers because they have different operations and costs. The marketer can estimate the savings each car manufacturer will make by using the computerized machine and set a price making it worthwhile for the manufacturer to buy this machine rather than continue with the old technology.

The way to set price by applying perceived-value pricing is stated in the following:

First step: Set original price according to product quality, functions, service level and other factors.

Second step: Estimate sales volumes and assumed target profit.

Third step: Forecast target costs.

Total target cost = Sales − Total target profit − Total tax

OR: Target cost per unit = Price per unit − Target profit per unit − Tax per unit

Fourth step: Make decision.

If real costs ≤ target costs, target profit can be achieved, the original price can be set as selling price; if real costs > target costs, target profit cannot be achieved, the company should decrease real costs or target profit level.

2. Reversely Pricing

Reversely pricing involves setting an acceptable final consumer price and working backwards to calculate what a producer can charge. It is commonly used by producers of final consumer products, especially shopping products, such as women and children's clothing. It is also used for toys or gifts, on which customers will spend some predetermined amount, such as $15, $20 or $50. Here, a reverse cost-plus pricing process is used – also called 'market-minus' or 'retail-minus' pricing.

The producer starts with the real price for a particular item and subtracts the typical margins that channel members expect. This provides the approximate price that the producer can charge. The average or planned marketing expenses are then subtracted from this price to determine how much can be spent on producing the item.

Case 11.4

The retail price of a product is ¥100, retailers and wholesalers can get 30% and 10% discount respectively, then retailers pay $100 \times (1-30\%) = ¥70$ to the wholesaler, wholesalers pay $70 \times (1-10\%) = ¥63$ to the producer.

3. Discrimination Pricing

Discrimination pricing sells a product or service at two or more prices, even though the difference in prices is not based on those in costs but according to customer demands. By applying discrimination pricing, companies can adjust their basic prices to allow for differences in customers, products and locations.

There are several forms of discrimination pricing that are listed in the following:

(1) Customer-based pricing

Customer-based pricing charges different customers for different prices when they buy the same product or service. For example, companies may charge different prices for old and new customers, females and males, adults and children, deformed and healthy persons, business and consumer buyers.

(2) Location-based pricing

Location-based pricing charges different prices for different locations. For instance, theaters, airplanes and hotels vary their seat or room prices because of customer preferences for certain locations.

(3) Time-based pricing

Using time-based pricing, a company varies its price by the season, the month, the day, and even the hour. For example, cinemas vary their prices to customers by time of day versus night. For some seasonal products, prices may vary by busy seasons versus slack seasons.

(4) Product-based pricing

Under product-based pricing, different versions of the product are priced differently according to different demands, even though there is no big difference in costs. For instance, public utilities vary their prices charged for water to business buyers, consumer buyers and agricultural buyers.

11.2.3 Competition-Oriented Pricing

Price setting decisions are made by applying appropriate pricing methods according to the competitive position in the target market. It considers not only costs and market demands, but also the competition structure and level of the target market. Competition-oriented pricing focuses on competition and sets prices according to prices charged by competitors. It adjusts pricing methods with the change of competition. The feature of competition-oriented pricing is that the price setting does not have direct relation with product costs and market demands. It sets prices with the consideration of the competitive power of a product's price in the market. There are some disadvantages of competition-oriented pricing. First, it pays too much attention to price competition and neglects competitive advantages that could be formed by other marketing mixes. Second, excessive competition on price will lead to little profit because of price war. Moreover, it is difficult to evaluate exactly changes of competitors' price.

1. Going-Rate Pricing

Every company faces competition sooner or later in the market of monopolistic competition and pure competition. When this happens, deciding how high or low a price is set may be relative not only to the market demand curve, but also to prices charged by competitors. Most companies choose to obtain average profits by keeping their prices on the average market level.

Going-rate pricing avoids 'price war' and helps the sound development for the whole industry since organizations keep the same price to obtain the average profit when costs, product functions and deal conditions are nearly the same. It is easy to set prices by applying going-rate pricing because it does not consider costs and market demands. Meanwhile, it saves time and money of marketing research and reduces risks of price fluctuation.

In practice, the price is formed by two ways. In the pure competition market, no one has the right to decide the market price. Therefore, the price is formed when price agreement is reached between organizations. In the monopolistic competition market, a few large organizations in the industry set price first, and then others follow it or use it as reference price.

Organizations may lose profit when applying going-rate pricing when costs increase higher than the average cost of the industry. Non-price competition becomes the major competition method if prices are set nearly the same. Companies should keep their competitive advantages by competing on quality, brand, service, and advertisement and distribution channel.

2. Offensive Pricing

Offensive pricing sets prices lower or higher than competitors' prices to build different product image. Product-based pricing is one type of it. The application of offensive pricing requires that organizations are capable of gaining large market shares in an industry or in a certain area and customers have realized the relation between the organization and its products. A large amount of money spent on advertisement, package and after-sale service is necessary to the companies which have established 'best quality and high price' image. All in all, in order to win the competition, companies should keep enhancing product quality to gain customer trust in the long term.

3. Sealed-Bid Pricing

Sealed-bid pricing involves offering a specific price for each possible job, rather than setting a price that applies for all customers. The customer will obtain several tenders, often accepting the lowest. For example, building contractors tender on possible projects and many companies selling products must submit tender for contracts.

The first step of sealed-bid pricing is to estimate costs and provide several tendering plans to choose. The tender price must include an overhead charge and a charge for profit.

The second step is to assure the likelihood of success of different tendering plans by analyzing the competitive capability and possible tender prices of competitors. The competitive capability is determined by product sales, market share, brand image, prestige, quality, service level, etc.

Furthermore, it needs to calculate expected profits of every tendering plan according to its possible profit level and likelihood of success. The formula is set as below:

Expected profit of every tendering case = Possible profit level × Likelihood of success

Lastly, choose tendering plans according to the tender object of the company.

Sealed-bid pricing is a fair way to do business, and the customer chooses the best tender by comparing quality, service and price of tender providers. However, it can be complicated and expensive on the other hand. Organizations can spend thousands or even millions of dollars to develop tenders. Therefore, it is applicable to the contracts of expensive products, raw materials and building projects.

11.3 Basic Pricing Strategy

As a complicated process, pricing should be well designed to meet customer demands. Marketing managers must develop pricing strategies as well as pricing objectives to get the right product price. There are many factors such as psychological, social and cultural effects should be taken into account in price setting. The pricing strategy for a particular product may vary in different markets or during different product life cycles. Organizations must choose pricing strategies according to their pricing objectives, market environment and product features. There are some pricing strategies shown in the following.

11.3.1 Pricing Policies over the Product Life Cycle

When marketing managers administer prices, they must set introductory prices and consider where the product is in its life cycle and how fast it is moving through the cycle. They must also decide if their prices should be above, below or similar to market price levels.

1. Market Introduction Stage

Consider a new product in the market introduction stage of its product life cycle. Decisions about price should focus first on the nature of market demands. There are few or no direct substitute products for a new product. Depending on the demand curve for the product, a higher price might lead to a higher profit from each sale but fewer units being sold. Conversely, a lower price might appeal to more potential customers.

(1) Skimming pricing

A skimming pricing policy aims to sell to the top of a market at a high price. Skimming policy may maximize profits in the market introduction stage for a true innovation, especially if there is little competition. For example, early mobile telephone sellers, such as Motorola skimmed the market with an average price of more than $2,000 in 1987, targeting professionals and affluent consumers.

Advantages of skimming pricing include the following:
- Gaining as much profit as possible in the first introduction period and reducing investment risks;

Chapter 11 Price Strategies

- Creating prestige image of the product;
- Being capable of reducing price over time to keep competitive capability;
- Exploring new target markets by cutting price to attract potential customers and even price-sensitive customers.

Disadvantages of skimming pricing can be as follows:

- High price may lead to limited market demands which have negative effects on market exploration, sales volumes and new product introduction;
- High profit will attract competitors entering market in short time and bringing substitutes. Consequently, price can be dropped dramatically and prestige image of product may be damaged accordingly;
- Excessive profit will cause public objection and negative feeling of customers, sometimes, even government will take actions to reduce prices.

Skimming pricing is quite useful when

- Products are unique and there are only a few or no direct substitutes in the market;
- Products are hard to copy by competitors during a certain period of time;
- Target customers are not price sensitive or market demand is quite inelastic.

(2) Penetration pricing

A penetration pricing policy represents an attempt to sell to the whole market at low price. Such an approach might be wise when customers who are willing to pay a high price are small. It can sell large quantity of products, attract more customers and achieve comparatively high market shares. Furthermore, a low penetration price discourages competitors from entering the market. However, if market share occupation is quite slow, low price will lead to low target returns. Moreover, brand image will be damaged by setting low price.

Penetration pricing is useful when

- Producing larger quantities results in lower costs because of economies of scale;
- Demand is elastic and market demands can be enhanced dramatically by lowering prices.

2. Market Growth Stage

In the market growth stage, sales are growing quickly and most companies will not cut prices. However, if the introduction price is high and aggressive competitors are emerging, companies might cut price to increase market shares.

In the stage, customers focus on costs and unique features of different brands instead of product utility. Marketing managers can adopt product differentiation or cost leadership strategies to decide prices of products according to corporate objectives.

3. Market Maturity Stage

In the market maturity stage, both customers and sales volumes achieve the highest levels and then begin to decline. Competition is even tough and companies might cut prices to attract business. If there are only a few competitors, companies can keep original prices by

(1) Separating product or service line instead of binding together;

(2) Improving cost management;

(3) Exploring and expanding product line;

(4) Reevaluating distribution channels and other marketing mixes to create competitive advantage and keep profits.

4. Market Decline Stage

During the market decline stage, new products replace the current offerings. Price competition from dying products becomes more vigorous, most companies choose to cut prices accordingly. If industry competitors move out of the market or current products are valuable, prices can be kept and even be increased. Generally speaking, there are three choices shown in the following:

(1) Go selective: It refers to give up some or all the segmented markets and then refocus on markets which have more competitive advantages;

(2) Harvest: Company leaves the industry step by step. It gives up some weak markets at first and leaves the market finally. The target of pricing is not to retain the left markets but gaining the most incomes;

(3) Maintain: It tries to gain profits from strengthening competitive advantages in the decline stage.

11.3.2 Discount and Allowance Pricing

Most price structures are built around a price list. Basic list prices are prices that final customers or users are normally asked to pay for products. Discounts and allowances are reductions from basic list prices which intent to attract customer buying. They can be useful in marketing strategy planning. There are several ways of discounts and allowances, such as quantity discounts, cash discounts, seasonal discounts, functional discounts and promotional allowances.

1. Quantity Discounts

Quantity discounts are those offered to encourage trade members and other customers to buy in larger quantities. The more customers buy the more discounts customers can get. This helps a seller to obtain more of a buyer's business, shifts some of the storage function to the buyer, or reduces shipping and selling costs. Such discounts are of two kinds – cumulative and non-cumulative which can be used together or separately.

(1) Cumulative quantity discounts

Cumulative quantity discounts are reductions in price for larger purchases over a given period, such as a year, and the discount usually increases with an increase in the total amount purchased. Cumulative discounts are intended to encourage repeat purchases by a particular customer by reducing the cost of additional purchases. This is a means of developing close and ongoing relationships with existing customers, thus ensuring their loyalty.

(2) Non-cumulative quantity discounts

Non-cumulative quantity discounts are reductions in price when a customer purchases a larger quantity in a single order. They aim to encourage customers to buy large quantities of products in a single order.

The difficulty of application is how to define appropriate discount policies. As we can see, the bad defined discount policies cannot encourage larger purchases if only a few buyers can get discounts or they are not attractive to buyers. Therefore, marketing managers must develop right discount policies according to product features, sales targets, cost level, market demands, purchase frequency and competition.

2. Cash Discounts

Cash discounts are reductions in the price when buyers make payments before due days or the buyers make the payment by cash. They aim to encourage the buyers to pay their accounts quickly. The terms for a cash discount usually modify the 'net' terms. For example, '3/20, net 60' means that 3% discount on the face value of the invoice is allowed if the invoice is paid within 20 days – otherwise, the full face value is due within 60 days.

3. Seasonal Discounts

Seasonal discounts are those offered to encourage buyers to purchase earlier than current demand requires. By applying seasonal discounts, producers can shift the storage function further along the channel, smoothes sales over the year and therefore permits year-round operations. For example, beer producers offer wholesalers a lower price if they buy in winter when sales are slow.

4. Functional Discounts

A functional discount is a reduction in the price given to channel members for the task they undertake. A manufacturer might allow retailers a 30 per cent trade discount from the suggested retail list to cover the cost of the retailing function and their profit. Similarly, the manufacturer might allow wholesalers a chain discount of 30 per cent plus 10 per cent off the suggested retail price.

5. Promotional Allowances

Promotional allowances are price reductions given to organizations in the channel to encourage them to advertise or otherwise promote the supplier's products locally. For instance, Coca-Cola may give an allowance to its wholesalers or retailers. They, in turn, would be expected to spend the allowance on local advertising.

Discounts and allowances provide pricing flexibility and enhance suppliers' profits. However, marketing managers must use discounts and allowances to all customers on equal terms to avoid charges of price discrimination.

11.3.3 Geographical Pricing

Geographical pricing defines details of delivery and its costs. Usually, purchase orders specify place, time, method of delivery, freight costs, insurance, handling and other charges. There are many possible variations and some specialized terms that have developed.

1. F.O.B. Pricing

A commonly used transportation term is F.O.B., which means 'free on board' of some vehicle at some place. Typically, it is used with the place name, often the location of the seller's factory or warehouse, as in 'F.O.B. Taiwan' or 'F.O.B. mill'. This means that the seller pays the cost of loading the products onto some vehicle, then title to the product passes to the buyer. The buyer takes responsibility for freight charges and damage in transit, except as covered by the transport company.

If the organization wants to pay the freight for the convenience of customers, it can use 'F.O.B. delivered' or 'F.O.B. buyer's factory'. In this case, title does not pass until the products are delivered. If the seller wants the title to pass immediately but is willing to prepay freight, 'F.O.B seller's factory-freight prepaid' can be used.

Since the delivered cost varies depending on the buyer's location, organization can apply F.O.B pricing when buyers are not far away.

2. Regional Pricing

Regional pricing involves making an average freight charge to all buyers within a specific

Chapter 11 Price Strategies

geographic area. The seller pays the actual freight charges and invoices each customer for an average charge. For example, an organization in New Zealand might divide Australia into 5 regions. All customers in the same region are billed the same amount for freight.

Regional pricing reduces the wide variation in delivered prices that results from F.O.B shipping point pricing policy. It also simplifies charging for transportation.

3. Uniform-Delivered Pricing

Uniform-delivered pricing means making an average freight charge to all buyers. It is a form of regional pricing in which an entire country may be considered as one zone and the price includes the average cost of delivery.

Uniform-delivered pricing is used most often when transportation costs are relatively low, and when the seller wishes to sell in all geographic areas at one price.

4. Basing-Point Pricing

Under basing-point pricing, the seller selects a given city as a basing point and charges all customers the freight cost from that city to the customer location, regardless of the city from which the goods are actually shipped.

5. Freight-Absorption Pricing

Freight-absorption pricing means absorbing freight cost so that an organization's delivery price can match the nearest competitor's price. This amounts to cutting list price to appeal to new market segments. These absorbed costs reduce profit on each sale, but the additional business may increase total profit.

11.3.4 Portfolio Pricing

Most organizations product a variety of products, therefore the whole company line needs to be priced. Portfolio pricing involves setting prices for a whole line of products.

1. Product Line Pricing

Product line pricing sets a few price levels for a product line according to different quality, customer needs and competition. For example, a brand of jeans can be priced between ¥100 and ¥400. In the product line pricing, jeans are priced at three levels, such as ¥120, ¥240 and ¥360. Customers will choose different jeans according to their incomes and how much money they wish to pay on the clothing.

When applying the product line pricing, the bottom price of a product should be determined first to attract customer attention on the whole product line, then the ceiling price of a product should be set. Lastly, price other products according to different product classes.

2. Optional-Product Pricing

Using optional-product pricing, companies offer to sell optional or accessory products along with their main product. For instance, car dealers sell power window and CD player besides cars. Prices of optional-products affect their main products' sales volumes. There are two kinds of optional-product pricing. One is pricing optional-product at high level to gain profits. And the other is attracting customers by setting low optional-product price.

3. Complements Pricing

Complements pricing sets prices for several products, as a group. This may lead to one product being at a very low price so that the profits from another product will be greater, thus increasing the product group's total profit. A new razor from Gillette, for example, may carry a low price to encourage the sale of blades, which must be replaced regularly.

4. By-Product Pricing

In some industries, like producing processed meats or petroleum products, there are often by-products. The value and disposal cost of by-products affect the pricing of main products. Using by-product pricing, the company will seek a market for these by-products and should accept any price that covers more than the cost of storing and delivering them.

5. Product Mix Pricing

An organization that offers its target market several different products may use product mix pricing by setting one price for a set of products. Organizations that use product mix pricing usually set the overall price so that the customer pays less by buying all products at the same time, rather than separately. For example, McDonald's offers a product mix price for a hamburger, French fries and a soft drink. Product mix pricing encourages customers to spend more to buy products that they might not otherwise have bought, because the added cost of the extras is not as high as it normally would be.

11.3.5 Psychological Pricing

Psychological pricing involves setting prices that have special appeal to target customers.

Chapter 11　Price Strategies

1. Odd-even Pricing

Odd-even pricing involves setting prices that end in certain numbers. For example, products selling below $50 often end in the numbers 5 or 9, such as $0.49 or $24.95. More expensive products are often $1 or $2 below the next even dollar figure, such as $99 rather than $100.

Some marketers believe that consumers react positively to such prices, perhaps viewing these as substantially lower than the next higher even price. Odd-even prices were originally used by some retailers to force sales assistants to provide change, so the assistants had to record the sale and could not pocket the money. Today, it is not always clear why such prices are used or whether they work. Perhaps it happens simply because 'everyone else does it'.

2. Prestige Pricing

Prestige pricing involves setting a relatively high price to suggest high quality or high status. Some target customers want the best and will buy at high prices. At cheaper prices, they become concerned about quality and do not buy. Prestige pricing is most common for luxury products, such as furs, jewelry and perfume.

3. Customary Pricing

Most customers have a reference price that the price they expect to pay for many of the products they purchase. For a consumer, the reference price for a loaf of bread may be $2. He or she may expect home brands to cost less than $1.6 and premium brands to cost more than $2. Different customers may have different reference prices for the same basic type of purchase. Demands may increase if customers feel that a product is at good value because the price is below their reference price.

4. Loss Leader Pricing

Loss leader pricing involves setting some very low prices to attract customers into stores. The aim is not to sell large quantities of the leader items, but to attract customers into the store to buy other products.

The right way of applying loss leader pricing includes the following:

(1) Loss leader products are usually well-known, widely used items that customers buy regularly, such as milk, eggs and drinks.

(2) Loss leader items should be priced low to attract customers' attention but still above cost.

11.4　Summary

　　价格是市场营销组合中最重要的因素之一，它直接决定产品的销量和盈利率。因此，企业必须重视定价策略的选择和使用，使之与产品特征、分销渠道选择和促销策略完美地结合。影响定价的因素包括定价目标、产品成本、市场需求、竞争状况、其他市场营销组合因素和政策法律等。定价目标可分为利润导向型、销售导向型以及竞争导向型三种。企业定价的方法有成本导向定价法、需求导向定价法和竞争导向定价法。定价策略包括产品生命周期定价策略、折扣与让利策略、地理定价策略、产品组合定价策略和心理定价策略。

Key Terms

Cost-Oriented Pricing　Demand-Oriented Pricing　Competition-Oriented Pricing　Skimming Pricing　Penetration Pricing　Discount and Allowance　Leader Pricing　Odd-Even Pricing　Geographical Pricing　Product Line Pricing

---

【案例】新产品定价策略

　　汕头罐头厂生产橘子罐头，剩下的橘子皮九分钱一斤送往药品收购站，尽管价格便宜，但销售依然困难。经研究发现橘子皮只有入中药做成陈皮才有用。最后他们开发出"珍珠陈皮"小食品，具有养颜和保持身体苗条的功能。以何种价格出售这一产品成了当前的问题。经市场调查他们发现妇女和儿童尤其喜欢吃零食，在此方面不吝花钱，但惧怕吃零食导致肥胖，而珍珠陈皮正好可解其后顾之忧，且市场上尚无同类产品。于是他们果断决定每15克袋装售价1元，合33元一斤，该产品投放市场后销售火爆。

（资料来源：圣才学习网. 新产品定价策略. [2010-06-18].
http://www.100guanli.com/HP/20100618/DetailD1154032.shtml.）

【案例分析】

　　这一案例运用了取脂定价策略。取脂定价是指在产品生命周期最初阶段把产品价格定得很高以攫取最大利润。本案例中罐头厂将"珍珠陈皮"这一新产品定价为33元/斤能最大限度为企业赚取利润。

　　之所以要采取这种定价策略是因为：

　　1. "珍珠陈皮"这种小食品生命周期短，生产技术一般比较简单，易模仿，即使是专利产品也被竞争对手加以改进成为市场新产品，故应在该产品生命初期趁竞争对手尚未进入市场之前以高价赚取利润，尽快弥补研制费用和回收投资。

　　2. "珍珠陈皮"之所以敢采取取脂定价策略还因为有如下保证：(1)市场需求大；(2)产品质量高，配料和包装均较考究；(3)产品迎合了消费者追求健美的心理，既能防止肥胖，又可以养颜；(4)该产品是新产品，无竞争对手。这些都为企业制定高价奠定基础。

在此案例中企业不能制定低价，否则将导致利润大量流失。若实行低价，一方面使"珍珠陈皮"名不符实，让消费者怀疑产品的质量，也很难与其他廉价产品区别开来，需求量不一定比高价时大；另一方面，该产品生产工艺并不复杂，很快就会有竞争对手进入，采取低价根本无法收回投资。

【思考题】
1. 简述定价在营销组合中的作用。
2. 比较成本导向、需求导向和竞争导向这三种定价法的优缺点。
3. 讨论不同定价策略的适用条件。

Chapter 12

Place Strategies

Focus on:

1. Features and basic types of place.
2. Main types of wholesalers and retailers.
3. New orientation of the marketing system.
4. Design and management of place.

12.1　Basic Types and Features of Place

12.1.1　Concepts of Place

Place, also called distribution channel, is a general designation for the route, channel and link of how products or services go from manufacturers to consumer. It is a whole set of organizations that bring out the successful use or consumption of certain products or services.

The target of place's specific task is to move goods from manufacturers to consumers or users so that they can buy goods in the proper time and place to satisfy their needs. In commodity economy, the realization of product value is done in transaction in which the product generally has two ways of movements. One is the movement of the value as the result of buying and selling. It is a transfer or series of transfers of product ownership from one owner to another and finally to the consumer. This is called business flow. The other is the special movement of product entity with business flow. This is commodity flow. Business flow and commodity flow normally center on the final realization of product value and help form changeable routes from manufacturers to consumers. Those routes are called Place in marketing.

12.1.2　Basic Types of Place

Place can be classified in different angles.

Chapter 12 Place Strategies

1. Long Channel and Short Channel

Place can be classified into long channels and short ones in terms of the number of intermediate links. If a product goes through one marketing institution that transits the ownership of the goods either directly or indirectly, we may call this process as one intermediate link. In the distribution of goods, the more links, the longer the channel; and on the contrary, the less links, the shorter the channel. Apparently, it is just a comparatively speaking term. Taking consumer market place as an example, there exist the following basic types (see Figure 12.1):

(1) Direct channel: manufacturers ⟶ consumers
(2) One-layer channel: manufacturers ⟶ retailers ⟶ consumers
(3) Two-layer channel: manufacturers ⟶ wholesalers ⟶ retailers ⟶ consumers
(4) Three-layer channel: manufacturers ⟶ agents ⟶ wholesalers ⟶ retailers ⟶ consumers

Figure 12.1 Place in the Consumer Market

The place in which the producer sells goods to its consumer through two or more than two intermediate links is called the long channel. In this kind of channel, the region can have a wide extension whereas more links result in huge circulating costs, so it is suitable for the commodities with optimum yield to expand market coverage.

The place in which the producer sells goods to its consumer through only one intermediate link is called the short channel. This kind of channel has fewer links and fewer circulating costs, but its regional extension is narrow, so it is suitable for local market commodities. The length of the channel should be determined by the commodity, which does not mean the shorter channel the better. Producers should try to reduce unnecessary sale links. However the necessary sale links that can extend market should be increased rather than reduced.

2. Wide Channel and Narrow Channel

According to the number of intermediates in each link, the place can be divided into wide and narrow channels. If a manufacturer asks for more intermediates of the same type to sell the product, this place is called the wide channel. The main feature of this channel is that goods are concentrated in distribution so that it can help expand market coverage and be convenient for consumer purchasing.

If a manufacturer asks for only one intermediate to sell the product, this place is called the narrow channel. This kind of place has a comparatively clear production and marketing relation. Its circulating formality is simple and convenient. However producer's market coverage and market share both depend on exclusive agents' sales network. So narrow channel is only used in selling particular commodities.

3. Direct Channel and Indirect Channel

According to having intermediates or not, the channel can be divided into direct and indirect one. In the direct channel, manufacturers use no intermediate. They have the functions of producing and circulating and make production meet directly with market needs. The direct marketing channel is the main type of channel that sells industrial products. It includes (1) Accepting the user's order. Companies sign contracts or agreements with key users, then produce and sell goods according to the contracts. (2) Setting up retail stores. Some companies set up retail stores or distributing firms to sell products. (3) Door to door promotion. Companies send out salespersons to have individual visits with customers and sell their products. (4) Selling in the communicating or electronic ways, such as order by mail, television and telephone or on line.

The indirect channel is a channel that producers sell products to consumers through intermediate links in the circulation domain. There exists switch transaction activity between producers and consumers in this kind of link. The intermediaries undertaking the circulating function mainly are retailers, wholesalers and agents. There may be one intermediate link or several. Sometimes there is more than one intermediary in an intermediate link, so the number of intermediaries involving in the commodity transaction should not be greater than that of the intermediate links. Since the producer may choose different types of intermediaries and the number of intermediaries may also be different, there are different kinds of indirect channels. Most of the products go from production field to consumer field through intermediate links. The indirect channel is the main channel in commodity circulation especially in consumer goods circulation.

4. Traditional Channel and Emerging Channel

According to the strength of relationship between members in the channel, the channel can be divided into traditional channels and emerging channels. The traditional channel is the one that consists of independent producers, wholesalers, retailers and consumers. "Independently" means every member does things in one's own way and does what one thinks is right. They carry out cutthroat competition in pursuit of self-interest maximization regardless of the profit of the whole channel system.

The emerging channel is a network in which management specialization and central planning is implemented and every member in the channel adopts integrated business or joint operation. In this way, scale operation is formed. Exchange capacity is strengthened. Operating efficiency is enhanced. Adaptability and market competitiveness is reinforced effectively.

The emerging channel includes the following:

Vertical marketing system (also known as VMS): This is a unified system made up of

Chapter 12 Place Strategies

producers, wholesalers and retailers. The channel members of this system either belong to the same corporation or sell the franchise to other members or have adequate capacity to make other members to cooperate with each other, and thus by controlling channel members' activities they can eliminate conflicts caused by independent channel members pursuing ones' own targets. The channel members make profit through scale economy, bargaining power and reducing duplication of service. 50% of consumer goods market in Europe, America and Japan has adopted this VMS.

Horizontal marketing system: This is the channel system in which two or more companies join together to exploit new marketing opportunity. These companies make up the horizontal marketing system either because of capital, manufacturing technique and marketing resource shortage that they can not exploit market independently or because they do not want to take risks or because they see the synergy effects brought by joint operation. Their temporary or permanent cooperation can be regarded as a new company.

Multi-channel marketing system: A company adopting this kind of system uses several channels towards one or different submarkets. With the emerging of consumer submarket and the increasing of potential channels, more and more companies adopt multi-channel distribution. For example, GE sells household appliances not only through independent retailers (department stores, discount stores and mail-order houses), but also directly to building contractors. The multi-channel marketing system can be divided roughly into two types. One is that manufacturers sell the product of the same trademark through more than two competitive distribution channels. This mode usually leads to intense competition between different channels and brings estranging from the original channel. The other is that manufacturers sell diversified products of different trademarks via several distribution channels. For example, a winemaker in the United States sells one kind of whisky through various types of retail stores(supermarkets, independent food stores, discount stores, and convenient stores), but all these kinds of wine use different trademarks. There are even some companies that enlarge their sales in the way of forming several channels by providing different service contents and manners in the marketing process of one product.

12.1.3 Features of Place

The features of place are as follows:

(1) Place is the channel from which the value of certain product goes through. One side of the channel is connected with production and the other side is connected to consumption. It is the whole circulating process of the product going through producers to consumers.

(2) Place is a mix of some related operational organizations or individuals. These

organizations or individuals carry out marketing functions jointly to solve problems on product realization and form symbiotic partnership because of collective economic and social benefits. These members generally include producers, wholesalers, agents, retailers and consumers among which all kinds of intermediates are active members. Meanwhile channel members have their individual economic benefits, so contradiction and conflict sometimes might appear among them, and management and coordination are needed at that time.

(3) In place, the shift of ownership is the premise of product movement. Under certain conditions, producers can sell their products directly to consumers and realize one-time procedure of ownership shift. Here the distribution channel is the shortest. However in most cases, producers have to sell the product through a series of intermediates or agents and finish the transaction of product ownership in a longer distribution channel. The length of the channel depends on comparative profits.

(4) In place some other circulating forms exist apart from the flow of ownership. For example, the physical flow of products, information flow, capital flow and promotion flow. They supplement each other, but they vary in terms of time and space. So the efficiency of distribution not only depends on channel member itself but also its related support system, like commercial service units (transportation corporations, storehouses, banks, and insurance companies), sales service units (advertisement companies, marketing research companies, and consulting firms).

12.2 Choice Tactics of Place

12.2.1 Factors Impacting the Selecting of Channel Type

Selecting distribution channels is to make decisions on the length and width of the channel, and it is an important issue in channel strategy. It has a close relationship with the success or failure of a company's marketing, that is, how a company chooses the best way to send the product to the target market. Here "the best" means getting most profits with the same cost or using the fewest costs to get certain income in a settled structural and functional market. The length and width of a channel cannot go as you please, and they are restricted by various factors. Every marketing firm has to think over the main factors such as customers, products, intermediates, competitors, and company policy, etc. when choosing channels.

1. Products

(1) The price of the product: Generally speaking, the lower the unit price, the longer and wider the channel; vice visa. On the other hand, the profit is very low, and thus multitudinous

Chapter 12　Place Strategies

sale is needed. Only by adopting intermediates can the market be broadened and the product occupy a favorable market position. Usually the indirect marketing channel with multi-links is adopted. However if upscale durable consumer goods like color TVs and air conditioners go through too many intermediate links, this would add up to circulating costs, and the selling price would surely go up and then influence sales. Therefore most producers prefer to send their products to large retail stores or electrical shops for sale. The higher the unit price is, the smaller the number of channel levels should be. Producers should avoid sales drop resulting from increase of channel levels. The shortest channel is the most favorable one.

(2) The volume and weight of the product: The products with different volume and weight have direct influence on modes of transporting, storehouse conditions and circulating costs. Overweight or bulky products should choose as shorter distribution channels as possible. Transit supply should be the prior way of transporting as regard to the product that surpasses the stated restriction of traffic departments (super-elevation, super-wide, over-length, concentrated weight). Small and light products of large quantity with ready conditions to choose longer marketing channel may consider indirect distribution channel.

(3) The natural property of the product: Some products are perishable, fragile, losing effects easily or with short natural life cycle and need critical storage conditions or difficult to be transported many times. The channel for these products should be as short as possible; the channel for self-stable products, crashworthy products and controlled release, long natural life cycle products can be longer and wider; and the vulnerable products should not adopt too many transfers between intermediate links to reduce possible damages caused by transporting process and temporary parking.

(4) Technicality of the product: Some products with especially high technical nature (precise instrument, complete plant) need install, debug and regular technical service and maintenance, and the producer might just as well sell them directly to users or sell only through intermediates with high expertise so that the producer can insure timely nice sales and technical service to users. For the products with low technical nature that do not need technical service, the producer can choose both long and wide marketing channel.

(5) Articles made to order and standard samples: The article made to order generally needs both production and demand parties to discuss about technical factors like specifications, quality, styles, etc. Standard samples have specific quality standard, specification and style, so the distribution channel can by either long or short. When users are dispersive, selling via intermediates would be a better choice; some can be sold directly according to the sample or the product catalog.

(6) Product market life cycle: For the product in input time, in order to open a sale as

quickly as possible and dominate the market, the producer should adopt synthetically various kinds of channels. For the product in period of saturation, the producer should try to find new channels to dominate new market.

(7) Product consumptive utility value: The necessities that are closely related to people's life are required to choose wide channels and bigger commercial networks so that consumers could buy the product whenever and wherever they are. Non-daily-necessities that are not closely related to people's life can apply narrow channels and often there are only few stores that sell this kind of products.

2. Markets

(1) Size of batch purchase. For large batch purchase, direct sale is used. For example, manufacturers surpass wholesalers and sell the product directly to retail chains and cooperative institutions with large order and small frequency; as for small batch purchase, apart from setting-oneself retail department, manufacturers adopt a longer indirect channel.

(2) Consumer distribution. Consuming regions of some commodity have a relatively narrow distribution which is suitable for the direct sale. On the other hand, it is suitable for indirect sale. For sales of industrial products, local users are very convenient in production and demand connection, and the direct sale is suitable. Non-local users are scattered thus the indirect sale is more suitable.

(3) Quantity of potential customers. When the potential demand of consumers is big and the market scope is large, intermediates are needed to provide service to satisfy consumers' demands, so in this case producers should choose the indirect distribution channel. If potential demands and market scope are small, producers can choose the direct sale.

(4) Buying habits of consumer. Some consumers prefer to buy commodity directly in the company while others prefer to buy in stores. So producers should sell both directly and indirectly to meet different consumers and enlarge sales of products.

3. Manufacturers

(1) Reputation and financial situation of the corporate. The corporate with good reputation, abundant funds and strong financial capability is free to choose distribution channels. It can have control over some of the important market, set up its own commercial network, introduce the operating mode of integrating production with marketing and control marketing, and reinforce the connection with consumers. Producers may also choose the indirect place. As for companies with weak funds, it must rely on the intermediate to sell and provide service, so the indirect channel is the only choice.

(2) Marketing capacity. The allocation of marketing mechanism and marketing personnel, familiarity and experience on marketing as well as storing and transporting capacity all restrict the choosing of the marketing channel. The company with strong marketing capacity should choose the direct marketing channel. Conversely, the company has to turn to the intermediate and choose the indirect channel. Furthermore, if a company cooperates well with the intermediate or has efficient control over the intermediate, the indirect channel can be used here. However, if the intermediate can not cooperate well or is not reliable, this will influence the market development of the product, so it had better execute the direct sale.

(3) The company's desire to control the channel. In order to have efficient control over the marketing channel, some companies would rather spend higher direct selling costs to build short and narrow channels; others might do not want to control the channel, and this would adopt the longer and wider channel according to such factors as the cost of sales.

(4) Potential service levels to provide. The intermediate generally hope manufacturers to provide as many service items like advertising, exhibition, maintenance and training as possible to create conditions for sales. When the manufacturer has no intention or capability to meet the requirements, agreement is difficult to be reached. In this instance, the manufacturer is forced to sell by himself. On the contrary, the higher the service level is provided; the intermediate would be more pleased to sell this product. In such case, the company should choose the indirect channel.

(5) Limitation of consignment. Manufacturers will prescribe limitation for some products to arrange the production. Higher consignment is beneficial to the direct channel; lower consignment is beneficial to the indirect channel.

4. Environmental Factors

(1) Policies and regulations. National policies and laws like monopoly system, antimonopoly law, provisions for importing and exporting, tax law, etc. may also affect the choice of marketing channels. Company's selecting of distribution channels should be in conformity with stipulations of relevant national policies and laws. Apart from this, tax policy, pricing policy, exporting law, commodity inspection provision, etc. also influence the choice of distribution channels.

(2) Economic situation. The better the economic situation of the society is and the more rapid the development is, the bigger the choice of the marketing channel; however when it comes to economic depression, there is a decline of the market demand. Companies must try to reduce unnecessary supply chain and use shorter channels.

5. Economic Returns

Another key factor that influences marketing choice is that different channels have different economic returns. Analysis concerning economic returns mainly focus on three aspects: cost, profit and sales volume.

6. Features of Intermediates

The advantages and disadvantages of different types of intermediates handling various kinds of work should be taken into account. Generally speaking, intermediate's capability in executing transporting, advertising, storage and getting in touch with customers, credit terms, right to refund products, personnel training and delivery frequency, etc. are quite different. Apart from these differences, the number, location, scale of intermediates and product classification and so on would all influence the choice of channel.

7. Nature of Competition

The manufacturer's choice of distribution channels is also affected by the channel competitor use. In some industries, producers may wish to either sell in the similar or even the same channel of the competitor to compete with competitor's product, or obtain brand effectiveness, or gain the same attracting profit.

12.2.2 Choosing Place

When designing distribution channels, the company has to choose between ideal channels and potential channels. This decision making process usually has to go through steps of analyzing consumers' needs, setting up the channel objective, assuming main alternative channel proposals and evaluation of the proposals.

1. Analyzing Customers' Requirements on Channel Service

Business firms should understand that in the chosen target market, what products the consumer buys, and where, why, when and how to buy them; they should also analyze the service requirements that consumer's purchase brings towards the channel members. The requirements are normally shown in the following four aspects: (1) batch size of each purchasing; (2) length of delivery time; (3) accommodations of purchase place; (4) varieties of product.

2. Setting up Channel Objectives

The channel objective is the service output objective that should be accomplished under the

Chapter 12 Place Strategies

general requirement of a company's marketing target when deciding distribution channels. This objective generally requires that the distribution channel should reach the service output level settled in the entire marketing and at the same time minimize the total channel cost. The marketing channel objective is the basis of channel design. Following factors should be considered when setting channel objectives: performance of the marketing channel, degree of the marketing channel control, financial expenses, etc. The performance of the marketing channel includes sales volume, market share, and target rate of returns; the degree of the marketing channel control is determined by the company's role in coordinating channels and its desire to control channels; financial expenses are set according to how much financial resources the company wants to spend on establishing and controlling the channel.

3. Identifying Alternative Channel Proposals

Suppose a company has defined its target market and ideal market positioning, it should next identify its major channel alternatives. The channel alternatives consist of three elements: the type and number of intermediates, the conditions of every channel members and their mutual responsibilities.

(1) Selection among different types of intermediates. A company should first of all determine the type of intermediates available. It can design its own channel scheme according to the situation of target market and existing intermediates, and at the same time refers to the existing experience of product's operators. If there is no suitable intermediate to use or if the direct sale can bring more economic returns, the company can design a direct channel, i.e. to send its own sales personnel or set up its own distribution channels to sell the product directly to users.

(2) Decide the number of intermediates. A company has to decide the number of intermediates to use at each level to form wide types of distribution channels. There are three types: intensive distribution, selective distribution and exclusive distribution.

Intensive distribution is the place in which the producer chooses lots of sales agents to sell products. Generally speaking, the articles for daily use seek this distribution method. Common raw materials for industrial products, small tools and standard articles, etc. also use this method. In this circumstance, wholesalers and retailers usually do not want to share advertising costs but ask manufacturers to pay for them. However, the manufacturer can have the maximum brand exposure and consumer convenience.

Selective distribution is the place in which the producer chooses one or more intermediates in the target market to sell the product instead of choosing all of the intermediates who want to sell the product. This will be helpful in increasing the company's effectiveness of operation. In most cases, for free choice of goods and specialty goods in consumer products, spare and accessory parts of industrial products should use this distribution method.

Exclusive distribution is an approach that in certain target market, at certain time, the producer chooses only one intermediate to sell this company's product. Both sides sign the contract provided that the intermediate should not sell the product of the manufacturer's competitor and the manufacturer should only supply goods to selected distributor. The exclusive distribution is used in the distribution of automobiles, large size house appliances and some distinctive products.

(3) Set requirements and responsibilities for channel members. Manufacturers should set the requirements and responsibilities for channel members to urge them to execute their channel functions with enthusiasm and effectiveness. Main elements of this business connection are pricing policy, sales terms, right for regional classification, mutual service and responsibility.

4. Evaluating the Major Alternatives

Because of permutation and combination of intermediates, likely extent of market demonstration, possible assignment of marketing work among channel members and different business connection sets, a company might confront with many kinds of choices among channel plans. Every transaction channel plan might be the route that the manufacturer goes to the end-user. The company always chooses one that can best satisfy its long-term goal among all these channel plans.

Normally, evaluating channel schemes may undergo economical efficiency, controllability and adaptability.

(1) Economical efficiency. Evaluating channel schemes should first of all start with economical efficiency. This means to compare the sales and cost level of each scheme.

(2) Controllability. Evaluation on economical efficiency may offer guidance whether one channel plan is better than the other one. This evaluation must be extended and considered in light of the incentives, controllability and conflicts of these two feasible alternatives. The degree of the producer's control over the channel could affect economic results, and thus the control problem should be taken into account after evaluating every feasible channel's economical efficiency.

(3) Adaptability. Suppose a particular channel plan is very advantageous from the economic perspective, and at the same time has no special control problems, the manufacturer's flexibility to adapt to environment changes would be another standard for consideration. If a channel plan takes too much time, then it would lose elasticity and can not adapt to the future change of objective environment.

Chapter 12 Place Strategies

12.3 Wholesalers and Retailers

Wholesalers and retailers are the main institutions of establishing the marketing channel as well as performing transfer of product ownership. The wholesaler and the retailer should come to understand how to hold a marketing campaign successfully to accomplish the divided marketing function and develop the institution.

12.3.1 Retailers and Marketing Decisions

1. Features of Retailers

Retailing includes all the activities involved in selling products and services directly to final consumers. Every institution-producers, wholesalers, retailers-might do retailing. However retailers are mainly organizations or individuals who do retailing. Retailers, the nearest intermediate institution with consumers or users, are the intermediate link between producers and consumers or between wholesalers and consumers. It is the last link of the goods circulating. The main task of the retailer is to serve final consumers. It dismounts products, provides customers with various services. Retailers have a large sum and extensive spread. They are in different types.

2. Types of Retailers

Retailers come in all shapes and sizes, and new retail types keep emerging. Division standards have not been unified. According to store-based or not, they can be classified into the following types:

(1) Store retailing. Brick-based retailers can be divided into specialty stores, department stores, supermarkets, combination stores, superstores, hypermarkets, convenience stores, discount stores, ware house stores, catalog sales exhibition rooms, etc.

(2) Non-store retailing. Non-store retailing includes direct selling, direct marketing, automatic vending, purchase by mail or telephone, door to door selling, etc.

(3) Retail organization. Although most of the retailers have independent ownership, more and more stores are selling through group retailing. Cooperative sale has five main types: corporate chain store, voluntary chain, retailer cooperative, consumer cooperative, franchise organization, merchandising conglomerate.

3. Retailer Marketing Decisions

(1) Target market decision. Choosing the target market is the retailer's most important decision. Many retailers have no specific target market or have too many markets to target and end up with satisfying no market well. Retailers should first of all make clear what group is the target consumer. Should the store focus on upscale, mid-scale, or downscale shoppers? Only when the retailer has defined its target market can it make consistent decisions on store location, product assortment, store decoration, advertising and pricing, etc. So, retailers should carry out marketing research on a regular basis to make sure that it can approach and fulfill target consumers. Where the store locates; what kind of customers it serves, general public, high-income level or particular group; what kind of image it should take to have successful access to the target market; all these are the problems retailers should solve.

(2) Product assortment decision. Product assortment has become a crucial factor to compete among similar retailers. Product assortment should match with shopping expectation of the target market. The width and depth of product assortment should be decided. Thus in a restaurant, it may provide a narrow-shallow mix (small lunch counter), narrow-deep mix (cooked food store), wide-shallow mix (buffet dinner) and wide-deep mix (large eating house). Another dimension of product assortment is product quality. A customer might be fond of the scope of choice and value very much the quality of a product.

(3) Service mix and store atmosphere decision. The department store offers as many services as possible for people while the supermarket cancels nearly all of these services. Service mix is a main means for a retailer to realize differentiation with competitors. Table 12.1 shows some of the service items a retailer with full service provides.

Table 12.1 Typical Retailing Services

Pre-sales Services	After-sales Services	Accessorial Services
1. Accepting Telephone Order	1. Delivery	1. Check Encashment
2. Accepting Mail Order	2. Conventional Packing	2. Regular Service
3. Advertising	3. Gift Wrap	3. Free Parking
4. Window Display	4. Transfer of Goods	4. Restaurant
5. In-store Display	5. Replacing Goods	5. Repair
6. Fitting Room	6. Return of Goods	6. Interior Decoration
7. Saving Shopping Time	7. Tailoring	7. Credit
8. Fashion Show	8. Installation	8. Restroom
9. Coupon	9. Sculpture	9. Babysitting

Store atmosphere is another element in the competition. The store's layout and pattern, music, smell, etc. form the unique style and characteristic of the store, i.e. store atmosphere. Some department stores that are good at operation pay special attention to the store atmosphere and design the atmosphere that fits with target consumer's features and psychology. They know how to integrate stimulating factors like visual, auditory, olfactory, and tactual to generate the expected impact.

(4) Price decision. A retailer's price is a key positioning factor which must be decided according to the target market, product and service assortment and competition. All retailers hope to sell at high price and achieve expansion of sales. However it can not be completed in both respects. Most retailers are divided into high make-up on lower volume (like high level specialty stores) and low make-up on high volume (like integrated shopping malls and discount stores). The retailer should also pay attention to pricing strategy. Most retailers price some of the products low to attract customers. And sometimes they will sacrifice sales for all the products. They sell the product of a slow turnover with deduced price.

(5) Promotion decision. The promotion that retailers use should support and reinforce its image location. High-grade stores will advertise graciously in rather influential magazines or newspapers. Popular stores mostly hype their products with a low price and characteristics in radio, TV, newspaper. They also have their own features in hiring sales personnel and sales promotion. They always apply various kinds of promotional methods to attract customers.

(6) Place decision. Place is a crucial element in successful retailing. It means whether a retailer can successfully attract customers because the customers generally prefer to purchase at a nearer place. Consumer's shopping habits are quite different in different countries and regions, so full consideration should be taken when choosing location. When picking the place for the department store, chain store, supermarket, gas station, fast food restaurant, a retailer should be more careful.

Moreover, large retailers have to solve another problem, i.e., whether to set up several small branches in separate places or to set up a larger store at a large region. Generally speaking, a retailer should set up enough stores in every city to achieve scale economy in promotion and distribution. The larger scale the store has, the larger its sale scope. The retailer always confronts with the conflict between large customer flow and high rent. They must select the most favorable place for their stores. They use various ways to evaluate the store location, like counting traffic flow, investigating the customer's shopping habit, analyzing competitive places and so on.

12.3.2 Wholesalers and Marketing Decisions

1. Features of Wholesaling

Wholesaling includes all the activities involved in selling goods and services to those individuals or organizations buying for resale or producing other products or services. The features of wholesaling are quite different from those of retailing.

(1) Service object of a wholesaler is non-final-user organization or individual.

(2) Business feature of a wholesaler is bulk buying and bulk selling while the retailer buys in bulk and sells separately to meet individual or family need.

(3) Because wholesalers are in the different position in commodity circulation, and have different service objects, they generally gather in big cities with comparatively advanced industry, commerce, finance, transportation, and parochial economical centers. The number of wholesalers is smaller than that of retailers and their distribution is narrower than that of retailers.

(4) Business volume of wholesaling is bigger than that of retailing and the region coverage is larger than that of retailing.

(5) Government imposes different law and tax policies on wholesalers and retailers.

2. Types of Wholesalers

Wholesalers fall into three categories: merchant wholesalers, agents and brokers, manufacturer's wholesale institutions.

(1) Merchant wholesalers. They are independent companies that have ownership with the commodity they sell, i.e., the wholesale institutions buy and sell by themselves. The quantities or sales of independent wholesalers play a very important role in the wholesale establishment. The independent wholesalers are divided into two types: full-service wholesalers and limited-service wholesalers.

Full-service: wholesalers provide customers with all-around service like keeping inventory, hiring fixed sales personnel, offering credit, delivering goods, assisting management.

Limit-service: The wholesaler provides the limited service to his suppliers and customers.

(2) Agents and brokers

An agent is a wholesaling institution that serves clients (usually suppliers). It has no product ownership and just represents the buyer to talk with the seller. Its main function is to promote transactions. After the deal is done, an agent gets certain commission from the client based on its sales. The biggest advantage of an agent is that it is very familiar with the market, has professional knowledge, has great endeavor with promotion and charges less. Thus many

manufacturers prefer to adopt the agent to sell products. The agent has special effect when a product enters into a new market. The agent has the following types:
- Manufacturer's agents: It represents a manufacturer to sell the product in certain region. Usually, the manufacturer can use several agents of this type to sell the product. However an agent often sells several manufacturers' products, but the products are complementary instead of competing with each other.
- Selling agents: It is an agent that represents a manufacturer to sell some products or entire outputs. This kind of agent is not limited by the region and has also decisive words in pricing, sales terms, advertising, product design and so on.
- Commission merchants: The commission merchant is an agent that has a control power over commodity substance and handles product sales. It usually does not have long-term relation with consignors.
- Auction houses: An auction house is an agent that provides transaction site and various kinds of service items for both buyers and sellers and concludes the transaction in the way of determining price by public auction.
- Import and export agents: The import and export agent is the one with offices in main ports that seeks source of supply from abroad and promote the product to abroad.

The broker is similar with the agent in that it also has no product ownership, and has no control over product substance, pricing policy and sales terms. The principle functions of the broker are to serve as a bridge, help with negotiation, and facilitate transaction. When the transaction is finished, the broker gets its commission from consignors. It has no fixed relation with both buyers and sellers. The most frequently seen brokers are food brokers, real estate brokers, insurance brokers and bill brokers and so on.

(3) Manufacturer's wholesale institutions. The ownership and management right of manufacturer's wholesale institution belong to the manufacturer. It includes distribution institutions and sales offices. The distribution institution is engaged in various businesses such as collecting orders, storing, and delivery and so on. The sales office is mainly responsible for collecting and transmitting orders. Apart from this, manufacturers may also set up wholesaling windows in booths and space in the trade fair and wholesale market.

3. Wholesaler Marketing Decisions

(1) Target market decisions

Wholesalers like manufacturers also need to clear their target market instead of serving everyone. They will choose a target consumer group formed by retailers according to consumer scale, consumer type, service demand or other criteria. Among the consumer group, the wholesaler can find out those profitable retailers and provide them with better products or establish good marketing relationships.

(2) Marketing-mix and service decision

The wholesaler often has to sell a full product line and maintain sufficient stock to cope with fast delivery when facing with prodigious pressure. However this will impair profit. At this time, the wholesaler should reassess how many product lines to operate will be better. ABC classification method may be used to organize his products: A stands for product or assortment of the highest profit; B stands for product or assortment of average profit; C stands for the product or the assortment of the lowest profit. In this way, the wholesaler decides the stock according to each product's profit level and the importance for the consumer. The wholesaler should also consider what service item is the most important for establishing good customer relationships and what service item should be abandoned or be charged. The key point is to find the unique service offers that the customer values most.

(3) Price decision

The wholesaler usually adopts traditional mark-up pricing, i.e., add cost plus to make up for all the other expenses. The profit of the wholesaler is relatively low and the wholesaler should seek new pricing method to shoot for new key account and cut the profit for some of the product lines. He ought to ask suppliers to offer special cut-rate supply to expand the manufacturer's sales.

(4) Promotion decision

The wholesaler mainly depends on sales personnel to meet his promotion target. As for non-personnel-promotion, the wholesaler uses some retailers to build his image. General promotion strategy should be worked out and the wholesaler should make the most of the commodity supply, assortment and (or) capital, etc. he has obtained to promote products.

(5) Place decision

The wholesaler generally sets up stores in the regions with low rent and low tax so that he can spend less on facilities and offices. Thus his material handling system and order processing system are behind the existing technology level. The advanced wholesaler has already worked on the relation of time and action in material handling process. The end result of this research is warehouse automation by entering the order into the computer; the machinery picks up various kinds of products; conveyor belt sends the product to dispatching platform; and finally it is loaded and transported together. In the process of being popularized, wholesalers handle accounting, payment, stock control and prediction by computers.

Chapter 12　Place Strategies

12.4　Summary

　　分销渠道，也称配销通路或分配渠道，是指产品(服务)从制造商手中传至消费者手中所经过的路线、途径、环节等的统称，它是促使产品或服务顺利地被使用或消费的一整套相互依存的组织。分销渠道体系中至少存在着五个流程：实物流、所有权流、付款流、信息流和促销流。分销渠道可以从各种不同的角度进行分类。根据流通环节的多少，可以将渠道划分为长渠道和短渠道；按各环节中间商数目的多少，将渠道分为宽渠道和窄渠道；根据有无中间商的介入分为直接渠道和间接渠道；按渠道成员相互联系的紧密程度，分销渠道亦可分为传统渠道和渠道系统。

　　分销渠道的设计受到顾客、产品、中间商、竞争者、公司政策等主要因素的影响。企业在设计分销渠道时，必须在理想的渠道和实际可能得到的渠道之间做出选择。一般要经由分析消费者需要、确立渠道目标、假定可供选择的主要渠道方案以及对其进行评估等几个阶段。企业还要对分销渠道进行动态管理，具体内容有：对中间商的管理、对渠道冲突的管理以及分销渠道的调整等。

　　中间商在分销渠道中起着重要作用。其中，零售商与批发商是组成分销渠道的主要机构，也是渠道中完成产品所有权转移的机构，零售商与批发商应该了解如何搞好自己的市场营销活动，从而完成由分工确定的营销职能，使企业不断得到发展。

Key Terms

　　Marketing Channel (or Distribution Channel)　Direct Marketing Channel　Exclusive Distribution　Intensive Distribution　Selective Distribution　Chain Store　Convenience Store　Shopping Center　Supermarket　Wholesaler　Agent　Discount Store　Department Store

【案例】　宝洁公司推分销新政

　　面对渠道上的窜货、假货等严重扰乱价格体系的问题，宝洁公司最近推出了分销新政。

　　新政的关键是，针对目前分销商的三类客户，即零售终端、大批发商和二级批发商，宝洁将制定出三个不同的价格区间，全国的分销商都必须按照规定的价格发货，不得逾越，否则，将受到宝洁的罚款处分，甚至取消分销资格。

　　宝洁有两大销售渠道：分销商渠道和大型连锁超市零售渠道。新政的施行，导致超市非法流出的低价产品冲击分销商渠道，两个渠道的冲突加剧。

分销新政

　　从2007年7月1日起，宝洁公司分销商对外发货执行全国统一价格。"宝洁是希望所有渠道的价格按照公司规定严格执行，现在市场价格体系有点儿乱。"一位业内人士表示：一是宝洁分销商迫于销售压力，跨区域低价窜货时有发生，扰乱了价格；二是不同价位的

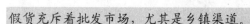

假货充斥着批发市场，尤其是乡镇渠道。

但分销商对此大都持观望态度。一位山东的分销商表示："宝洁把价格限制死了，分销商缺乏机动性。"宝洁对每一类客户的价格规定了最高、最低限价，只留3%的上下浮动区间。之前，如果有大型零售终端团购，分销商可以给 4%~5%的优惠，现在无法实行了。据一位分销商透露，有的分销商在宝洁的销售系统外，还有一本按自己价格走的账。不过宝洁的态度很坚决，公司会根据历史的销售记录，对订单明显增加的分销商进行评估，并让不同区域的分销商互相监管。

渠道冲突

在分销渠道限价后出现意外局面时，宝洁零售渠道的低价产品出现流窜，冲击了不少分销商的生意。同时，由于限价只针对分销商，直供终端如果做促销，对分销商则产生很大的压力。更严重的是，宝洁直供终端的产品还流向了分销商覆盖的批发市场。例如，河南信阳地区销售的宝洁产品60%是从武汉进货的，在这个过程中，批发商为中间人，产品从麦德龙、家乐福等大型超市流出。

据了解，宝洁分销商渠道与现代零售渠道的矛盾一直都存在，而这次限价政策使双方的冲突愈演愈烈。

(资料来源：1. www.cb.com.cn；2. www.pg.com.cn)

【案例分析】

分销渠道问题与产品销售关系重大，渠道政策直接影响分销商的积极性并进而影响产品的市场拓展，因此，企业必须制定既能调动分销商的工作热情又能以较低成本开拓市场的分销策略。否则，不恰当的分销策略将严重妨碍产品在市场上的有序流通。例如案例中宝洁公司推出的分销新政("制定出三个不同的价格区间，全国的分销商都必须按照规定的价格发货，不得逾越，否则，将受到宝洁的罚款处分，甚至取消分销资格")过于僵硬，导致渠道上的窜货、假货等盛行，严重扰乱了其价格体系。同时，宝洁的两大销售渠道是分销商渠道和大型连锁超市零售渠道。由于新政的施行，超市非法流出的低价产品冲击了分销商渠道，导致两个渠道的冲突加剧。

【思考题】

1. 宝洁公司内部一定程度上存在"轻"分销商、"重"大型零售终端的情绪，你认为这种分销策略是否合适？
2. 宝洁公司对直供的大型零售终端的影响力是否能保证其分销目标的顺利实现？
3. 试为宝洁公司设计未来的分销商政策。

Chapter 13

Promotional Strategies

Focus on:

1. Definition and types of communication.

2. Contents of the marketing communication strategy.

3. Roles of sale promotion tools in the marketing.

4. Foundation to establish the public relationship strategy and the target group of the public relationship.

5. Aims to carry out the advertisement strategy.

13.1 Generalities

13.1.1 Communication

Communication is the exchange of information between two partners. Information can be defined as purpose-orientated news and purpose-orientated knowledge.

One distinguishes between one-sided and two-sided communication. We speak of one-sided communication when information is conveyed from a sender to a recipient.

In two-sided communication, the information flow goes both ways. The sender receives feedback from the recipient as a reaction to his information. To convey his message, the sender uses a medium called "channel". In verbal communication, the channels of speech and writing are used to address the sense organs of ear and eye.

In non-verbal communication, one appeals to the senses of ear, eye, nose, and touch by means of channels such as sounds and noises, images, body and smell.

Among the media for verbal communication, there are e.g. a newspaper, book, conversation, words on a billboard.

Examples of non-verbal communication are images and, above all, body language (facial expression, gestures).

Furthermore, we can differentiate between personal communication and mass communication.

If a sender communicates with one person or a limited number of people, we call it personal communication. If the sender communicates with a large number of recipients, we call it mass communication.

13.1.2　Term "Market Communication"

New communication technologies bring about significant changes in people's conduct.

If the sender and recipient are the offerer and the potential buyer of products, we call this market communication.

In the market communication, we differentiate

(1)　Mass communication (advertising, public relations, consumer information),

(2)　Individual communication (personal sale, telephone marketing, direct mailing).

A company has a choice of the following instruments of communicative policy:

(1)　Sales Promotion;

(2)　Public Relations;

(3)　Advertising.

13.2　Sales Promotion

Strategies of sales promotion are primarily meant to optimize and influence direct contact with the customer.

Sales promotion wants to inform sales staff, intermediaries and users about the benefits of the product and influence potential customers and sales agents in such a way that they prefer the product over others.

Instruments of sales promotion are as follows:

(1)　Staff Promotion;

(2)　Merchandising;

(3)　Consumer Promotion.

13.2.1 Staff Promotion

Staff promotion consists in sales promotion strategies that are directed at one's own or other sales agents (sales staff, sales representatives, travelling agents). It can be carried out by means of written information about the product (accurate product descriptions, test results, sales pitch, sales manuals), by means of sales staff training, or by means of incentive schemes (e.g. sales competitions). Often the three options are combined. In the producer and consumer goods industry, well-founded knowledge of the product, sales pitch, techniques for a successful sales negotiation, market information (such as client conduct and competitors' conduct) form an essential part of the training of qualified sales staff for the manufacturer and dealer. Clients appreciate it when they receive thorough information and when sales staff engage with the client's individual situation and offer suggestions for problem-solving.

13.2.2 Merchandising

Merchandising consists in sales promotion strategies that are targeted towards the intermediary. Instruments of merchandising are as follows:
(1) Written information (advertisements or supplements in trade journals, mail-shots);
(2) Preferred or second position (positioning the product at eye level, positioning the product in several places at once);
(3) Display materials (price tags, shelves for leaflets, billboards advertising a special offer, cardboard figures, etc.);
(4) Propagandists (e.g. hostesses).

13.2.3 Consumer Promotion

Consumer promotion describes measures of sales promotion that are directed at the user. The consumer promotion may happen before the sale (brochures, fliers, customers' magazines, vouchers, samples, product demonstrations, competitions, etc.) or at the sale itself (free gifts, special price schemes, carrier bags, etc.).

13.3 Public Relations

13.3.1 Position of Public Relations Within the Marketing Mix

Public relations are the strategic shaping of the relationship between a company and the various sub-sections of the public with the aim of gaining this public's trust and understanding.

Public relations support and facilitate the use of the other strategic marketing instruments. But public relations and advertising represent different instruments of communicative policy.

Product advertising has the clear purpose of enhancing the sales of a specific product or product group.

Image advertising comes before the product advertising. It is meant to positively influence the appearance (image) of the company among the customers, with the aim of increasing sales in the long term.

Public relations, by contrast, do not only address the customers. Their task is to also favourably influence all other sections of the public which the company has dealings with. They want to create a clear-cut, consistent image of the company which clearly differentiates it from the competition.

To reach this aim, it is necessary to have a public relations strategy that is based on a written verbalisation of "Corporate Identity".

(1) Corporate identity: Corporate identity is a company's self-image. The image of how a company wants to be perceived by the interested segment of the public is largely determined by the company's mission statement.

(2) Corporate design: Corporate design is the visual appearance of a company in public. The creative elements of the visual appearance are as follows: Brand name, Logo, Font, Skin color, and Architecture.

In this way, it becomes possible for the company to be identified quickly. The visual appearance is associated with other experiences the public has had with the company, and both combine to shape the desired company image.

13.3.2 Target Groups of Public Relations

The major sub-segments of the public which the company has relations with are shown in

Figure 13.1:

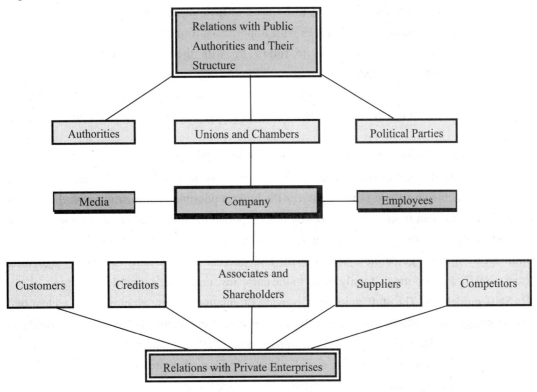

Figure 13.1 Major Sub-Segments of the Public

A strategic public relations plan has to take into consideration all of these sub-segments of the public. Specific Public Relations instruments are employed for each.

(1) Media relations: Media relations are the relations between the company and the representatives of the media (journalists). Media editors may take PR information on board without being paid for it, or they may ignore it. Through good personal relations with the representatives of the media, it becomes easier for the company to place in the media general information about itself, its successes, plans and new developments. In this context, the major PR instruments are press conferences, press releases, press events.

Press conferences: Press conferences are events to which interested journalists are invited and where the company presents information about its latest innovations, plans and decisions. The journalists are handed a written synopsis of the relevant information and are invited to ask detailed questions.

Press releases: Press releases are written summaries of interesting news, given to media representatives for their information and to be used at their discretion. On the one hand, their purpose is to supply media representatives with important information. On the other hand, they are meant to encourage the journalists to follow up with their own research and to place corresponding reports in the media.

Press events: Press events go beyond press conferences; they are spectacular events by means of which the company seeks to gain or improve the understanding and goodwill of the media.

(2) Human relations: Human relations are defined as the relations of a company to its own employees. Only if a company succeeds, through the way it shapes the relationship with its employees, in achieving among the employees the highest possible identification with the desired corporate identity, can it hope also to convey this corporate identity to other sub-segments of the public. To help reach this goal, the public relations can rely on the following means of corporate communication: staff guidelines, notice board and internal mail system, company magazines, letters to staff, works outings, family visits to the company, employee suggestion scheme.

Staff guidelines: The staff guidelines provide orientation to new employees in a clear and concise manner and inform them about the history of the company, its organisation, products and/or services. It also includes the mission statement and the most important company rules, and it contains information about available social schemes and how they are used.

Notice board and internal mail system: The notice board is used to publish the latest organizational information. Employees and union members, too, can use it to disseminate interesting information among the workforce.

Company magazines: The company magazine is meant to inform staff about all the measures and events concerning them in such a way that they feel a stronger sense of unity and gain a better understanding of the larger context in which the company operates.

Letters or e-mails to staff: Letters to staff are used to convey information of particular importance.

Works outings and works parties: Like sporting events, works outings and parties are particularly apt to improve the personal contact between management and staff.

Family visits to the company: An employee's family members can understand his worries and also his reasons for joy much better if they know his work environment. Therefore, family visits to the company premises have the potential of improving the social wellbeing of the staff, and can also serve to convey the business's corporate identity to employees' families.

Employee suggestion scheme: Within such a scheme, an employee has the opportunity to make suggestions for improving conditions and procedures in the workplace. Thus he can

Chapter 13   Promotional Strategies

participate in a manner that goes beyond his immediate sphere of action. If suggestions are acted upon and prove successful, it is crucial that the commitment of the employee is rewarded adequately.

(3) Industrial relations: Industrial relations denote the use of public relations instruments vis-à-vis all interested sub-segments of the public in private enterprise.

Among these sub-segments of the public are customers, associates or shareholders, suppliers, creditors, competitors.

Public relations vis-à-vis customers: Public relations vis-à-vis customers is defined as all activities of a company (organization) that serve the purpose of enhancing the customers' understanding of the company, and that help introduce its work to them.

This type of public relations comes very close to advertising. Its addressees must therefore be divided into target groups such as wholesalers, retailers and consumers, and these groups have to be treated individually according to their specific characteristics.

The major instruments of PR vis-à-vis the customers are correspondence and telephoning, publications, customers' magazines, factory tours, reception rooms, business reports, special service features.

Correspondence and telephoning: Correspondence, e-mail and telephone conversations have to be carried out in a winsome tone. This general rule also applies to e.g. reminders, negative replies, or when dealing with unjustified complaints. In order to ensure that the customers are treated courteously, all employees who are in contact with clients (not only the sales staff) should regularly undergo communicative training and special courses.

Publications: Besides launching positive reports in the mass media, a company may also try to elicit the trust, understanding, approval, goodwill and interest of the public by means of issuing documentaries, lectures, brochures, and even teaching materials for schools. Examples of such publications are reports to the media, documentaries, lectures, and brochures, teaching materials.

Customers' magazines: A customers' magazine reports about general developments on the respective market, new products launched by the company, the additional benefit offered by the new products, satisfied users, plans and activities of the company. Its purpose is to contribute to a climate of trust and thus promote customer loyalty.

Factory tours: The primary purpose of organizing factory tours is to demonstrate to the customers that the company is striving to uphold the highest level of technology and quality. At the same time the company may demonstrate that it adheres to rules of hygiene and to modern social standards, that measures for the prevention of accidents are in place, that there are training facilities, and similar.

Reception rooms: When a client enters the company building, he forms his first opinion of the company on the basis of the impression conveyed by the location. Therefore the company building should express the desired corporate identity in a visual and emotive form. The same applies to the portal and the factory premises.

Business reports: Business reports should have a good layout and enable clients, shareholders, creditors and journalists alike to gather essential information about business progress, company goals, and successes achieved.

Special service features: Special service features are customer services of any kind that go beyond the mere satisfaction of needs by the delivery of the goods and the customary services connected with this. Among them there are e.g. brochures with nutritional advice which the retailers can distribute to the buyers, and company sports facilities that are also open to the public.

Public relations vis-à-vis shareholders: Public relations vis-à-vis the shareholders or associates comprises all activities aiming to foster the shareholders' and associates' trust in the company's managing board. This type of PR attempts to raise awareness for the problems facing the management and the solutions proffered. The objective is to engender and sustain loyalty and trust that the chosen corporate strategy is right.

For instance, a managing board solicitous to maintain good relations with its shareholders will not limit information flow to the business report and general meeting, but will supply the shareholders with progress reports and information about important decisions that are imminent.

The most important instruments of public relations vis-à-vis shareholders are business reports, general meetings, progress reports, correspondence, preference share offers, documentary materials, factory tours and special events.

Public relations vis-à-vis suppliers and creditors: Public relations vis-à-vis suppliers and creditors comprise all of a company's activities serving to foster the trust and readiness for co-operation among these two sub-segments of the public. Most of the PR instruments described above can be employed here. A well-written business report can satisfy the belief of suppliers and creditors in the financial power of the business.

Public relations vis-à-vis competitors: Public relations vis-à-vis the competitors comprises all of the activities of a company which serve to achieve relations with the competitors that are the most conducive to realizing the company targets.

(4) Public relations with public authorities: Public relations vis-à-vis public authorities describe all of the activities of a company which serve to create good relations with public authorities. Public authorities are authorities of the state, political parties, unions and chambers.

As a prerequisite of good relations with the authorities, national regulations must be strictly adhered to so that a genuine relationship of trust can develop. The most important PR instruments towards authorities are personal contact, donations, sponsorship, foundations, continuous information.

Personal contact facilitates every kind of engagement with an authority. Donations, sponsorship and foundations are used above all to cultivate the relations with local authorities. They clearly show the joint interests and mutual interdependence.

The work of authorities is made easier if they receive continuous information about company policy, the expansion of social schemes, and workforce planning. Thus trust is strengthened. The relations with political parties are of particular importance because it is the parties that take crucial legislative decisions. Through continuous exchange of information, companies endeavour to create a political climate that is favourable to them.

For small and medium-sized enterprises, this type of PR may consist mainly in creating and maintaining good relations with their own professional association or the respective sub-body within the professional chamber. These then represent their members' interests vis-à-vis the political parties and the authorities in charge.

13.4 Advertising

Advertising is the deliberate, well-directed and cost-incurring employment of special communicative means with the aim of influencing customers. From this follows that advertising must not be a creative act alone. Instead, it has to be planned strategically and integrated in the overall marketing strategy. Above all, one should never engage in advertising without first having achieved clarity about the advertising objectives. Many managers disobey this rule when they decide to spend a good deal of money on advertising but have thought little about the actual objectives. The objective of sales advertising is to trigger positive reactions to the company's products or the company itself in the customers. In this respect we distinguish between product advertising and company advertising (image advertising).

It is important to bear in mind that every communicative utterance of the company reflects back on its image. Therefore product and image advertising, as well as all other communicative measures (e.g. product and packaging design, branding, stationery, etc.), have to be in tune with each other. The aim is to create a consistent, unambiguous corporate appearance, the so-called Corporate Identity.

13.4.1 Media Concept

The media concept consists of advertising objectives and advertising strategy, as well as their creative implementation in a bundle of communicative measures targeted towards influencing the clientele. The media concept can be characterised by posing the following questions:

(1) Who   (company, advertiser)
(2) Says what   (advertising message)
(3) Why   (advertising objectives)
(4) Under what circumstances   (environmental situation)
(5) Via which channels   (media, advertising vehicles)
(6) How   (advertising material)
(7) When   (timing)
(8) To whom   (target person, recipient, target group)
(9) At what cost   (advertising budget)
(10) To what effect   (advertising effectiveness)

If a company wants to keep the cost of its media concept (i.e. the ratio between advertising effort and advertising effect) to a minimum, it must solve systematically and unequivocally the questions raised while working out the media concept. Therefore advertising cannot be the result of an (accidental) creative idea, but must be planned strategically step by step as follows:

(1) Working out the advertising objectives;
(2) Working out the advertising strategy;
(3) Creative implementation of advertising objectives and strategy;
(4) Budgeting and implementation of the media concept;
(5) Reviewing advertising effectiveness.

13.4.2 Determining the Advertising Objectives

As a first step, in an analysis of the initial situation, internal and external framework must be determined. The internal framework of advertising results from the overall marketing strategy. It consists of basic information supplied by marketing planning, overall marketing concept, marketing objectives, as well as the marketing strategy and, in particular, the creative conceptual idea contained in it.

Chapter 13   Promotional Strategies

Besides, the following external framework has to be taken into account: advertising activities of the competition, results of media analyses, customers' buying and information patterns (socio-psychological principles of advertising).

The advertising objectives indicate the results one wants to reach by means of the advertising strategy. These results are ultimately defined in terms of the economic factors of turnover and profit, but they are preceded by the communicative implementation of marketing strategy (see Figure 13.2).

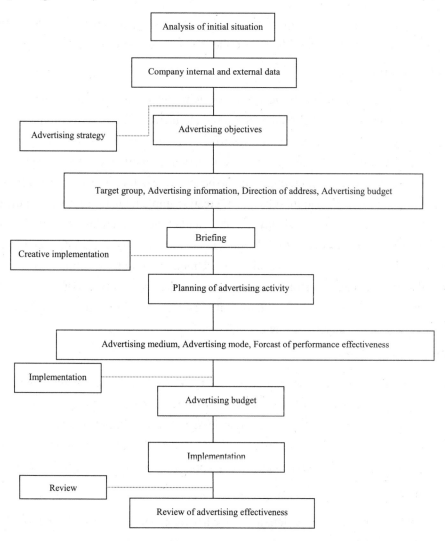

Figure 13.2   Communicative Implementation of Marketing Strategy

13.4.3 Advertising Strategy

On the basis of the advertising objectives, the advertising strategy determines the target group, advertising message, direction of address, and advertising budget. The result of advertising strategy is the briefing.

1. Target Group

We call target group the group of people the advertising message wants to address. For efficient advertising, it is indispensable to describe the target group clearly.

2. Advertising Message

Advertising message is the basic argument with which a company wants to gain the attention and goodwill of potential buyers and motivate them to purchase its products. By means of the advertising message, the company tries to express poignantly its marketing idea and the services which it wants to offer its buyers. The technical properties of the product take a back seat here, because the focus is on highlighting the benefit (the solution to a problem) for the user.

The advertising message and its subsequent creative implementation are used to differentiate the product clearly from others already on the market and to endow the product with an unmistakable profile. The aim is to find the unique characteristic of the product and to highlight this characteristic. In this connection we talk of the Unique Selling Proposition (USP).

The following main components of the USP have to be taken into account: every advertising medium must communicate a claim to the user; it must be a claim that the competition cannot or does not make; the claim must be strong enough to affect the target group.

3. Direction of Address

The direction of address is the framework for the creation of concrete advertising materials (text and image). For instance, with a product that requires a good deal of explanation, it may be necessary to put more emphasis on text than on image. The specific characteristics of the target group, too, can influence the direction of address. For example, a young, progressive and urban target group requires a different textual and visual approach than an older, conservative group.

4. Funds Allocated to Advertising

One of the major problems is determining what financial means to allocate to advertising. Basically there are two ways of doing this: creating an advertising account and creating an advertising budget.

Chapter 13 Promotional Strategies

The advertising account is the sum set aside for an advertising strategy in a specific period of time. The advertising account represents a financial restriction.

The advertising budget, on the other hand, is the advertising plan evaluated in terms of money. The amount of advertising budget is determined by the advertising objectives and the measures required.

5. Advertising Briefing

Briefing is the basic information which the advertising agency (or department) receives from the company (or marketing department) as a foundation on which to build the creative advertising campaign. Every advertising agency can tell you how poor the information flow coming from marketing experts is. The marketing experts have ideas in their heads about how they want to reach their objectives, but these ideas are not clearly put down on paper. The advertising expert therefore has to work hard trying to understand what others have thought up in over several months. This leads to repeated rejections and reviews.

A thorough and useful briefing should contain the following data:

(1) General market situation
- Representation of the general market and the sub-market
- Market development
- Market shares
- Survey of the most important goods and their major properties.

(2) General advertising situation
- Company's own activities so far
- Activities of the competition so far
- Current product image
- Current market positioning

The activities (one's own as well as those of the competition) should be defined in terms of budgeting, media, and quality.

(3) Involved decision-makers and co-ordinators
- in the company
- in the agency

(4) General situation of the end user
- Degree of saturation and penetration
- Socio-demographic structure of the owners and potential buyers.

(5) Goals
- Corporate mission statement

- General commercial and marketing-related objectives (sales, profit, market share, profit margin)
- Definition of sub-goals to be reached by means of advertising

The goals should be defined both short- and long-term.

(6) Target group

- Psychological and socio-demographic definition of the people to be reached (exact description of the group)

(7) Clues for the advertising strategy

- Time schedule of the campaign; Timing
- Media
- Existing results of market research
- Possible product benefits
- Central advertising message (USP)

(8) Marketing policy besides advertising

- Sketching all other marketing instruments (price, product, distributive organization, activities, sales promotion, service, etc.)

(9) Advertising account

Every dissemination plan needs to be adjusted to the resources available. This is usually an internal discussion during which the advertising expert has to stipulate minimum requirements. If available funds fall below a specific absolute value, an implementation no longer makes sense.

(10) Time schedule

Advertising activities are projects which necessitate a proper network planning technique – not only for one's own benefit, but also with a view to the continuous information of the internal departments.

(11) Performance review

Investments require supervision, and so does advertising expenditure. Have the proposed objectives been attained? If not, what is the deviance? The results in their turn inform future activities. The effectiveness of any creative advertising work grows if the briefing is as accurate as possible. Only in this manner can it be warranted that the creative work goes in the right direction and does not cut itself loose.

13.4.4 Advertising Media

An advertising medium is the representation of the advertising message which replaces or reinforces the personal contact between advertiser and target group. Since not all of the various advertising media are equally suited for a specific advertising message, one must make a choice from among the available media. For the advertising media selected, one must then make decisions about factors to be employed.

Starting from the style and manner of individual advertising media, we can distinguish between the following groups of advertising media:

(1) Media of mass advertising

(2) Media of direct advertising

1. Media of Mass Advertising

We talk of media of mass advertising when the target are consumers whose properties as a target group are known. These consumers are approached with the help of the mass media.

There are the following instruments of mass advertising:

(1) TV spots

(2) Movie advertising

(3) Radio spots

(4) Advertisements

(5) Slides

(6) Outdoor advertising

(7) Packaging advertising

2. Media of Direct Advertising

We talk of media of direct advertising when potential buyers are addressed whose target group characteristics as well as personal addresses are known. They can therefore be approached without having to resort to the mass media.

The advantages of direct advertising are as follows:

(1) Absolute accuracy: The addresses for mail shots etc. can be obtained from publishers of addresses, from the Yellow Pages and name registers. The target group is approached directly and the advertising medium selected is attuned to the needs of this group.

(2) Spontaneous employment: When addresses are known, the advertising medium can be employed at any time. No standby time has to be factored in.

(3) Sustainable effect: Catalogues and brochures in particular are often kept for a longer period of time and can help make the decision at the actual time of purchase.

(4) Versatility: There are hardly any limits as to contents, design, point of time or duration. Only the postal service operates with restrictions regarding size and format.

(5) Cost advantage: If one compares the number of reactions to mass advertising with

those to direct advertising, at equal employment of funds, the number can be larger with direct advertising.

(6) Performance review: Since measures of direct advertising are usually accompanied by coupons, vouchers and order forms, the success of the activity is easy to measure.

3. Choice of Advertising Media

Advertising media are those media (persons, objects) that convey the advertising message via a specific advertising mode to the target group. The choice of advertising media and mode of advertising is therefore closely connected. The choice for one entails the choice of the other. The following advertising media as shown in Table 13.1 may be used:

Table 13.1 Advertising Media

Modes of Advertising	Advertising Media
TV spot	Television
Movie advertising	Cinema
Radio spot	Radio
Advertisement	Newspapers, magazines
Slide	Cinema
Outdoor advertising	Billboards, pillars, facades of buildings, gables, cars
Packaging advertising	Packaging
Direct advertising	Mail, distributors of flyers, sales personnel, customer service representatives

Product placement and sponsoring: Product placement and sponsoring offer additional new ways of carrying out advertising activities for products and businesses.

Product placement means that specific products are presented in TV broadcasts or other media so that a positive communicative effect for the product and/or company is created. For the viewer, the situation is different from "normal" advertising spots in so far as the advertising intention is not highlighted. Product placement wants to increase not only the familiarity with a product but also, and above all, the identification with the actors and the products they are using so that in the long run the viewers will begin to copy the actors and buy the products. The reasons for the success of product placement are, among others

(1) the relatively high cost of "classic" advertising;

(2) the relatively low cost of product placement;

(3) higher credibility than advertising;

Chapter 13 Promotional Strategies

(4) longer time of contact with customers;

(5) different kind of effect;

(6) can reach people who do not watch adverts.

With sponsoring, the sponsor provides money and/or material expenses destined to contribute to the attaining of marketing objectives. Sponsoring is possible for all areas of communicative policy (advertising, sales promotion and public relations).

The beneficiaries of sponsoring are e.g.

(1) Sportsmen and -women, sports teams, sporting events (sport sponsoring),

(2) Theatre, music, the fine arts, literature (cultural sponsoring),

(3) Social institutions and events (social sponsoring).

Research into Advertising Media:

Net Coverage: Each issue of an advertising media that is sold or distributed for free reaches not only the buyer or recipient but beyond that also a number of other people called co-readers. Therefore, the overall number of people reached by the medium (= net coverage of the advertising medium) consists of the number of circulated issues plus co-readers. For the net coverage we also use the term "readers per issue" (RPI).

Gross Coverage: If modes of advertising are used in several media (media combinations), it may happen that the target person is reached by several media at the same time. In this case we talk of media interference. The ranges of coverage of the individual media added together result in the Gross Coverage. The Net Coverage can also be determined by subtracting from Gross Coverage the people who were in contact with several media ("multiple recipients").

Interference Coefficient: The interference coefficient can be calculated by dividing Gross Coverage by Net Coverage.

Cumulated range of circulation: If one advertising medium is used several times in a row, the number of people reached becomes larger than indicated by the Net Coverage, because with every additional posting more people are targeted (accretion of coverage). The result is cumulating or a cumulated range of circulation of the advertising medium.

Media analysis: In media analysis, the consumer and media habits of a number of target groups are examined. For example, media analysis may try to find out the target groups that are interested in gardening and which media they use. The advantage of this is that the advertising planner knows which media to book in case he wants to address e.g. gardening devotees. Media analysis examines the press, radio and television. The benefit is that after successful identification of the target groups, one can determine the media with which to reach these groups.

Since enterprises have limited advertising funds at their disposal, they may not be able to make use of all advertising media that are appropriate for the target groups. The advertising budget has to be divided up among the eligible media. This procedure is called media planning. It is concerned with ascertaining the advertising media that are suitable for communication with the target group. On the basis of the results, the advertising media are selected (media selection). Media selection aims to establish a media plan that can achieve the best possible effect with the given advertising budget.

The main factors influencing media selection are as follows:

(1) Spatial coverage (e.g. how many people living in a province can be reached via the advertising medium?)

(2) Temporal availability (e.g. limited advertising time on TV)

(3) Quantitative coverage (e.g. Net Coverage, Gross Coverage, cumulated range of coverage)

(4) Qualitative coverage (strength of target group in relation to overall readership)

(5) Usage fees

The main determinant for media selection is cost per thousand (CPT) which is calculated as follows:

$$CPT = \frac{Price\ of\ an\ advertising\ page\ *\ 1,000}{Circulation}$$

Cost per thousand becomes more meaningful if circulation is replaced by readership per issue (net coverage).

$$CPT = \frac{Price\ of\ an\ advertising\ page\ *\ 1,000}{Readership\ per\ Issue}$$

A further option is to consider only that segment of the readership is part of the target group.

$$CPT = \frac{Price\ of\ an\ advertising\ page\ *\ 1,000}{Readership\ per\ Issue\ *\ Qualitative\ Coverage/100}$$

13.4.5 Service Enterprises of Advertising

Service enterprises of advertising are autonomous enterprises as well as freelancers who take over advertising tasks. These tasks may involve the following:

(1) Support with establishing an advertising concept
- Marketing and advertising consultants: providing advice for the working out of the marketing and advertising concept.
- Market research institutes: supplying customer-related data for the creation of the

Chapter 13 Promotional Strategies

advertising message and for performance review and prognosis.
- Market research institutes specializing in media data: providing data about reading, listening and viewing behaviour.
- Media observation institutes: analysing the competitors' advertising.

(2) Performing specific parts of the creative implementation
- Designers and producers of modes of advertising (graphic artists, copy-writers, repro institutes, printers, designers, advertising photographers, film and sound studios)
- Advertising brokers: arrange advertising media in the course of the dissemination plan
- Advertising media: broad spread of advertising through daily newspapers, magazines, TV and radio stations, bill boarding businesses, postal service, cinema advertising companies, etc.
- Address finder businesses and institutes for direct advertising: procurement of personal addresses of the selected target group

(3) The overall planning, design, distribution and review of advertising concepts
- Advertising agencies

The list shows that there is a variety of advertising service enterprises, which, according to their degree of specialization, may take charge of specific subtasks or of the overall implementation.

(4) The core questions to be addressed by businesses using advertising are
- Should an internal advertising department be installed?
- Should an agency be hired at all, or should only a few subtasks be outsourced?
- If one decides to hire an agency, how does one select the right one?

A. Internal advertising department

An internal advertising department is advantageous if
- the enterprise is large enough to bear the operating costs of such a department;
- advertising budgets are relatively high;
- advertising is a continuous remit;
- the product ranges are so diverse that an internal department is required to attune all advertising statements with the joint corporate identity;
- the emphasis of the advertising efforts is put on technical brochures for which a thorough knowledge of the products is required.

The cons of internal advertising departments are
- very high current costs such as can only be borne by a larger company;
- the implicit danger that the creativity of the internal department gets stuck in a rut and thus fails to lead to innovation.

Very large and advertising-intense corporations (e.g. manufacturers of washing detergents, cigarettes, cosmetic, and beverages) therefore frequently choose a middle course, i.e. they install their own advertising agency which develops the advertising objectives and strategies and co-ordinates and reviews the advertising activities. However, the creative implementation of the concept is outsourced to an external advertising agency.

B. Employment of an advertising agency

Before a business hires an advertising agency it should ask itself the following questions:

- Do the tasks really require an agency?
- Can the advertising budget cover the cost of hiring an agency? The costs comprise the fees for the developing of modes of advertising, for the brokerage and surveillance of other outsourced services, and for the agency's own work (market research, sales promotion, public relations). Furthermore, the media pay the agencies a commission. In case of larger budgets, the agency uses the media commission to cover the cost of creating the modes of advertising.
- Is the company willing to share a good deal of internal information with the agency?
- Should only subtasks be outsourced or should the agency develop the whole concept?
- Is it a non-recurring advertising activity or does one aim to co-operate in a long-term advertising strategy?

Experience shows that even in cases of smaller advertising budgets, it can be rewarding to make use of (smaller) advertising agencies because they possess creative potential that should not be underestimated.

C. Choice of suitable advertising agencies

When choosing a suitable advertising agency, three crucial questions have to be answered:

- The most important factor when choosing an agency is its creativity, because as a rule the advertiser co-operates with an agency exactly because he wants to benefit from its creative talent.
- Second, the agency must be user- and target-group orientated.
- Third, the agency must be able to fulfil exactly the tasks with which the advertiser requires support.

13.5 Summary

促销指企业用一定的手段说服、促进和引导顾客购买某种商品或服务并使顾客对商品或服务产生好感的行为或活动。企业在实施促销活动中，常采取的策略主要有销售促进、公共关系的沟通以及广告等。

Chapter 13 Promotional Strategies

销售促进可以通过人员推销、中介推广以及消费者促进等手段实现产品或服务的宣传与销售。公共关系沟通既包括宏观公共关系的沟通，又包括微观公共关系的沟通，前者主要指与政府当局、工会和社会团体以及金融机构等的沟通，后者主要包括与员工、股东、客户、供应商以及竞争者等利益相关者的沟通。广告作为一种传递企业及其产品信息的重要手段，是企业普遍重视且广为应用的促销方式。电视、杂志以及网络等各种媒体是广告得以迅速发展的重要工具。广告策略旨在确立受众群体、广告信息内容以及广告预算等主要问题。

Key Terms

Communication   Market Communication   Staff Promotion   Merchandising   Consumer Promotion   Public Relations   Advertising   Media   Advertising Media

【案例】 一次失败的广告策划——巩俐所做的"盖中盖"广告

曾有一段时间，数家电视台轮番播出一则广告：一封展开的信，纯真的童音在朗诵："巩俐阿姨，你寄给我们希望小学的'盖中盖'口服液，现在同学们都在喝……"画面上巩俐在捧读孩子们的感谢信，接着是朱唇轻启，曼声道出一句："盖中盖口服液，真是不错。"广告播出后，立即在全国掀起轩然大波。

任何广告对企业所起到的作用有两个层次：从表面上看，是提高了企业的知名度；从深层次上看，是提高了企业的美誉度。但知名度不一定等于美誉度，二者不一定成正比，知名度的提高并不代表美誉度的提高。通过近年来大量的广告投放，哈尔滨制药六厂(简称"哈药六厂")本来已经有了很高的知名度，但经过巩俐广告事件之后，由巨额广告费堆积出来的知名度可能会变成负面的知名度，现在看来，哈药六厂正想法取消这样的负面影响，但一般稍有思想的人都不会轻易谅解这种做法。

具体地说，巩俐向希望小学赠送"盖中盖"口服液这件事是假的，是属于一次营销策划行为，是十足的商业运作。退一步讲，即使巩俐确实向希望小学赠送了一些"盖中盖"口服液，对哈药六厂来说也无多大意义。这样的行为应该当作一项公益行为来策划。当作商业行为来运作就会与公益行为产生冲突，一旦到了这一地步，那么知名度越高，美誉度就越低，而美誉度是企业立足市场的根本。

(资料来源：曹刚，李桂陵，王德发等. 国内外市场营销案例. 武汉：武汉大学出版社，2003.)

【案例分析】

哈药六厂的这次广告行为明显属于一种社会营销行为，既然是社会营销行为，就涉及社会伦理问题，在这方面无论是广告主、广告公司还是发布媒体都必须十分谨慎。

根据国际惯例，一些涉及社会伦理的营销行为是不涉及金钱的，例如反腐败、禁毒等问题，各国都有一些明星参与宣传，但都是一种义务行为，明星本人并不从这种行为中得到报酬。巩俐为哈药六厂所做的涉及希望工程的广告之所以在社会上引起如此巨大的反响，是由于这种社会营销行为明显是一种商业运作，而这种运作与希望工程这一公益事业联系在一起，必然引起预料中的麻烦。

作为明星，也存在一个品牌维护问题，他参与社会公益行为或商业运作都会给他的形象带来正面或负面的影响。在这次广告风波中，巩俐不能说此事与她无关，她应该考虑，为什么做别的广告时没有人找她的麻烦，而唯独这次做药品广告才引起这么大的风波？这一事件的出现也同时促使明星们反省，做任何广告时是不是都要考虑一下其带来的后果？

巩俐广告事件表明了哈药六厂的一贯做法，就是利用名人效应进行营销，但明星效应要和社会效益结合起来才会有效果。广告策划者如果换一个角度思考，将广告投入的一半捐献给希望工程，建一批希望小学，并请巩俐做形象大使的话，就可以达到既有明星效应又有社会效益的目的，也完全可以解决广告受众与目标消费人群不一致的矛盾。

【思考题】
1. 选择广告代言人时应注意哪些问题？
2. 成功的广告策划具有哪些特点？
3. 你认为这则广告应怎样修改？
4. "巩俐广告事件"给我们以何启示？

Part V Relative Marketing Issues

Chapter 14

Marketing Management

Focus on:

1. Definition and roles of the marketing plan.
2. Types of the marketing organization and how to reengineer it.
3. Control approaches of marketing activities.
4. Contents and basic methods of marketing audit.

14.1 Marketing Planning

14.1.1 Generalities

Marketing plans refer to the detailed marketing tactics and steps. They are established on the base of studying the current marketing conditions such as market conditions, product conditions, competitive conditions, distribution conditions and macro-environmental conditions, etc. and mainly include strategic ones and tactical ones. The former generally lasts three or five years while the latter means the concrete activities that must be carried out within a year for the purpose of implementing the strategic plans.

14.1.2 Basic Process in Developing the Marketing Plan

The marketing plan of a company should be established in analyzing the marketing opportunities and threats, its advantages and disadvantages, determining its marketing aims. Also, the company's aims and the departments' target ought to be well coordinated. Besides, the fixed plans must be able to be implemented and controlled (see Figure 14.1).

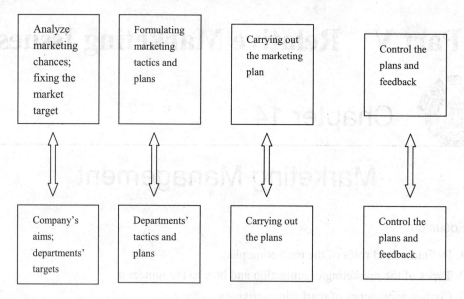

Figure 14.1　Basic Process of Developing the Marketing Plan

14.2　Marketing Organization

　　The marketing plan needs being implemented by certain organizations and requires the relative departments to input the resources into the marketing activities. The marketing department is a functional one to carry out the plan and serve the customer. Enterprises should pay much attention to the construction of the marketing organization. In general, marketing organizations can be divided into two main types: professional marketing organizations and structured marketing organizations.

14.2.1　Professional Marketing Organizations

　　The professional marketing organization includes the following four types: the functional organization, the product organization, the market-based organization and the district-based organization.

　　In the functional organization (see Figure 14.2), marketing activities are focuses, and advertising, product management and research functions are of less importance. This form of organization has the advantage of being easy to be managed. With the increase in the product variety and market expansion, the uneven development and the issues difficult to be coordinated may happen to this organizational form. Firstly, there will be some product or market planning imperfect conditions; Secondly, the functional units are trying to demand that their departments have been more important than the others, which may make coordination between the various functional departments more and more difficult.

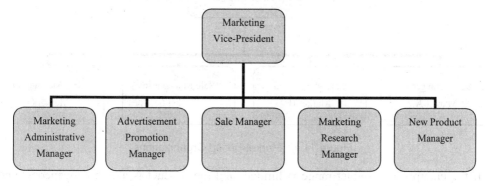

Figure 14.2 The Functional Organization

In the product-based organizations, business product strategy is embodied in setting goals, developing product marketing plans, pricing, advertising, promotion, and crisis management. Different products need different management style and content (see Figure 14.3).

Figure 14.3 Product Management Organizations

The market-based organization (see Figure 14.4) is to meet the various kinds of customers' needs, which will help enterprises to increase sales and raise the marketing capacities. Its disadvantage is that there exist ambiguous division of responsibilities and some contradictions. Besides, in order to serve more and more diversified customers' needs, enterprises must employ a large number of sale staffs.

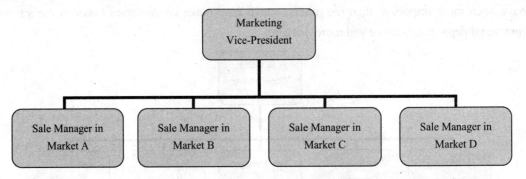

Figure 14.4 Market-Based Organizations

If the enterprise's product range is limited, and the product is also homogeneous, and the need able to cover many areas quickly, the district-based organization can be used (see Figure 14.5).

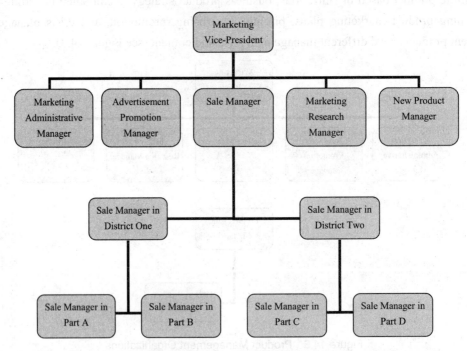

Figure 14.5 District-Based Organizations

14.2.2 Structural Marketing Organizations

The structured marketing organization means various marketing organizational systems formed on the interrelationships among the different marketing organizations and functions inside the enterprise.

The structural marketing organization system comprises four categories:

1. Vertical Organizations

It means a kind of organization of which the communication is from the manager to the general staff and the relationship between them is vertical. It is characterized by clear lines of authority and responsibility, and its communication is rapid and more efficient. The framework of the organizational structure is just like a pyramid.

2. Matrix Organizations

It integrates the features of vertical and horizontal organizations in marketing and managing the organization. Its structure is similar to the matrix form.

3. Division Organizations

Different products or regions are regarded as independent accounting units and they can be divided into different institutions. This structure is known as the division system.

4. Project Management Organizations

The business case is based on specific projects set by the marketing manager so as to complete the temporary project task. This structure is also called the project management system.

14.3 Marketing Control

Marketing control means that the marketing manager often checks the implementation of the marketing plan so as to test the adaptability of the plan to the actual performance and to take the corresponding measures to revise the plan.

14.3.1 Annual-Plan Control

Check the actual performance and the business plan if there are any deviations, and then the improving measures to ensure the implementation of annual marketing plans will be taken.

The main purpose of the annual plan control is to (1) ensure continuous production; (2) ensure that results controlled can be used as the basis for annual performance evaluation; (3) help companies resolve potential problems; (4) help the senior management to effectively monitor all departments' work.

Corporate managers may use three ways: sales analysis, financial analysis, tracking customer attitude.

1. Sales Analysis

Sales analysis is mainly used to measure and assess the relationship between the actual sales and the sales objectives that the managers have developed. Usually there are two main methods: market share analysis and marketing expenses and sales ratio analysis. The former means that the company's market share increase indicates that it lies in a better market situation than its competitors; otherwise, a worse situation. The latter refers to those ratios between the expenses of the sales team and the sales volume, between the advertisement cost and the sales volume, between the promotion expenses and the sales volume, and between the sales management expenses and the sales volume, and so on.

2. Financial Analysis

Marketing managers should conduct a comprehensive financial analysis to determine how and where to start business activities for the purpose of obtaining profits. In particular, the financial analysis is used to determine the factors affecting the rate of return of the corporate capital net value.

3. Tracking Customer Attitude

Enterprises need to establish a system to track the attitude of their customers, dealers and other market participants. If you find that the attitude of the customers to your products and your company is changing, business managers must take early action to gain the initiative. Enterprises generally use such systems as complaint and suggestion system, fixed customer samples, customer survey, etc. to track customers' attitude.

14.3.2 Profitability Capacity Control

Enterprises need adopt the profitability capacity control to evaluate the capacities to obtain the profit of different products, different sales regions, different customer groups, different channels and different order sizes. The information got by the profitability capacity control can help managers determine which products or marketing activities are to be expanded, reduced or

Chapter 14 Marketing Management

canceled.

1. Marketing Costs

Marketing costs directly affect corporate profits. They mainly comprise direct promotion costs such as salary, award, training expenses of sales personnel; promotion expenses such as advertisement costs, exposition costs, etc.; inventory costs and transportation expenses, and so on.

2. Indicators Evaluating the Profitability Capacity

The indicators that are often used to evaluate the profitability capacity include profit ratio of sales, return on assets, returns on equity (ROE), and asset management efficiency.

Profit ratio of sales = profits of the current period/ sales volume *100%

Return on assets = profits of the current period/ average asset total *100%

Returns on equity = after-tax profits/average net asset balance *100%

Asset management efficiency can be indicated by asset turnover, stock turnover, and so on.

Asset turnover = net sales returns of products/average asset use volume

Stock turnover = product sale costs/average stock balance

14.3.3 Efficiency Control

The profitability capacity control reflects the profit situation of a certain product, region or market while the efficiency control shows us whether the company manages its sales persons, advertisements, promotion and distribution with high efficiency.

1. Sales Person Efficiency Indicators

These indicators mainly include average daily sales visits for each salesman; the average visiting time; average revenue per sales visit; the average cost per sales visit; hospitality costs per sales visit; order percentage per hundred sales visit; the number of new customers per period; the number of customers lost per period; percentage of marketing costs / total sales.

2. Advertising Efficiency Indicators

The indicators refer to the following: advertisement costs needed by a thousand buyers for each mass medium; percentage of attention, association and reading to each mass medium by customers; customers' idea to the advertisement content and effects; attitudes to the product before and after the advertisement; inquiry times caused by the advertisement.

3. Promoting Efficiency Indicators

The promoting efficiency indicators aim at recording the sales promoting costs and their influence on sales. The concrete indicators include sales percentage from privilege; exhibition costs for each sale; percentage of gift coupon return; inquiry times caused by demonstration.

4. Distribution Efficiency

The distribution efficiency mainly analyzes and improves the stock level, the warehouse position, and the transportation mode so as to optimize the resources allocation and to seek for the best transportation mode.

The efficiency control aims at raising the efficiency of marketing activities such as personnel promotion, advertisement, sales promotion and distribution. Marketing managers should concern the above indicators in order to upgrade the validity of the marketing mix factors and the implementation of the marketing plan.

14.4 Marketing Audit

Marketing audit is to make a comprehensive, systematic, independent and periodic check to the marketing environment, targets, strategy, organization, methods, process and business, etc. so as to locate where difficulties and opportunities are and to improve the marketing plan and the management effectiveness. Actually, the marketing audit is also a complete evaluation to the whole marketing business of the firm and its main feature is to assess the total marketing activities and not to limit some issues.

14.4.1 Characteristics of Marketing Audit

1. Systematic

Marketing audit is a systematic process: first, determine the audit objectives and audit methodology; then determine the organizational form, personnel labor division and the breadth and depth of resources involved, the report form, beginning and ending time.

2. Comprehensive

Business activities of a comprehensive marketing audit aim at finding the real cause marketing problems more effectively.

3. Diversified

Various ways can be used in the marketing audit, such as internal audit, external audit and cross-auditing.

4. Institutional

Marketing audit should be conducted regularly to form a system of regular audits. It is necessary either for the company in normal development or for the one which lies in a very poor business situation.

14.4.2 Contents of Marketing Audit

1. Macro-Environmental Audit

Macro-environmental audit refers to the audit to the population, economic, cultural, technological, political and natural environment.

2. Micro-Environmental Audit

Micro-environmental audit refers to the audit to customers, competitors, distributors, suppliers, the company, and public relations.

3. Marketing Strategy Audit

Marketing strategy audit refers to the audit to the new product development strategy, marketing goals and objectives, marketing strategy, and so on.

4. Marketing Management System Audit

Marketing management system audit refers to the audit to marketing control systems, marketing planning systems and marketing information systems.

5. Marketing Efficiency Audit

Marketing efficiency audit means checking the profitability and costs of the marketing.

6. Marketing Mix Factors Audit

Marketing mix factors audit is to check the status of the product, price, distribution and promotion, and sales team.

Through regular audits, the company can detect the problems in the marketing in time and put forward improvement proposals and the foundation for formulating and revising the corporate marketing strategy, and constantly raise the marketing skills.

14.5 Summary

市场营销管理包括市场营销计划、市场营销组织、市场营销控制和市场营销审计多项活动。市场营销管理中，计划是出发点，其目的就是把各项营销活动结合起来。为了实现企业目标，企业必须选择建立合适的市场营销组织。市场营销计划的执行能否取得理想的成效，还需要看控制工作进行得如何。进入20世纪70年代后，许多工商企业开始从单纯关注利润和效率发展到全面核查经营战略、年度计划和市场营销组织，高瞻远瞩地改善企业经营管理和更有效地扩大经济效果。他们对市场营销活动的核查范围逐步扩大，确立了核查标准并采用计分办法加以评估。市场营销审计开始成熟，并逐步发展成为加强市场营销管理的一个有效工具，从而为市场营销理论增添了新的篇章。

Key Terms

Marketing Plan   Marketing Audit   Marketing Control   Marketing Organization

【案例】娃哈哈集团市场营销过程控制

杭州娃哈哈集团公司前身是杭州市上城区的一家校办企业，成立于1987年。经过近20年的发展，公司已经发展成为在全国十省市建有40余家全资或控股子公司、总资产40多亿元的中国最大食品饮料企业，其主导产品"娃哈哈"果奶、AD钙奶、纯净水和营养八宝粥的销量稳居全国第一，其中乳酸奶饮料、瓶装饮用水的产销量已跻身世界前列。取得如此辉煌成绩，娃哈哈独特的营销策略是其驰骋市场成功的关键，本案例分析了娃哈哈市场营销链的控制方法、解决冲货问题的策略以及营销体制等方面的问题。

一、控制与促销

(1) 对"最后一公里"的营销概念的理解各异，有的说是服务，有的说是质量，有的说是品牌，而娃哈哈却认为是"利益的有序分配"。有序必然就要有控制，控制在营销渠道中最重要的就是价差、区域、品种和节奏。

(2) 价差指的是产品从厂家到消费者手中经过的所有批零通路。就饮料、家电等产品而言，一般有3~4个环节之间的利益分配。有序地分配各级经销层次的利益空间，不但是生产商的责任，更是其控制市场的关键所在。

(3) 娃哈哈认为，生产商推出任何一项促销活动或政策，首先应该考虑的便是设计一套层次分明、分配合理的价差体系。

(4) 娃哈哈的促销重点是经销商，公司会根据一定阶段内的市场变动、竞争对手的异动以及自身产品的配备，而推出各种各样的促销政策，常年循环，月月如此。针对经销商的促销政策，既可以激发其积极性，又保证了各级销售商的利润，因而可以做到促进销售而不扰乱整个市场的价格体系。

二、冲货与竞争

(1) 区域冲货问题，是所有企业面临的共同问题，娃哈哈也不能避免。娃哈哈成立了一个专门的机构，巡回全国，专门查处冲货的经销商，其处罚之重为业界少有。一旦发现编号与地区不符，便要彻查到底。

(2) 彻底解决冲货问题的治根之策，是要严格分配和控制好各级经销商的势力半径。一方面充分保护其在本区域内的销售利益，另一方面则严禁其对外倾销。娃哈哈精选合作对象，从众多的经销商中发展、扶植大客户，同时有意识地划小经销商的辐射半径，促使其精耕细作，挖掘本区域市场的潜力。

(3) 对于竞争，娃哈哈则体现出作为一家成熟的市场强势企业的自信和能力。运用"弹钢琴"的策略：当对手以低价策略进行市场抢夺的时候，娃哈哈往往不会进行针对性的对抗。对抗无疑会玉石俱焚，得不偿失，而且还很容易陷入对手的陷阱——它很可能是以一个非主力产品的牺牲来扰乱和摧毁你的整个市场体系。娃哈哈会避开直接的对抗，而利用自己的广告和品牌优势，在别的产品上进行推导。当对手在抢得一定市场，实力耗尽并开始把价格提上去之后，它则迅速做出反应，突然开展强有力的促销。如此一来一往，一纵一收，如果对手的综合实力和市场基础原本就不稳，主动权和控制权很快便又回到娃哈哈手中。

三、联销体

(1) 娃哈哈的营销队伍走的是一条"联销体"路线。娃哈哈的营销组织结构是这样的：总部——各省区分公司——特约一级批发商——特约二级批发商——二级批发商——三级批发商——零售终端。娃哈哈保证在一定区域内只发展一家一级批发商。

(2) 任何营销都是建立在信用基础上的危险游戏。相对于生产商自己招聘人马、全资编织市场网络，娃哈哈的联销体模式似乎更为经济和高效。各级大大小小的经销商一方面可以使娃哈哈迅速地进入一个陌生的市场，大大降低市场的导入成本，更重要的似乎还在于，这些与娃哈哈既为一体又非同根的经销商团队，是保证市场创新、增长和降低风险的重要力量。娃哈哈其实通过这种"制度建设"，实现了市场的制衡。而尤为重要的是，它避免了娃哈哈营销队伍的巨型化。

四、营销安全

对一个成熟的经销商而言，与超额利润相比，他更渴望的是一个长期而稳定的合作同盟和收益来源。营销安全的根本是市场的秩序，是整个营销体系中的每一个环节的有序互动和相互职责的确定化，而这一秩序的发起和治理者，便应当是品牌生产商。娃哈哈悄然开始了一场雄心勃勃的营销网络建设工程：构筑起一个全封闭式的全国营销网络，在企业内部，这个计划被命名为"蜘蛛战役"。

娃哈哈认为，中国市场的终端之争，首先将在批零渠道展开。娃哈哈的目标，是把目前国内最具实力的县域级饮料销售商都聚集到自己的旗下。理想中的娃哈哈网络是这样的：娃哈哈在一个区域内只选择一个批发商，该一批商只卖货给自己的二批，二批只向划定区域内的三批商和零售店铺销售。整个销售网络是在一个近乎全封闭的、规范化的系统内进行的。这可能是当今中国市场上最具雄心和创造力的一个营销试验：娃哈哈试图把数十年如一的自然性流向变为控制性流向。一旦这一营销网络大功告成，价格的规范和产品的推广自然可以收发自如。

(资料来源：吴晓波，胡宏伟. 平常渠道非常控制. 中国经营报，2001年11月.)

【案例分析】

研究娃哈哈，可以研究其战略，也可以研究产品的创新，但最值得研究的还应该是娃哈哈在市场营销中对"控制"的理解。与许多企业庞大的营销队伍相比，娃哈哈的营销队伍只有两千多人，并且不打算进一步扩大。如此之少的人，却要将毛利并不高的产品撒遍全中国，可见与其合作的各级经销商及零售终端是营销链上的关键。对付经销商并不是件简单的事情，他今天可以帮你打击对手，明天也可以帮着对手打你，对此，娃哈哈采取了"让利首先要让利经销商"、"设立区域独家经销商制度"等策略，有效地对各级经销商及零售终端进行了控制。为了更加完善这个"闭环"的营销体制，目前，娃哈哈正在实施"蜘蛛战役"，准备将全国最具实力的县域级饮料经销商都聚集到自己旗下，完成自己"想怎么打，就怎么打"的营销梦。恐龙级企业是依靠许多外力的支持才能生存的，"恐龙"也需要合作。这个道理，如今再次被娃哈哈验证。

【思考题】

1. 娃哈哈是如何实现营销中的"利益有序分配"的？
2. 娃哈哈的营销组织结构有什么特点？
3. 你认为使娃哈哈营销网络支撑下去的决定性因素是什么？

Chapter 15

Other Marketing Orientations

Focus on:

1. Connotation of service marketing.
2. Composition and features of experience marketing.
3. Localization and adaptability of international marketing.

15.1 Service Marketing

Service marketing was really drawn attention in the late 80s of 20th century. During this period, the products of service content, that is, service-intensive products were increasing on the one hand; On the other hand, with the increase in labor productivity, market turned to the buyer's market, and also for the level of income was increased, consumers' demands had been changing, and demand levels had been increasing and diversified due to the advance in science and technology, significant improvement of social productivity, increasing speed of industrial upgrading and production professional development.

15.1.1 Contents of Service Marketing

1. Definition of Service and Service Marketing

(1) Service

Services are one or a series of remunerative activities available which have intangible characteristics and can bring some kind of benefit or satisfaction. Compared with the physical products, services have characteristics of non-sensory, non-separation, diversity, non-storability and the absence of ownership and so on, which determines service marketing is different from the physical product marketing.

(2) Service marketing

Service marketing is a process of business activity that takes a set of strategies to make deal in the marketing process, to fully meet customer needs, maintain and enhance relationships with customers under the premise of full understanding of customer needs. Good service is the next best pre-sale promotions, the main form to enhance consumer satisfaction and consumer loyalty, and an important way to establish corporate reputation and disseminate corporate image. Its main target is to provide customers value-exceeding services, namely, the service able to meet not only customers' normal needs, but also some beyond the normal requirements of the service, so that the quality of service can be beyond the customers' normal expectations. The value-exceeding service exists in the whole process from research and development to production and sales, that is "customer-oriented", to provide users with the most satisfactory products and service. Its idea lies in the following points:

- Beyond user's psychological expectations;
- Beyond conventional services;
- Beyond the value of the product so that customers can enjoy long-term, multiple forms of high-quality services;
- Beyond time limit so that the services are ever-present and everywhere;
- Beyond the personnel boundaries, to treat staff as customers;
- Beyond sector boundaries, to ask each department and mobilize all members from top to bottom in enterprises into value-exceeding service chain;
- Beyond economic limit, beyond economical social value and aesthetic value to melt material things into spirit category.

Service marketing is a qualitative leap of the concept of enterprise marketing, based on a profound understanding in business-to-consumer demand. With the development of social division of labor, progress of scientific and technological improvement of people's living standard and quality, the position and role of services marketing is more and more important in the enterprise marketing management.

2. 7Ps Service Marketing Mix

As services marketing theory and practice is deepened, the traditional 4Ps marketing mix elements are also re-considered from the service point and expanded into 7Ps, namely, Product, Price, Place and Promotion, People, Physical-evidence and Process, in order to better address marketing and service management issues derived from the characteristics of service products.

15.1.2 Characteristics of Modern Service Marketing

1. Behavior Consistency

It means that the service organization must be accurate to fulfill commitments to customers

Chapter 15 Other Marketing Orientations

to enable consumers to create a sense of trust to companies, which many large international company service marketing organization see as a corporate reputation protection today.

2. Activities Adaptability

Adaptability refers to the right and quick respondence to customer requirements. Therefore, business operators should have a strong sense of responsibility and good preparation, so that they can deliver timely services to customers. Especially the service means should be conducive to consumer acceptance. For example, many beauty institutions have opened telephone booking service, and customer's service can be provided via the telephone booking an appointment for their time and beauticians.

3. Competent Ability

The size of service capabilities, to some extent, affects the positioning range of competitive strategy. As the service capabilities include the number and quality of service people, advancement level of service tools and facilities, wide-ranging and intensive service outlets, all these determine whether the strategies of services competition are wide or short, new or old, cheap or expensive.

4. Communication of Emotion

The key that the service marketing is different from product marketing is that service marketing is a kind of emotional interaction between people, namely, whether suppliers and demanders can achieve mutual trust, so mutual understanding has an important effect on the efficiency of the service marketing.

5. Consumption Conductive

Wide development of modern marketing practice requires that services give full play to delivery and creation of the standard of living in the social function, that is, service marketing should be conducive to social economy development, improvement of people's material and cultural living standards and environmental quality.

6. Joy of the Product

Joy is to make customers worry-free when consuming services, mainly meaning that there are no insecurity concerns facilities, no financial risk concerns, and no troubles to customers in and after the service.

15.2 Experiential Marketing

15.2.1 Connotation of Experiential Marketing

1. Definition of Experience and Experiential Marketing

Experience means a person reaches the emotional, physical, mental and even spiritual level of a particular in his consciousness produced by the good feeling and it is the internal psychological reactions of customers generated by certain stimuli (such as marketing tools). In the consumer angle, the experience is the "experience" (feeling) after the customer has consumed (purchase or experience) a certain product; from a business perspective, it means that the enterprise supplies the customer economic consumption goods.

The experiential marketing means the marketing experience, and is a process in which the enterprise meets customers' mental or spiritual demands with the provision of experience by regarding the customer as a center, the product as a prop, and the service as stage.

2. Composition of Experiential Marketing

(1) Experiential marketing subjects: consumers are the main body of the experiential marketing. The experiential marketing means that consumers are both rational and emotional, consumers buy commodities with the same probability because of the reason, of the pursuit of pleasure, and of the stimulation impulse. Therefore, the experience of consumers before, in and after consumption is the key of their purchasing behavior and the brand management.

(2) Experiential marketing objects: products and services. According to different product features, the appropriate modification or products easy to be used will give the product the value of experience. Some products can give people the pleasant feeling (such as toys), so, they can be added to other products as ornaments in order to highlight the sensory characteristics of other products, make them easy to be felt by consumers, and increase the experience of feeling.

(3) Experiential marketing environment: to create an experiential marketing environment, the first task is to define a theme of experiential marketing. On the analysis of customers' needs, companies need to design experience theme of the event, namely, the first part of experience design. The experience theme refers to the concept that the enterprise provides customers with a mixed experience of the most central and resonant part from customers, and the entire experience marketing strategy will be carried out closely around the experience themes.

Chapter 15 Other Marketing Orientations

The experiential marketing environment includes all aspects of the physical environment in the occurrence of experience. It fulfills the important function of the external transmission of information, can lay the foundation for the whole experience process, and embodies the experience quality effectively. Therefore, enterprises usually take the experiential marketing environment as a marketing tool to be used. For example, the Hard Rock Cafe's success depends on the rock music playing, and Hollywood Hotel's success depends on providing customers with the service of playing classic video and celebrity documentary.

(4) Experiential marketing process: Experiential marketing process is the process of interaction between customers and brand. From the moment that the customer has been attracted by a product or the publicity of a service, a high-quality customer experience process is started. There is an opportunity to establish emotional ties in every experience process, such as store shopping, visiting the website, staff contracts, communication and the use of products and enjoying the services, etc. This requires that enterprises must carry out a detailed plan for the interactive experience process to improve customer and enterprise's experience value.

15.2.2 Features of Experiential Marketing

The experiential marketing is different from the traditional marketing in the following four main aspects.

(1) Concerned about customers' experience

Compared with the traditional marketing, the experiential marketing concerns the customer experience. Experience is a result that is produced only after running into, suffering, or having experienced certain scenarios. These scenarios tend to inspire a certain feeling, touch hearts, and stimulate the inspiration. Experience also links the company and brand to consumer lifestyles, and moreover, puts the consumer behavior and the purchase scene into a wider social environment. In short, the experience provides a sensory, emotional, cognitive, behavioral, and related value instead of the functional value.

(2) Consumer scene investigation

Compared with the product category and the competition which focus on the narrow definition, experiential marketing practitioners never consider the product itself. On the contrary, they take into account the consumer scene, and they'll ask themselves what kind of product is suitable for this kind of consumer scene and how to use these products. Product package and advertising before consumption can strengthen the consumer experience.

(3) Customers are a rational and emotional combination.

For an experiential marketing, the customer is both rational and emotional. In other words, although customers may frequently make a rational decision, they are also often affected by emotions. Because the consumer experiences often "tend to pursue the dream, feeling, and pleasure". This view has great significance for today's marketing practitioners: do not put the customer just as rational decision-makers. Customers need fun, exciting, felt emotional touch and acceptance of creative challenges.

(4) Methods and tools are a compromise.

Compared with the traditional marketing, which is strongly analytical, quantitative and dealing with linguistic information, experience marketing methods and tools are more changeable and diversified. All in all, the experiential marketing is not limited to a single method. It is a more compromise, and just uses the method more effective. Experiential marketing methods and tools are more exploratory, so we should take into account the reliability, availability, and rationality.

In short, the experience marketing is different from the traditional marketing in the following four key areas: focusing on consumer experience; regarding consumption as a whole experience; drivers of consumption being both rational and emotional; adopting a compromising method.

15.2.3 Analysis of the 6Es Mix of Experience Marketing

The 6Es mix of experience marketing is an experience marketing strategy which is carried out from the view of customers. The aim of the experience marketing is to produce and execute the experience by the events of customer joining. Therefore, the experience marketing mix should build around the production and consumption experience. The mix is divided into six elements: Experience, Environment, Event, Engaging, Effect, and Extension. Its combination is presented in Figure 15.1:

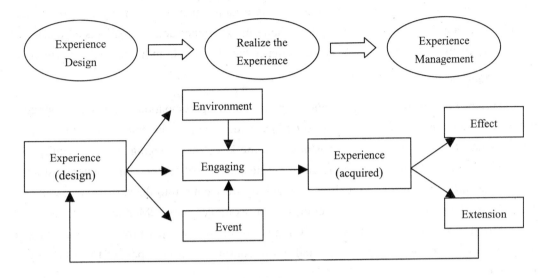

Figure 15.1 6Es Mix of Experience Marketing

1. Experience

Experience is the most basic element of the experience marketing mix, and it describes what kind of experience the enterprise should provide for customers. The experience is created by customers which is the mixture of these five types: senses, emotions, thinking, action and association. When we carry out the experience strategy, we should first find out the connection of all kinds of types, and then expand and combine on this basis to make a whole customer experience.

2. Environment

Environment is an acting stage which is created for the customers by the enterprise. It is an outer environment of experience. It can be designed into the real scene like the experience center of Amway which is the 5th term project in China. It can also be designed into the unreal world like some unreal communities designed by some internet managers. During the environment design, we can learn from the knowledge of opera theory, psychology, and sociology and so on. But the environment strategy must serve the experience strategy.

3. Event

Event is a series of performing procedures which are set for customers. The enterprise must carry out a special design for the process of performing to form the event strategy. According to a loose degree, the event can be divided into two models: one is the establishment of strict procedures, such as online games; the other is the establishment of relatively lax procedures, which is of certain flexibility. For example, in the farm experience activity which is organized by "Disneyland Birthday Club", children can experience the old-style farm life by their imagination.

4. Engaging

Experience marketing concerns about customers' active participation, and engaging strategy enables customers to immerse into the event which is designed by the enterprise for marketing, so what kind of role is designed for customers is the key. The engaging strategy requires the design of certain roles should make the customer become a real "actor." Only when customers really participate in the event can their mental activity truly enter into the scenario and will they finally be willing to pay for the experience. For example, most "Mediterranean clubs" of industrialized countries have designed all kinds of impromptu performances according to customers' different purchase purposes, and allow consumers to take part in their strategy of immersion.

5. Effect and Extension

Effect strategy is the strategy of management impression. Experiential marketing delivers the experience to the customer, and at the same time, should note the lifetime value of customers rather than a value arising from single transaction. Therefore, the enterprise must pay attention to the problems about repeat customers. Experience produces an unforgettable impression of the process which will become an important factor that is long-term maintenance in customer relations, such as saving the video of the experience process, taking photos, presenting the experience souvenirs, and establishing the experience clubs, etc.

Customer experience can be extended to the company's other products, different regions and periods, and be spread to others in order to achieve the maximization of customer value. The experience marketing completely implements the extension strategy by all kind of measures, which enable the effectiveness of experience to be maximized.

With the improvement of living standards, the experience marketing is being a new marketing system in the nowadays economical society. To win the future competition, it is very important to understand and carry out the experience marketing.

15.3 International Marketing

As long as there is a good deal of catching-up to do in the home country, the domestic market will suffice. The first exports then take place in the raw materials sector. The quality of

Chapter 15　Other Marketing Orientations

exported goods rises only when there is an advanced market.

By means of export, one can enlarge the market. The world is largely open nowadays. The same rules that apply to working the domestic market also apply to working the international market.

The image of the product exported is closely connected to the image of the country it comes from. If the world was a village of 1,000 inhabitants, there would be 60 North Americans, 80 Latin Americans, 86 Africans, 210 Europeans and 564 Asians living in it; 300 would have fair, 700 coloured skins; 60 people would own 50% of the overall income of the 1,000; 700 would be illiterate; 500 would not have enough to eat; 600 would be living in slums.

15.3.1　World Trade Triangle

The world economy is dominated by the three regions: USA, the European Union, the Far East. China is fast becoming a leading trade power on the globe. For marketing, not only the needs of the market have to be established but also the financial viability. The crucial factors in this are as follows:

Factor	Indicator
Affluence	Gross Domestic Product per capita
Growth	Gross Domestic Product in percentage of previous years
Life Expectancy	in years
Joblessness	percentage of active population
Investments	percentage of GDP
Population	in millions
Exports	percentage of GDP

15.3.2　Multinational or Global Marketing

On the one hand, there are aspirations for products to be uniform the world over; on the other hand, there are national idiosyncrasies. Certain products are unsalable in certain countries, Italians will not buy German spaghetti and Americans will not buy Italian steaks. Only a very few manufacturers can afford the products that are uniform worldwide. Regional products are usually easier to sell. A prime example of an international product is Coca-Cola. "Coke" is standardised the world over, but the distribution is adapted to national requirements.

What direction should one's marketing strategy take? Three possibilities present themselves:

- Homeland Orientation
- Host-Country Orientation
- World-Market Orientation

1. Homeland Orientation

This "international marketing" has an "ethnocentric" orientation. Starting from one's strong position on the domestic market, one builds up and strengthens one's position. According to the motto "what has been successful at home can also be sold internationally", one tries to conquer the world market.

2. Host-Country Orientation

First experiences will soon show that not all ideas are transferable from one country to another. Especially at a time when regional thinking regains importance, not all products can be offered to everybody alike. If carried to an extreme, one regards "every country as different" and does not take over any of the experiences or modules from another export country. One develops an individual strategy for each country. This "multinational marketing" has a "polycentric" orientation. In real life, it can only be implemented with a local partner and by using increased effort.

3. World-Market Orientation

The world is seen as a unified whole. There is only one world market. This is "global marketing" with a "geocentric" orientation. This method is inexpensive but not suitable for many products because national idiosyncrasies are neglected. Modules and sales-supporting facilities are only developed once, for all countries. Wastage is low, too, because the same strategy can be applied in all countries. International products have a great cost benefit. The consumers of all countries in the world are addressed with the same message. One example of global marketing is Coca-Cola. But in this case, too, the product, though internationally standardised, is distributed via different regional distribution partners.

But even internationally successful products can suffer setbacks with this method in some countries. Barbie dolls are an example of this. They have trouble being accepted in Japan because the chest size and the colour of the skin and eyes do not match the local culture.

15.3.3 Decision for International Activities

Internationalizing one's business can be motivated by the fact that the domestic market has become too small for the production, and one wants to expand beyond it. A too-small domestic

Chapter 15 Other Marketing Orientations

market can also have an adverse effect on the competitiveness of one's own production. Often a larger manufacturing volume is needed if one wants to be able to keep up with the competition.

With electronic goods in particular, production is concentrated in one spot in order to benefit from economies of scale. The distribution itself, however, is decentralized. Wherever the impetus for internationalizing the business may come from, it has to be well-founded. Therefore two analyses are necessary:

1. Analysis of the Foreign Market

For a first reconnaissance of the new market, the following information has to be ascertained:
- Market volume
- Potential of market growth
- Competition (number of competitors and market shares)
- Possible distribution channels for one's product
- Buyer groups (which sectors; how large are they; etc.)

So much for the knock-out criteria and also decisions:
- Duration of market entry (how long does it take for the product or enterprise to be accepted on the market)
- Cost of market cultivation
- If required, adapting the product to the national market
- Mentality
- Distance between target country and domestic market
- Price level
- Tax and duty barriers

In order to become familiar with the needs of the American market, the Chief Designer of Nissan spent several months living with an American family. His experiences influenced the development of the car that was destined for the American market.

2. Analysis of One's Own Company

Which market does one want to target with which products? What are the conditions at home that one starts out with? Here criteria such as the following come into play:
- Language skills of one's employees,
- Previous successes in foreign markets,
- Image and degree of popularity of one's enterprise or product on the targeted foreign market,

- Image of one's own country on the target market,
- References already gained through supplying via third parties, and
- Acceptance shown by one's employees of the mentality of the target market.

Based on these prerequisites, a decision for venturing abroad can be taken. This is followed by choosing the market strategy and the distribution channel. The choice of distribution channel determines the composition of the marketing team. One either wants to participate in the market through a partnership (joint venture) or one wants to sell via a local representative. Does one put the emphasis on building up local manufacturing and distribution activities of one's own company, or rather on a co-operation? The team is staffed accordingly. It has proved rewarding to commission those managers with drawing up the business plan who are later going to be in charge of the operative side of the business. It has not proved successful to use theoreticians for the business plan and pragmatics for the operational business. Too much information gets lost in the transition.

Large enterprises also have to come to an arrangement regarding internal co-ordination. Different departments and sections operate more or less successfully in different markets. Everybody only sees his own goal before him. While one department is closing down a sales office, another is considering entering into this market. Successful departments can facilitate market entry for each other.

When implementing a programme of action, it needs to be defined who does what, when, and under what circumstances. The operative marketing team must also be given targets such as quality and quantity and be equipped with corresponding competencies and responsibilities.

In order to be able to measure the progress and success of the international project, an exact timetable is indispensable. Whereas one should work consistently towards reaching the goal once set, one must abandon the activities without delay when the goals turn out to be unattainable.

15.3.4　Framework of International Marketing

Every market is embedded in a natural, economic, social and legal environment which exerts a particular influence on the conditions of this market.

1. Natural-Technological Environment

Environmental factors resulting from nature influence strongly the international business world. Needs manifested as demands very often result from such conditions, e.g. the demand for fur coats, parasols, four-wheel drives, etc. Climatic conditions such as air temperature, humidity, wind, precipitation, clouding and sunshine should be taken into account. Furthermore one should

Chapter 15 Other Marketing Orientations

consider topographical factors such as flora and fauna and soil conditions. Mountain ranges, deserts, primeval forests and other similarly impassable features of the land pose an obstacle to traffic and can therefore strongly influence the physical distribution, if not make it impossible for reasons of cost.

Before investing in a foreign market, one should research very thoroughly the state of technological development, the technical infrastructure and, above all, the energy supply.

2. Political-Legal Environment

The international marketing of a product or service largely depends on the current stage of development of the partner country. A developing country certainly needs different products from a highly developed industrial nation. One also has to bear in mind that the economic structural shifts have accelerated and are changing continually. The techniques of international marketing in countries that are ruled dictatorially are very different from the ones used in democratically ruled and market-orientated countries.

The range of political-economic policies, especially at the level of national governments, is extremely variegated. Basically, we distinguish between general economic and foreign-economic policies.

General economic policy comprises e.g. statutory laws regulating cartels, pricing and rebates, types of enterprises, market regulation, etc.

Foreign-economic policies are concerned with trade-, payment- and shipping treaties, agreements about technological and economic co-operation, customs regulations, import quotas, etc.

The legal system of a country is a very tricky determinant in international marketing. Since international law is rather feeble, the manager abroad has to study very carefully the legal system of the partner country.

The factor of politics is particularly delicate and at the same time very decisive. As long as the political system of a country is stable, one can adjust to any political situation. The problem lies in instability, i.e. the possibility of political reversal. Examples of this occur regularly every year.

A company interested in foreign expansion will therefore examine carefully the political situation of the partner country and carry out political analyses. Socio-political ideologies have an enormous potential for disruption and must therefore be observed with care and responsibility.

3. Socio-Cultural Environment

(1) Individual: The individual, as the carrier of needs and desires, has the strongest

influence on economic events. In international marketing, we deal with a large variety of people and therefore have to ask ourselves with each marketing measure whether it meets with a favourable response or not. The following factors need to be taken into account:

- Height
- Skin colors
- Growth of hair
- Education
- Emotions
- Lifestyle

For instance, a Chinese enterprise delivering spectacle frames to Europe must take into account that the bridge of the nose of European is different from that of Chinese people.

(2) Religion: Especially when exporting to Islamic countries, it is extremely important to consider the aspect of religion. For example, alcohol must not be exported to Islamic countries, and livestock has to be slaughtered according to the religious rites. State and society are subject to the religion. The situation of women is totally different from that of non-Islamic countries.

(3) Language: Language, as we know, is the best key to the culture of a people. Therefore one should ideally be able to speak the foreign language. Nothing offends a foreign business partner more than a business letter which, through poor translation, misuses his language. Besides being a key to the culture of a country, it can also be said that language opens the doors to the people of that country. Knowledge of a world language such as English is important, but it is even more advantageous to speak the business partner's native language. Besides the audible language, there is also the non-audible one ("silent language"). It is only possible to acquire this "silent language" after having lived in the country for a longer period of time.

(4) Esthetics and art: Aesthetics expresses itself in people's style and tastes. Some people prefer bold colors, others subdued ones. What some people find beautiful is unattractive to others. But not just color, the perception of forms and shapes, too, plays a large role in international marketing. Consequently designers must take the national taste into account. This applies to hifi devices and fashion alike.

(5) Way of life: "Way of life" describes a specific lifestyle, such as the customs and traditions that rule everyday life. Every people has its own ideas of how life should be lived. US Americans, for instance, have a different way of life from the Europeans. And within Europe, the people in Mediterranean countries certainly have a different idea of how life should be lived than Germans or Scandinavians. Thus the people of different nations have different attitudes to time, money, manners, communication, and work.

Chapter 15　Other Marketing Orientations

(6) The social system: The social structure of the host country may differ considerably from that of the home country. The division of Rich and Poor is different in each country. The relationship between men and women is different in Asian countries compared with Europe or the Arabic world. In the one place, women are allowed to go first; in the other place, they have to walk behind the man. Experienced international managers usually admonish us not to inquire after the wife's wellbeing in some countries, or even to touch upon family issues.

In conclusion, let us turn to some typical examples from Great Britain:

The Department of Trade and Industry in London carried out a survey and collected examples of business deals that fell through on the international market. The list of gaffes culminates in the realization that one in four businesses suffered losses in revenue because learning foreign languages was considered a waste of time. Some businesses even go bankrupt due to this misconception. Thus, for instance, a liquidator found (written) orders of extraordinary value in the desk of a bankrupt businessman, which could have saved the business. The potential buyer, however, never received a response because the letters were written in German. Nobody had attempted a translation.

Another company had to destroy 15,000 leaflets that were totally misdirected for the Brazilian market. The leaflets were written in Spanish; in Brazil, however, they speak Portuguese. The car manufacturer Vauxhall was for a long time puzzling over the difficulty that their "Nova" car had being accepted on the Spanish market. Presumably, the mistake was made as early as when the name was chosen: "nova" in Spanish means something like "no go".

Other barriers emerge in direct contact with foreign business partners. An English manager missed an important business dinner because he had mistranslated "half past eight" as 9:30.

All of this pales in comparison with the washout a notable British manufacturer of laundry detergent experienced in an Arabic country. The costly campaign revolved around the "before" and "after" formula, and – like in the home country – the dirty shirt was seen on the left, the dazzlingly white end product on the right hand side. Unfortunately, though, Arabs read from right to left.

15.4　Social Marketing

Recently there has been an addition to Producer Goods Marketing and Consumer Goods Marketing, namely, "Social Marketing".

In the Social Marketing, the "product" does not consist in a purchasable commodity or service but instead in the conveying of an idea that is accepted by society. Social Marketing makes use of the same tools as marketing in the business world. In this manner, governments and special interest groups can carry out campaigns to achieve social change.

An example of a Social Marketing campaign was the switch from left- to right-hand traffic in Sweden in 1967.

The same techniques as in the Product Marketing come into play, the only difference being that the objects are ideas, convictions, places and regions, persons, and organizations.

With the help of strategic marketing, organizations can attempt to recruit members, convince people of a specific idea, or influence people. This can happen with profit in mind or regardless of it.

"People marketing" is especially used in politics where a person campaigns to be elected for a specific office and therefore has to market him- or herself in order to gain the people's trust and votes. But also freelance "one-person-businesses" have to market themselves in this way, e.g. doctors, lawyers and tax consultants.

Places and regions market themselves as attractive tourist destinations and, for example, as attractive places for future investments by government and the economy.

But Social Marketing can also market ideas, such as measures for the protection and the improvement of the environment.

15.5　Summary

　　市场经济的迅速发展、市场竞争的激烈竞争带来了市场营销活动的繁荣。市场营销实践的繁荣加速了市场营销理论体系的进一步完善，同时也促成了诸如服务营销、体验营销、国际市场营销以及社会市场营销等众多市场营销新观念的产生。这些观念从不同视角探讨了市场营销实践活动的特性，密切了营销理论与营销实践的关系，深化了营销理论发展的内涵。

　　服务营销是企业在充分认识顾客需求的前提下，为充分满足顾客的需求，维护和增进与顾客的关系，在营销过程中采取一系列策略而达成交易的商务活动过程。体验营销是指企业以客户为中心，以产品为道具，以服务为舞台，通过提供体验来满足顾客心理或者精神上的需求的过程；其主体是消费者，客体是产品和服务。国际市场营销是市场全球化、经济一体化的产物，它探讨营销实践与理论在不同国家和地区的本土化与适应性问题。社会市场营销则强调市场营销思想在社会中的传播，其"产品"超出了一般商品或服务的范畴，政府和特定的社会团体往往可以通过市场营销工具和手段实施其活动并达到推动社会变化的目的。

Chapter 15　Other Marketing Orientations

Key Terms

Service Marketing　　Experience Marketing　　International Marketing　　Social Marketing

【案例】花旗银行，服务营销的创始者

　　花旗银行(Citibank)迄今已有近 200 年的历史。进入新世纪，花旗集团(Citigroup)的资产规模已达 9022 亿美元，一级资本为 545 亿美元，被誉为"金融界的至尊"。时至今日，花旗银行已在世界 100 多个国家和地区建立了 4000 多个分支机构，在非洲、中东，花旗银行更是外资银行抢滩的先锋。花旗的骄人业绩无不得益于其 1977 年以来银行服务营销战略的成功实施。服务营销在营销界产生已久，但服务营销真正和银行经营相融合，从而诞生银行服务营销理念，还源于 1977 年花旗银行副总裁列尼·休斯坦克的一篇名为《从产品营销中解脱出来》的文章。花旗银行可以说是银行服务营销的创始者，同时也是银行服务营销的领头羊。花旗银行能成为银行界的先锋，关键在于花旗独特的金融服务能让顾客感受并接受这种服务，进而使花旗成为金融受众的首选。多年以来，银行家们很少关注银行服务的实质，强调的只是银行产品的盈利性与安全性。随着银行业竞争的加剧，银行家们开始将注意力转移到银行服务与顾客需求的统一性上来。银行服务营销也逐渐成了银行家们考虑的重要因素。

　　自 20 世纪 70 年代花旗银行开创银行服务营销理念以来，就不断地将银行服务寓于新的金融产品创新之中。而今，花旗银行能提供多达 500 种金融服务。花旗服务已如同普通商品一样琳琅满目，任人选择。1998 年，花旗与旅行者集团的合并，使花旗真正发展成为一个银行金融百货公司。在 20 世纪 90 年代的几次品牌评比中，花旗都以它卓越的金融服务位列金融业的榜首。今天，在全球金融市场步入竞争激烈的买方市场后，花旗银行更加大了它的银行服务营销力度，同时还通过对银行服务营销理念的进一步深化，将服务标准与当地的文化相结合，在加强品牌形象的统一性的同时，又注入了当地的语言文化，从而使花旗成为行业内国际化的典范。

　　一、花旗服务营销的新内涵

　　金融产品的可复制性，使银行很难凭借某种金融产品获得长久竞争优势，但金融服务的个性化却能为银行获得长久的客户。著名管理学家德鲁克曾指出："商业的目的只有一个站得住脚的定义，即创造顾客。""以顾客满意为导向，无异是在企业的传统经营上掀起了一场革命。"花旗银行深刻理解并以自身行动完美地诠释了"以客户为中心，服务客户"的银行服务营销理念。在营销技术和手段上不断推陈出新，从而升华花旗服务，引领花旗辉煌。

　　花旗通过变无形服务为有形服务，提高服务的可感知性，将花旗服务派送到每一位客户手中。花旗银行在实施银行服务营销的过程中，以客户可感知的服务硬件为依托，向客户传输花旗的现代化服务理念。花旗以其幽雅的服务环境、和谐的服务氛围、便利的服务流程、人性化的设施、快捷的网络速度以及积极健康的员工形象等传达着它的服务特色，传递着它的服务信息。

花旗在银行服务营销策略中，鼓励员工充分与顾客接触，经常提供上门服务，以使顾客充分参与到服务生产系统中来。通过"关系"经理的服务方式花旗银行建成了跨越多层次的职能、业务项目、地区和行业界限的人际关系，为客户提供并办理新的业务，促使潜在的客户变成现实的用户。同时，花旗还赋予员工充分的自主服务权，在互动过程中为客户更好地提供全方位的服务。

通过提升服务质量，银行服务营销赋予花旗服务以新的形象。花旗在引导客户预期方面决不允许做过高或过多的承诺，一旦传递给客户的允诺就必须保质保量地完成。如承诺"花旗永远不睡觉"，其实质就是花旗服务客户价值理念的直接体现。花旗银行规定并做到了电话铃响10秒之内必须有人接，客户来信必须在两天内做出答复。这些细节就是客户满意的重要因素。同时，花旗还围绕着构建同顾客的长期稳定关系这个主旨，提升针对性的银行服务质量。通过了解客户需求，针对此提供相应的产品或服务，缩短员工与客户、管理者与员工、管理者与客户之间的距离，在确保质量和安全的前提下，完善内部合作方式，改善银行的服务态度，提高银行的服务质量，进而提高客户的满意度，提高服务的效率并达到良好的效果。

二、花旗银行服务营销的启示

花旗银行服务营销的成功实施，拓展了服务领域，强化了服务质量，从而使得花旗品牌深入人心，客户纷纷而至，以至每四个美国人中就有一个是花旗银行的客户。在当今信息技术引发的金融创新浪潮中，各个银行之间试图通过网点优势、人员优势、技术优势、产品优势拉开与竞争对手差距的时代已成为过去。银行服务营销开展的优劣将成为银行竞争成败的关键。

在当前我国积极实施国有商业银行市场化改革的进程中，花旗的银行营销给我国国有商业银行的市场改革进程带来许多重大的启示。诚然，银行大楼是越盖越高，装修越来越好，服务项目也越来越多，但人们总能发现某个储蓄网点不是 ATM 机不好用，就是 POS 机出了问题；不是大堂经理不在，就是窗口暂停服务。由此可见，缺乏现代银行服务内涵的金融产品竞争已失去了先前的魅力。因此，在推进国有商业银行市场化体制建设的同时，要给宛如希腊神庙般的银行建筑、深色凝重的银行摆设、冰冷的面容、单调的语言等，注入现代银行的服务内涵，这也将成为国有商业银行能否真正与市场接轨的关键问题。

国有商业银行在推行银行服务营销的过程中，要积极地将"以产品为中心"的产品推销观念转化为"以客户为中心"的银行服务营销观念。在实践中，要将银行服务营销观念与策略导入银行服务业，通过差别化、个性化的服务，营造具有自己特色的金融品牌。同时，要根据客户需求的变化相应调整银行的服务。正如花旗银行合理引导客户预期并提供迎合客户预期的银行服务一样，国有商业银行也要在推行银行服务营销的实践中根据客户需求，积极开发与之相符的并具有自身特色的便利服务和支持性服务，从而将银行服务营销真正融于具体的银行经营实践中。

(资料来源: 酷思路—国际公关整理. 花旗银行, 服务营销的创始者. [2006-09-16]. marketing.kusilu.com.)

【案例分析】
　　作为银行服务营销的创始者和领头羊, 花旗银行以其独特的金融服务成为金融受众的首选。随着银行业竞争的加剧, 银行服务与顾客需求的统一成为了银行家们关注的焦点, 尽管银行产品的盈利性与安全性也是银行家们考虑的重要因素。在全球金融市场步入竞争激烈的买方市场后, 花旗银行更加大了它的银行服务营销力度, 同时在管理上进一步深化银行服务营销的理念, 将服务标准与当地的文化相结合, 既注重品牌形象的统一性, 又注重其产品在不同地区的差异性与适应性, 从而使花旗成为业内国际化的典范。

【思考题】
1. 你认为花旗银行服务营销成功主要体现在哪几个方面?
2. 结合该案例与2008年全球金融危机的原因, 讨论花旗银行金融创新的利弊。
3. 花旗银行服务营销成功的事例给我国银行业的启示有哪些?

参 考 文 献

1. 梁东，刘建堤等. 市场营销学[M]. 北京：清华大学出版社，2006.
2. 周朝琦，孙学军，侯龙文. 企业定价方略[M]. 北京：经济管理出版社，2001.
3. 胡其辉. 企业定价决策[M]. 大连：东北财经大学出版社，2001.
4. Nagle T T, Holden R K 著. 赵平，杜晖，潘欣译. 定价策略与技巧[M]. 北京：清华大学出版社，1999.
5. David F R. 战略管理——概念与案例[M]. 第 10 版. 北京：清华大学出版社，2008.
6. Keegan W J, Green M C. Global Marketing [M]. 4th ed. 北京：中国人民大学出版社，2005.
7. Kotler P, Armstrong G. Principles of Marketing[M]. 11th ed. 北京：清华大学出版社，2007.
8. Quester P G, McGuiggan R L, Mccarthy E J, Perreault W D. Basic Marketing: A Managerial Perspective[M]. 4th ed. The McGraw-Hill Book Company, 2006.
9. Kotler P. Marketing Management[M]. Millenium Edition. Tenth Edition[M]. Prentice-Hall, Inc., 2000.
10. Kotler P. Marketing Management[M]. 11th ed. Upper Saddle River, NJ: Pearson Education, 2003.
11. Kotler P, Keller K L. Marketing Management[M]. 12th ed. Upper Saddle River, NJ: Prentice Hall, 2006.
12. [2009-12-05]. http://open.xsrtvu.com/media_file/2008/12/17/4528eb6d-3d48-4c51-8d9d-ece6757274df/001.html.
13. [2010-03-02]. www.scuec.edu.cn.